China - Sierra Leone Relations

Friendship, Co-operation and
Win-Win Diplomacy

Adonis & Abbey Publishers Ltd
Third Floor
207 Regent Street
London W1B 3HH
Website: http://www.adonis-abbey.com
E-mail Address: editor@adonis-abbey.com

Nigeria:
Plot 2560, Hassan Musa Katsina Street, Asokoro, Abuja, Nigeria
Tel: +234 (0) 7058078841/08052035034
Website: http://www.adonis-abbey.com
E-mail Address: editor@adonis-abbey.com

British Library Cataloguing-in-Publication Data
A catalogue record for this book is available from the British Library

ISBN: 9781913976293 (PB)

ISBN: 9781913976309 (HB)

China - Sierra Leone Relations

Friendship, Co-operation and
Win-Win Diplomacy

David J. Francis (Ed.)

ADONIS & ABBEY
PUBLISHERS LTD

Table of Contents

About the Contributors

Professor David J. Francis is currently a Senior Visiting Research Professor at the Institute of African Studies, Zhejiang Normal University, China. He is a distinguished international academic who previously served as Head of the Department of Peace Studies at the University of Bradford, UK. Professor Francis also held a Research Professorial Chair and the UNESCO Chair at the University of Bradford. He is extensively published, with 12 books focusing on Sierra Leonean and African politics, peace, security, international relations, and development issues. As a statesman and policy practitioner, Professor Francis has served as both Chief Minister and Foreign Minister in the Government of the Republic of Sierra Leone.

Professor Joe A. D. Alie is a professor of history at Fourah Bay College, University of Sierra Leone (USL). He holds a PhD and a Postgraduate Certificate in African Studies from the University of Wisconsin-Madison (USA). He is an accomplished textbook author who have written over a dozen books and published scholarly papers in refereed journals. Professor Alie has lectured at universities in the United States and Europe and was recently a Visiting Professor at the Institute of African Studies, Zhejiang Normal University in Jinhua, China, the premier Institute of African Studies in China.

Mr. Abraham John is a Dongfang Scholar at Peking University in China. He has written and presented papers on democratic governance in post-conflict Sierra Leone, with a particular focus on the 1996 and 2002 elections. Mr. John previously served as Director of Ministerial Coordination & Follow-up in the Office of the Chief Minister at State House in the Government of Sierra Leone. He also worked as Director of Asia and the Middle East in the Ministry of Foreign Affairs and International Cooperation of the Republic of Sierra Leone.

Dr. Lansana Gberie is Sierra Leone's Ambassador to Switzerland and Permanent Representative to the United Nations and other international organisations, including the World Trade Centre. He is currently the President of the Arms Trade Treaty (ATT) and Vice President of the Governing Bureau of the International Organisation for Migration (IOM). Prior to his appointment in 2018, Dr. Gberie worked for the United Nations for many years, including as Coordinator and Finance Expert of the United Nations Security Council Panel of Experts on Liberia. He also served as a senior researcher at the Institute for Security Studies in Addis Ababa, Ethiopia. An academic and writer, Dr. Gberie is the author of several books and numerous scholarly articles in various peer-reviewed journals.

Mr. Sahr L. Jusu served as Financial Secretary in the Ministry of Finance of the Government of Sierra Leone. He is a Harvard University Edward S. Mason Fellow in Public Policy & Management. Mr. Jusu is currently the managing partner of the Centre for Consulting & Advisory Services in Sierra Leone.

Dr. Edward Hinga Sandy is currently the Chairman for the Executive Director of the National Investment Board (NIB) of the Government of Sierra Leone. Dr. Sandy served as Minister of Trade and Industry from 2019 to 2023. He was awarded a doctorate degree by the School of Environmental Sciences and Engineering, China University of Geosciences, Wuhan.

Dr. Mohamed Combo Kamanda is the current Secretary General of the Sierra Leone National Commission for UNESCO, based at the Ministry of Technical and Higher Education. He is an educationist specialising in teacher education, English language, literature, and communication skills. Dr. Kamanda has published extensively on politics and language planning, language in Education and linguistic human rights. He has consulted widely, including developing curricula for the Ministry of Foreign Affairs—Foreign Service Academy as well as creating new curricula for creative writing and English literature for senior secondary schools in Sierra Leone.

Professor Aiah A. Gbakima served as the first Minister of Technical & Higher Education in the Government of Sierra Leone between 2018 and 2021. He held several significant positions, including Vice Chancellor of the University of Sierra Leone, Country Director of the USAID Ebola Project in Sierra Leone, Country Director of the

Washington, DC-based Metabiota Inc. in Sierra Leone, Editor-in-Chief of the Sierra Leone Journal of Biomedical Research (SLJBR) and Chair of the Sierra Leone Health & Biomedical Research Association (HBIOMED). Professor Gbakima is currently an adjunct professor of microbiology at COMAHS-USL. He is widely published in refereed journals.

Dr. Memunatu B. Pratt is the former Minister of Tourism and Cultural Affairs in Sierra Leone. Before her appointment, she served as Senior Lecturer and Head of the Department of Peace and Conflict Studies at Fourah Bay College, University of Sierra Leone. Dr. Pratt has also been a visiting professor at several universities in Africa, Asia, Europe, and the United States. She is a recipient of several honours, awards, and recognition, as well as a number of publications to her name. Since the completion of her five-year term as Minister, she has returned to academia and is currently at FBC-USL, where she is involved in teaching, research, and supervision.

Dr. Emmanuel Saffa Abdulia is currently the Executive Director of the National Sports Authority of the Government of Sierra Leone. He is also the Head of the Department of Law at the Faculty of Law, University of Sierra Leone. Dr. Abdulia also serves as a civil society practitioner and pro-democracy activist. He is currently the Chair of the African Union Economic, Social, and Cultural Council, which monitors several elections in Africa. Dr. Abdulia is extensively published, including works on *Electoral Politics, Laws, and Ethnicity in Africa*. He is the managing partner of Abdulia and Associates, Luawa Chambers.

Mrs. Isatu J. Kabbah currently serves as the Presidential Adviser on Gender to the Government of President Julius Maada Bio. She is Chief Executive Officer of the Ahmad Tejan Kabbah Foundation for Peace & Democracy. Mrs. Kabbah holds a Bachelor of Science in Sociology, a Postgraduate Diploma in Public Administration at the Institute of Public Administration and Management (USL), and a Master's degree in Gender and Development Studies from Fourah Bay College, University of Sierra Leone.

Dr. Mohamed Abuja Sherriff is an agricultural economist and retired Chief Agriculture Officer who served as Director General at the Ministry of Agriculture and Food Security. Dr. Sherriff is a senior director at the Economic Policy Research Development & Statistics Consulting (EPRDS) and an associate lecturer at Njala University in Sierra Leone.

Professor Xu Wei holds a PhD in Anthropology and is the Deputy Dean of the Institute of African Studies, Zhejiang Normal University, China.

Map of Sierra Leone (political). Source: www.worldmeters.info/ma

Map of China (political). Source: www.worldmeters.info./ma

Preface

China and Sierra Leone share a traditional friendship. The establishment of diplomatic relations was the brainchild of then Sierra Leonean President Siaka Probyn Stevens and Chairman Mao Zedong. Amid the bitter Cold War rivalries and animosities, these two men made the courageous and foresighted decision to establish diplomatic relations at the ambassadorial level. Over the past 50+ years since the establishment of diplomatic relations, our two countries have firmly supported each other on issues concerning each other's core interests, engaged in effective cooperation in areas related to economic and social development, and maintained close coordination on international affairs. In particular, the people of both countries have fought Ebola and COVID-19 together, which further strengthened our bond. Chinese President Xi Jinping even said that ties between the two nations can be regarded as a model of China-Africa unity and cooperation during Sierra Leonean President Julius Maada Bio's visit in Beijing in January/February 2024.

People-to-people bonds play a crucial role in building the shared future between China and Sierra Leone. Driven by the Belt and Road Initiative, our two countries have engaged in pragmatic cooperation in the fields of culture, investment, economy, trade, infrastructure, and agriculture, thereby strengthening the friendship between the Chinese and Sierra Leonean people. The Institute of African Studies at Zhejiang Normal University (IASZNU) was founded in September 2007 under the auspices of China's Ministry of Education and China's Ministry of Foreign Affairs. Moving in lockstep with the state's overall development and the general trend of China-Africa cooperation, IASZNU has been conducting comprehensive research on both basic theory and practical strategies, focusing on contemporary African development and Sino-African cooperation in the new era. Since its establishment, the institute has established cooperative relations with more than 20 universities and research institutions across Africa. From 2015 to 2016, Professor Joe Anthony Dominic Alie, Dean of the Graduate School of the University of Sierra Leone and a renowned specialist in African history, was invited to take an academic visit to IASZNU and conducted field research on the development of the relationship between China and Sierra Leone since 1971. Hon.

Professor David J. Francis is the most recent former Minister of Foreign Affairs and International Cooperation of the Republic of Sierra Leone, appointed in April 2021, as well as a former Chief Minister of the Government of Sierra Leone. He is an internationally recognised academic with extensive scholarly publications, including 12 books and more than 30 refereed journal articles and book chapters.

To further promote cooperation between our two sides, in December 2023, Professor Francis was invited to visit IAZNU. During his stay in Jinhua, China, he was appointed as an Honorary Professor at IASZNU, and invited to speak at the opening ceremony of the Fourth Zhejiang Belt and Road Think Tank Forum, deliver a keynote speech for our researchers and students, and visit other research institutions in Beijing and Shanghai.

We are pleased to announce that this book project is published by the London-based Adonis & Abbey Publishers Ltd. and will be formally launched in Freetown, Sierra Leone, at the Chinese Embassy on 1st October 2024. I would like to take this opportunity to thank the Embassy for the great support they have offered.

In order to further promote African region and country studies, IASZNU is currently undertaking the compilation work for the Series Books of African Region and Country Studies. We believe that, with the joint efforts of both sides, we will achieve fruitful results in African studies in China, and Chinese studies in Africa.

Professor Liu Hongwu
Director General
Institute of African Studies (College of African Area and Country Studies), Zhejiang Normal University, P.R. China
1ˢᵗ September 2024

Foreword

I would like to extend my warm congratulations to Professor David J. Francis on the publication of his seminal book, **China-Sierra Leone Relations: Friendship, Co-operation and Win-Win Diplomacy**. Starting from the background of our shared struggle for national liberation and independence in the mid-twentieth century, the book reviews the glorious journey China-Sierra Leone relations have travelled over the past 53 years. It presents a panoramic view of our exchanges and cooperation in the fields of politics, trade, health, agriculture, education, culture, youth, sports, and poverty alleviation. The book not only shows us the enduring friendship, fruitful results, and special significance of China-Sierra Leone relations but also points to the broad prospects of the relations in the future. Professor Francis served as the Chief Minister and then Foreign Minister of Sierra Leone from 2018 to 2023 with profound academic knowledge and broad international vision. He is a good friend of the Chinese people and has visited China several times. The contributors of this book include former Sierra Leonean cabinet ministers, officials from the Ministry of Foreign Affairs and International Cooperation, heads of current government agencies, and think-tank scholars from Sierra Leone. Professor Liu Hongwu and other scholars from the Institute of African Studies at Zhejiang Normal University also made significant contributions to the publication of this book. I would like to express my sincere gratitude for their hard work.

On July 29, 1971, the People's Republic of China and the Republic of Sierra Leone formally established diplomatic relations. Over the past 53 years, regardless of changes in the international situation, this relationship has consistently maintained sound momentum on development and has remained filled with vigorous vitality. During talks with President Julius Maada Bio in February 2024 at the time of his State Visit to China, President Xi Jinping described China-Sierra Leone relations as "a good example of China-Africa solidarity and cooperation". This high appraisal vividly reflects the enduring strength and success of 53 years of China-Sierra Leone relations.

"A good example" is reflected in the high degree of political mutual trust. In 1971, with the support of Sierra Leone and other peace-loving countries that stood up for justice in the world, the 26th United

Nations General Assembly adopted Resolution 2758 to restore the lawful seat of the People's Republic of China in the United Nations. Since then, Sierra Leone always firmly adhered to the one-China principle and supported the efforts of the Chinese government to achieve national reunification. China also firmly supports Sierra Leone in safeguarding national independence, sovereignty, security, and development interests. This provides a strong political foundation for our bilateral relations.

"A good example" is reflected in the fruitful win-win cooperation. Boosting common development has always been an important goal of China's policy towards Africa. While pursuing its development, China has extended support and assistance to the limits of its capacity to support Sierra Leone to improve people's livelihoods and seek development. The Friendship (Youyi) Building, National Stadium, China-Sierra Leone Friendship Hospital, and Foreign Service Academy play important roles in Sierra Leone's social development. Since the "Belt and Road" initiative was proposed by President Xi, our practical cooperation has been expanded to various fields such as fisheries, mining, agriculture, and infrastructure, which have brought tangible benefits to the people of the two countries.

"A good example" is reflected in the close cooperation in international and regional affairs. China and Sierra Leone are both developing countries with extensive common interests and similar positions. We are important partners in advancing the reform of the global governance system and working for a more just and equitable international order. We jointly advance multilateralism and steadfastly support the international system with the United Nations at the core, the international order underpinned by international law, and the basic norms governing international relations based on the purposes and principles of the UN Charter. China has always championed the principle of Africans solving African issues in their own ways, and firmly supports an increase in the representation and participation of African countries in the international governance system. China supports making special arrangements for the U.N. Security Council reform to meet Africa's aspiration as a priority.

"A good example" is reflected in the deepening traditional friendship. China and Sierra Leone have enjoyed a long history of profound friendship and have lent a helping hand to each other whenever in need. When the Ebola epidemic broke out in May 2014, China was among the first to provide medical assistance and send groups of public health experts. After the outbreak of the COVID-19 epidemic in 2020, the Chinese government provided multiple batches of anti-epidemic materials and vaccines to Sierra Leone. A friend in need is a friend indeed. The friendship forged through standing together to overcome difficulties will forever be a precious treasure and an important source of strength for our bilateral relations.

Here, I briefly shared some thoughts on why China-Sierra Leone relations are a good example of China-Africa solidarity and cooperation. I believe that reading this book will contribute to a better understanding of these ties.

After more than half a century of development, our relations have achieved a great deal and shown high-level robustness. As a Chinese saying goes, 'the fire burns high when everyone brings wood to it'. It is the loving care and hard work of the national governments, local authorities, friendly organisations, and people from all walks of life in both countries that have made China-Sierra Leone relations flourish. Let me extend high tribute and express my heartfelt gratitude to all who have dedicated themselves to the cause of China-Sierra Leone friendship. It is hoped that people in both countries will continue to take active and vigorous steps in contributing to our relations.

Today, China-Sierra Leone relations are at a crucial point where we can build on our past achievements and open up a new future. In the face of complex challenges in the world, China-Sierra Leone relations have gained further strategic significance and present important opportunities for further development. We must align and synergize in our development strategies in order to expand shared interests in delivering greater benefits to our peoples. We need to deepen exchanges and mutual learning to cement the foundation for people-to-people affinity and strengthen the bonds between our citizens. We also need to reinforce solidarity, coordinate to address global challenges together, and jointly build a community with a shared future for humanity. Standing at a new historical perspective, let us unite while sticking to our original aspirations, to continuously enrich the substance of China-Sierra Leone comprehensive strategic cooperative partnership, and create a better future for China-Sierra Leone relations.

Ambassador Extraordinary and Plenipotentiary of the People's Republic of China to the Republic of Sierra Leone
WANG Qing. 29th July 2024.

Introduction

50 Years of China-Sierra Leone Relations

David J. Francis

The primary objective of this book is to document the 53 years of China-Sierra Leone relations and, in particular, to commemorate the 50th anniversary of the excellent bilateral partnership between the two countries, within the geopolitical framework of South-South cooperation at bilateral and multilateral levels.

To mark the 50th Anniversary/Golden Jubilee of the China-Sierra Leone engagements and the establishment of diplomatic relations on 29th July 2021, the President of China, Xi Jinping, of the Government of the People's Republic of China, and the President of Sierra Leone, Julius Maada Bio, held a long telephone conversation on strengthening bilateral relations between the two countries. The question is, why would a major world leader like President Xi Jinping, in charge of one of the most powerful and influential countries in the world, even make the valuable time to hold a telephone engagement with a rather small, poor, and relatively insignificant country in world affairs such as Sierra Leone? Why is China, a developed and advanced First World economy that still modestly describes itself as a 'Developing Country', with a GDP of USD 17.96 trillion and population of 1.4 billion, interested in a small country like Sierra Leone with a GDP of USD 4 billion and population of 7.8 million? Though China is one of the most important bilateral partners of Sierra Leone, with significant development cooperation assistance and infrastructural projects implemented across the country through the China Aid programme, not much is known as to why and how Sierra Leone is important or became important to China in the geopolitical and geoeconomics context, and in the process, has emerged as a model partnership of China-Africa relations and cooperation.

This book, outlined in 13 chapters, critically examines the history, nature, scope, trajectory, and key players in terms of the structure-agency debate, the context and complexity of bilateral and multilateral diplomacy, and the overall impact of Sino-Sierra Leone relations on both countries. Chapter 1 critically outlines the context and debates of the Sierra Leone-China win-win diplomacy and relations within the broader context of the Sino-Africa engagements. In Chapter 2, Joe A.D. Alie, examines the evolution and history of the China-Sierra Leone engagements. Abraham John in Chapter 3 outlines the diversity and importance of the political, economic, and development engagements between China and Sierra Leone since establishing diplomatic relations. In Chapter 4, Sahr Jusu assesses the broad and specific nature and scope of China's development and financial assistance to Sierra Leone. Lansana Gberie, in Chapter 5, evaluates the relevance of the China-Sierra Leone multilateral diplomacy within the context of cooperation at the United Nations Human Rights Council. Edward Hinga Sandy in Chapter 6 examines how the Chinese Government's Belt and Road Initiative and infrastructure diplomacy have contributed to infrastructural development, trade, and investment in Sierra Leone. In Chapter 7, Mohamed Combo Kamanda critically outlines the importance of the Chinese Scholarship programme to the educational development of Sierra Leone and how China uses Education Grants to exercise 'soft power'. Aiah Gbakima in Chapter 8 focuses on the diverse and important contributions of China's health and medical contributions at the national level in Sierra Leone, especially during the period of the Ebola epidemic and the COVID-19 global pandemic. Memunatu Pratt in Chapter 9 evaluates the evolution of the people-to-people China-Sierra Leone engagements within the context of the Friendship Society, the establishment of the Confucius Institute, and the broader cultural diplomacy between the two countries. Isatu Jabbie Kabbah, in Chapter 10, draws from the historic Beijing Conference on Women Development in 1995 to illustrate China's contribution to women's empowerment in Sierra Leone. In Chapter 11, Saffa Abdulia examines the role, contribution, and impact of China on youth and sports development and empowerment in Sierra Leone. Mohamed Abuja Sherriff in Chapter 12 assesses how China's food/rice aid and agriculture capacity building have contributed to poverty alleviation in Sierra Leone. Xu Wei, in Chapter 13, reviews the history and current situation of Chinese immigrants in Sierra Leone.

The book project was developed out of the partnership with the Institute of African Studies at Zhejiang Normal University in China, supported by the African Directorate of the Ministry of Foreign Affairs of the Government of the People's Republic of China in Beijing. The African Studies Institute is the premier African studies centre of excellence in China, and as principal editor, I am delighted that the leadership of the African Studies Institute, Professor Lui Hongwu, and his team supported this book project. Sierra Leone becomes the second country in Africa, the first being Nigeria, to document and publish a book project commemorating 50 years of bilateral relations.

The unique feature of this book project is that it is the first academic and policy-practice publication, documenting the evolution, nature, dynamics, and complexities of Sino-Sierra Leone relations framed within the Win-Win Diplomacy. Two-thirds of the chapter contributors have visited China, and an additional three contributors have studied in China as well as served in the Government of Sierra Leone. In effect, the contributors have sound, credible, and first-hand experience of China-Sierra Leone relations as well as the broader Sino-Africa engagements. As principal editor, I have developed strong, in-depth, and credible relations with the government of the People's Republic of China based on political trust. In my capacity as the former Chief Minister of the Government of Sierra Leone between June 2018 and April 2021 and former Foreign Minister of Sierra Leone between April 2021 and July 2023, I visited China on several occasions and held high-level meetings with senior government officials in China. I have attended two Forum on African–China Cooperation (FOCAC) summits and held several high-level meetings with the Foreign Ministers of the Government of China. As a Visiting Senior Research Professor at the African Studies Institute at Zhejiang Normal University in China, I have developed strong academic and research collaborative network partnerships with premier Chinese universities, research centres and policy-relevant think tanks. I am therefore well placed, with the academic, research, and policy-practice knowledge to lead on and edit this seminal book project, documenting 50 years of Sierra Leone-China relations.

This book was published by *Adonis & Abbey Publishers Ltd., London,* and launched in Sierra Leone at the Chinese Embassy on 1st October 2024 as part of the commemoration of the 53rd-anniversary celebration of China-Sierra Leone diplomatic relations and the National Day of the People's Republic of China. Let me commend the leadership and vision of the Directorate of African Affairs, H.E. Wu Peng, at the Ministry of Foreign Affairs in Beijing, and H.E. Wang Qing, the Ambassador of the People's Republic of China to Sierra Leone, for their committed support for this book project.

CHAPTER ONE

China – Sierra Leone Win-Win Diplomacy: context & debates on Sino – Africa Engagements

David J. Francis

Introduction

On 29th July 1971, Sierra Leone formally established diplomatic relations with the government of the People's Republic of China. To mark the 50th anniversary of the cordial, trusted, mutually respectful, strong, and win-win partnership between China and Sierra Leone, the two leaders of both countries, President Julius Maada Bio and President Xi Jinping, held a telephone conversation on 29th July 2021, to consolidate the mutually beneficial bilateral, multilateral, and international cooperation between both countries. On this momentous occasion, President Xi Jinping stated that "despite changes in the international landscape, our two countries have always rendered each other understanding and support on issues involving each other's core interests and major concerns. Our cooperation in the economic field has yielded fruitful results. In the face of stern challenges posed by COVID-19, our peoples have stood with each other in pandemic response, demonstrating our brotherly bond, one that has seen us through thick and thin". On this 50th anniversary occasion, the Ambassador to Sierra Leone, Hu Zhangliang, stated that "50 years ago, our great leaders and forefathers, late Chairman Mao Zedong and late President Siaka Stevens, made the historic decision to establish ties between China and Sierra Leone. . . . Our two sides have not only deepened bilateral cooperation but also cooperated in appropriately addressing international and regional issues . . . . 50 years down the path, China-Sierra Leone friendship is full of vitality, presenting a flourishing and thriving scene. . . .China has never attached any political strings to its aid in Sierra Leone". President Bio, on his part, in commending the impressive gains of the 50 years of Sino-Sierra Leone relations, aptly stated that the immense contributions of China to the national development of Sierra Leone were evident in every sector of the country, including infrastructure, agriculture, mines, health, tourism, commerce and trade, sports, and education.

The historic Golden Jubilee was observed by both countries with week-long, high-level events in the capitals of both countries, including receptions and cultural celebrations in Beijing and Freetown, which started on 29th July 2021. The two heads of state, President Xi and President Bio, as well as the two foreign ministers, Wang Yi of China and David J. Francis of Sierra Leone, had already exchanged diplomatic letters of congratulations.

Since establishing the first diplomatic relations with Africa in 1956 with Egypt, Sierra Leone is one of the 52 African countries that have established diplomatic relations with China. In effect, Sierra Leone's diplomatic relations and international cooperation are part and parcel of the broader Sino-Africa engagements, dating back to ancient, modern, and contemporary times. By all indications, the Sino-Sierra Leone relation is very important to the broader China-Africa decades of engagement. It is important to state that the evolution of the China-Sierra Leone relations is situated within the broader context of the Sino-Africa engagements. Chairman Mao Zedong's concept of 'intermediate zones' in 1964, the five fundamental principles of China's foreign policy, the era of Modernisation with Chinese characteristics and the perception of Africa as a 'pivoting point' in China's relations with the rest of the external world, all provided the theoretical and policy-practice framework for Sino-Africa relations. These principles underpinned the foreign policy approach of the People's Republic of China to support decolonisation, self-determination, political independence, and liberation struggles to end the scourge of colonialism and imperialism in Africa. As this chapter will critically illustrate, the history and political economy of Sino-Sierra Leone relations are embedded in the common commitment to multilateralism and Third World solidarity as manifested by both countries' memberships and active participation in the South-South Cooperation Group, Non-Aligned Movement (NAM), Group of 77, and the commitment to a rule-based approach to world order, international peace, and security, as well as the post-Cold War Global South common solidarity. Additionally, it is important to stress, from the onset, that the evolution of the Sierra Leone-China relations in the

1970s emerged against the background of the struggle for decolonisation across Africa; the Cold War politics of conflict and confrontation between the Capitalist West and the Communist/Socialist East; the continuation of the scramble for access to Africa's vast strategic mineral resources and spheres of geopolitical interest in the superpower Cold War rivalry, which invariably converted Sierra Leone and Africa into mere tools and pawns in the hostile international politics of the Cold War. Far from being a mere object or pawn in its emerging relations with China, Sierra Leone shrewdly crafted its foreign policy practice that focused on the pursuit of strategic national interests in terms of benefits and 'win-win' relations.

Evolution of China-Africa Engagements

The China-Sierra Leone relation is part of the broader Sino-African engagements over the centuries and recent decades. To be clear, China has a very long history of engagement and relations with Africa. There are three distinct phases of the Sino-Africa relations. The first phase dates back to the ancient period. As far back as the imperial Han Dynasty (202 BC–9 AD, 25–220 AD), some 2,000 years ago, China established contact and indirect trade engagements with Africa. Historical records state that the first Africans to China were Acrobats from Egypt in 112 BC and the first Chinese to Africa was the legendary travel writer, Du Huan, in the mid-8th century, but direct official contact between China and Africa was only established during the Yuan Dynasty (between 1279–1368 AD)[1]. China-Africa trading relations increased during this period, in particular with the East African coast and Indian Ocean Island territories such as Zanzibar, Madagascar, and Mozambique. The second phase of the historic Sino-Africa engagements covers the modern era, starting with the 15th century. Despite the dominance of the Western colonial powers in the Indian Ocean trade and commercial routes, which significantly

---

[1] Government of China, Ministry of Foreign Affairs, www.mfa.gov.cn.eng

disrupted China-Africa relations, the 18th and 19th centuries saw increasing China labour migration, hired by the Western colonial companies to work in East and Southern Africa. The beginning of the 20th century saw more Sino-Africa engagements with the support from China, for African national liberation movements fighting to bring an end to colonial rule. The third phase is contemporary Sino-Africa relations, which effectively commenced with the founding of the new People's Republic of China in 1949. China established its first diplomatic relations in 1956 with Egypt and marked the beginning of increasing diplomatic and friendly relations with countries in Africa, especially the support for the political and economic liberation of African countries from Western colonialism and imperialism. It has been difficult to unearth historical evidence of Sino-Sierra Leone engagements dating back to the ancient and modern eras. Sierra Leone-China engagements started in the era of contemporary China-Africa relations.

The 21st century has seen remarkable progress in the relevance, development, and consolidation of the historic Sino-Africa relations and engagements. Some key highlights in Sino-Africa relations within the context of the new People's Republic of China include the deployment of the first Chinese Medical Team to Algeria in 1962, followed by the visit in 1964 of Premier Zhou Enlai to Africa and announced the 'Eight Principles' of China's Foreign Aid to Africa. In 1971, 26 African countries co-sponsored the United Nations General Assembly (UNGA) Resolution 2758, which adopted the restoration of China's legitimate seat at the United Nations and Security Council, and led to the famous statement by Chairman Mao Zedong that "It was our African friends that took us back to the United Nations". In 1974, Chairman Moa Zedong visited Zambia in southern Africa and announced the 'Three Worlds Theory', stating that "in my view, the United States and the Soviet Union belong to the First World. The in-between Japan, Europe, and Canada belong to the Second World. The Third World is very populous. . . . Asia belongs to the Third World. So does the whole of Africa and Latin America".[2] The first of China's

---

[2]Ministry of Foreign Affairs of the People's Republic of China, "Chairman Mao Zedong's Theory of the Division of the Three World and the Strategy for Forming an Alliance Against an Opponent" www.fmprc.gov.cn

infrastructure diplomacy and construction projects was opened in 1976: the Tan-Zam/TAZARA Railway and Friendship Road to Freedom that linked Tanzania and Zambia, two major post-independence socialist countries in Africa at that time. In 1996, President Jiang Zemin was the first Chinese leader to deliver a keynote address at the Organisation of African Unity (OAU), now African Union (AU).[3] Other major Sino-Africa developments include the Forum on China-Africa Cooperation (FOCAC), established in 2000 as a major platform for Sino-Africa political, diplomatic, economic, development, and security dialogue and an instrument of Chinese Foreign Policy engagement with Africa. The FOCAC Summit between African Heads of State and the President of China has been held every two years in China and Africa. The FOCAC Summit has, over the years, established strategic partnerships for 'win-win' cooperation based on political equality, mutual respect, and trust. Furthermore, the China-Africa Policy announced in 2006 served as the framework for the overall policies, objectives and principles for the China-Africa partnership. In 2008, China funded the construction of the new African Union Headquarters and Conference Centre in Addis Ababa, Ethiopia. The FOCAC Sharm el-Sheikh (Egypt) Action Plan in 2009 and the Chinese Government's 'New Eight Measures' became the major policy framework and principles guiding the Sino-Africa engagements in the 21st century. An important development is the announcement of the Belt and Road Initiative (BRI) by President Xi Jinping in 2013 and the invitation of African countries to participate in this major infrastructural diplomatic initiative.[4] In 2021, President Xi announced the following global initiatives and encouraged Africa to fully participate, such as the Global Development Initiative (GDI); of which Sierra Leone is a founding member; the Global Security Initiative (GSI); and the Global Civilisation Initiative (GCI)[5].

---

[3] Africa Union, https://au.int.Speeches
[4] Ministry of Foreign Affairs, China, "Declaration on Sharm El Sheikh of the Forum on China-Africa Cooperation, 12-11-2009 www.focac.org/eng/zywx
[5] Ministry of Foreign Affairs, www.mfa.gov.cn.eng

The China-aided infrastructure projects across Africa include the construction of sports arenas/stadiums, hospitals and clinics, schools, roads, seaports, railways, electricity power transmission and distribution/hydropower electric power plants, telecommunication Backbone networks, and Agricultural Projects. China has built more than 100 major sports arenas and stadiums across Africa as part of its infrastructural diplomacy. Sierra Leone is a primary beneficiary, as the country was one of the first African countries where China donated and constructed a Stadium, the Siaka Stevens National Stadium, to exercise its soft power influence and leverage in Africa. In March 2024, Kenyan and Tanzanian governments contracted Chinese companies to build a 30,000-seat stadium in Arusha, Tanzania, and a 60,000-seat stadium in Nairobi, Kenya, as part of the two countries' preparations to host the African Nations Cup Tournament (AfCON) in 2027.

China's new win-win outcomes diplomacy in bilateral relations and the tangible benefits in the form of major infrastructure projects constructed across Africa have significantly contributed to changing the negative and stereotypical perception about 'China in Africa', i.e., that Chinese investments are simply about access to and exploitation of Africa's natural resources and strategic minerals. Guided by the Chinese traditional proverb, 'If you want to get rich, build roads', the Chinese BRI and its infrastructure diplomacy have become a popular programme for African governments. In the process, it presents the superficially alluring impression in Africa and Sierra Leone that it is now the panacea, if not the magic wane, to solve all the economic growth and infrastructural development challenges the continent faces.

Even so, the new Sino-Africa cooperation includes areas such as tourism, culture, civil aviation, technology, and finance. Over the decades, we have seen increasing cultural, youth, and academic exchanges and research cooperation among Afro-Chinese think tanks, including the establishment of 61 Confucius Institutes in 46 African countries[6]. The people-to-people exchange regarding the Afro-Chinese engagements has increased exponentially, with an estimated one

---

[6] P. Jakhar, "Confucius Institutes: the growth of China's controversial cultural branch" www.bbc.co,uk, 7th September 2019, Ministry of Foreign Affairs, www.mfa.gov.cn.eng

million Chinese citizens residing in Africa and two million Africans living or working in China.

The Sino-Africa relations have also led to significant cooperation in peace and security. China has emerged as one of the most critical contributors to UN peacekeeping deployment in Africa among the United Nations Security Council (UNSC) 5 Permanent Members[7]. China has participated in UN peacekeeping deployments in Africa and joint naval military training and deployment operations in the Gulf of Aden and Somalia[8]. The Government of China has a dedicated Special Representative for Africa Affairs. The Chinese government's peace and security cooperation has significantly contributed to material, technical aid, and logistics in Africa in support of African peacekeeping and peace support operations. Currently, there are more than 30,000 Chinese peacekeeping forces deployed as 'Envoys of Peace' in 17 UN peacekeeping missions[9].

Regarding economics and trade, China is Africa's largest trading partner. China – Africa trade volume increased from USD 10 billion in 2000 to USD 282 billion in 2023. To appreciate the economic and financial scale, and the trading relations between China and Africa, 10 African countries are in the Top 20 countries indebted to China, including Angola (USD 21 billion), Ethiopia (USD 6.8 billion), and Kenya (USD 6.7 billion).[10] This has raised critical comments, especially in the Western media, of the so-called 'China Debt Burden' and 'China Debt Trap'. We now see what I call 'debt-mongering', not 'war-mongering' in Africa, by the West and its global financial institutions such as the World Bank and IMF. The criticism is that China's Belt and Road Initiative, for example, according to the World Bank and IMF, is creating a debt trap and burden for African countries that end up mortgaging their natural resources to China. However, this debt-mongering by Western governments and their IFIs is hypocritical,

---

[7] UN DPKO, http://peacekeeping.un.org

[8] Ibid

[9] Ibid

[10]Marcus Lu, (2024), 'Ranked: The Top 20 Countries in Debt to China', www.visualcapitalist.com/ranked 29th April

because it is a poor attempt by the West to scare off African countries from the China BRI infrastructure projects that Africa desperately needs for its development. What we know and the data and evidence available in the public domain is that two-thirds of the USD 1.8 trillion debt owed by Africa is mainly to the West and its IFIs, the IMF, and the World Bank[11]. Interestingly, we do not see much criticism of how the West and its IFIs have plundered Africa and kept it a highly indebted poor continent despite its abundant natural resources.

Chinese Modernisation & Fundamental Principles of Foreign Policy Approach: Impact on Sino-Sierra Leone Relations

The China-Sierra Leone relation is conducted within the context and framework of the broader Sino-Africa engagements and foreign policy approach. Five main fundamental principles of foreign policy guide China's interaction and engagements with Sierra Leone and the rest of the world, and they include: i. respect for political sovereignty and territorial integrity, with the 'One-China' principle at the core of this foreign policy approach; ii. friendly state relations and non-aggression in relation to other states; iii. non-interference in the domestic and internal affairs of member states; iv. respect for sovereign equality and mutual benefits in all relations; v. promote peaceful coexistence and shared values of humanity for peace, development, fairness, justice, democracy, and freedoms[12]. The focus of China's foreign policy is similar to that of Sierra Leone's objectives. The 1991 Constitution of Sierra Leone, Section 10, outlines the four critical foreign policy priorities, which include: i. the promotion and protection of national interests; ii. Pan-African Unity and Cooperation by promoting sub-regional, regional and inter-African cooperation and unity; iii. International Peace and Security through the promotion of international cooperation to consolidate international peace, security, mutual respect among all nations, and respect for territorial integrity and independence; iv. Rule-based international order is achieved

---

[11] Afriximbank, "State of Play of Debt Burden in Africa 2024: Debt Dynamics & Mounting Vulnerability' www.media.afriximbank.com

[12] Ministry of Foreign Affairs, www.mfa.gov.cn.eng

through respect for international law and treaty obligations, and respect for peaceful settlement and resolution of international disputes through negotiation, conciliation, arbitration, or adjudication. Based on the above, both countries have a similar focus on the foreign policy approach and the principles that guide the conduct of international relations and cooperation. It is therefore not surprising that the communiqué on the establishment of diplomatic relations between China and Sierra Leone on 29th July 1971 states:

> The Government of the People's Republic of China and the Government of the Republic of Sierra Leone, in accordance with the interests and wishes of the people of the two countries, decide to establish diplomatic relations at the ambassadorial levels as of today. The Chinese government and people firmly support the government and people of the Republic of Sierra Leone in their struggle against imperialism, colonialism, and neo-colonialism and in their efforts to safeguard national independence and state sovereignty. The Government of Sierra Leone recognises the Government of the People's Republic of China as the sole legitimate government representing the entire China. The two governments agree to establish diplomatic relations, friendship, and cooperation between the two countries on the basis of the principles of mutual respect for sovereignty and territorial integrity, mutual non-aggression, non-interference in each other's internal affairs, equality and mutual benefit, and peaceful coexistence.[13]

This communiqué established the core principles that have framed and guided the evolution of the Sino-Sierra Leone relations.

To critically understand the evolution of the China-Sierra Leone foreign policy and international cooperation engagements, we must review the history of the broader Sino-Africa relations and China's contemporary modernisation efforts over the decades. It is important to note that Sierra Leone established diplomatic relations with China during the era of Chairman Mao Zedong, who had launched a Cultural Revolution to transform China into a modern industrial power based

---

[13] Government of China, Ministry of Foreign Affairs, Beijing, Website

on anti-imperialist, anti-capitalist political, ideological, and economic development policies. This was followed by some measure of political reforms, the opening up of the Chinese economy and rapid development, economic liberalisation and then the gradual opening of its economy and domestic markets. On the part of Sierra Leone and at the time of establishing diplomatic relations with China, in 1971, President Siaka Stevens, against the background of the 1967/68 political turmoil and military coups in the country, introduced a Presidential Republic, declaring himself as President of the Republic, thereby abolishing the post-colonial British Parliamentary Republic. This in turn paved the way for President Stevens to introduce the 1978 Constitution that established a one-party state governed by the All Peoples Congress (APC) party and based on socialist political and ideological principles. During this period, Stevens presented himself and the APC One-Party government, now very similar to the Chinese Socialist Party, as an 'anti-capitalist' socialist administration. This astute diplomatic maneuvre on the part of Stevens further cemented the political and ideological affinities and friendship between Communist China and so-called socialist Sierra Leone. Sierra Leone became China's important ally, receiving ample development assistance, aid, and major infrastructural projects such as the Siaka Stevens National Stadium and the Youyi Ministerial Building Complex. It is clear that the 1970s and 1980s witnessed significant but modest development assistance from China to Sierra Leone because China was still a developing country and could not afford to grant aid away from its own domestic development and poverty eradication needs at home. The civil war in Sierra Leone between 1991 and 2001 led to the freezing of significant political engagements between China and Sierra Leone, except for the visit of the military regime Chairman and Head of State, Capt. Valentine Strasser, in 1994. China only renewed its partnership and politico-economic engagements after the formal end of the civil war when Beijing resumed diplomatic relations in 2003. The visit of the Sierra Leone Foreign Minister, Momodu Koroma, to Beijing for high-level talks with his counterpart Foreign Minister, Li Zhaoxing, led to renewed political, diplomatic, trade, economic, and development relations between both countries.

Today, Sino-Sierra Leone engagement has emerged as a successful model of China-Africa relations. During the State Visit of President

Bio to China, President Xi Jinping stated on 28th February 2024 that the China-Sierra Leone relations were a good example and a model of China-Africa solidarity and cooperation; "China has always regarded solidarity and cooperation with African countries as an important cornerstone of our foreign policy".[14] President Xi commended the historic friendship and strong bilateral relations between both countries and the mutual political trust and support for China's core national interests at multilateral levels, including the UNGA and UNSC, and invited Sierra Leone to participate in the new China-led global initiatives such as the Global Development Initiative, the Global Security Initiative and the Global Civilisation Initiative. President Xi further underscored the importance of high-level mutual political trust and mutually beneficial cooperation in international and regional affairs to safeguard peace, security, and developmental interests, and to advance amicable bilateral relations. President Xi committed to provide assistance to support Sierra Leone's development in infrastructure construction, agriculture, human resources, and investment in the business sector. President Bio, for his part, praised China as a trustworthy and reliable friend, partner, and ally that has consistently supported the development aspirations of Sierra Leone and, as such, Sierra Leone will always support China's strategic interests, in particular the 'One China' principle.

To underscore the importance of the history and evolution of the firm and cordial relations between China and Sierra Leone, we have to look at the high-level visits between both countries. Significant high-level visits have taken place, and almost all Presidents of Sierra Leone have visited China, starting with Siaka Stevens (four times in 1968, 1973, 1981, and 1985); Joseph Saidu Momoh (1986 and 1990); Capt. Valentine Melvin Strasser in October 1994; Ahmad Tejan Kabbah in May/June 1999; Ernest Bai Koroma (twice in 2008 and 2017); and Julius Maada Bio (twice in 2018 and 2024). These high-level visits to China include visits of Sierra Leonean officials, including Vice Presidents, Speakers of Parliament, and Foreign Ministers. On the part

---

[14] Xinhuanet, 'Xi holds talks with Sierra Leonean President' Huaxia, 2024.02.28 22:31:30

of China, the high-level visits to Sierra Leone included Chinese leaders such as Vice Chairmen, Vice Premier, Vice President, and Foreign Minister Wang Yi in 2015.

What does this overview say about Chinese modernisation in the context of the broader Afro-Chinese relations? The 20th National Congress of the Communist Party of China and its 20th Party Congress Report of October 2022 articulated the new Chinese modernisation framework for the government and the People's Republic of China. The critical elements of the new era of modernisation include:

i. Sets the blueprint to understand the future direction of China's politics, economy, geopolitics, and diplomacy. Essentially, it is the policy framework to position and understand China's future development path

ii. Outlines China's pathway to address the critical and multifaceted global problems and challenges

iii. Framework for building a new pattern of global partnership based on a multi-polar world order in that Chinese modernisation advances and promotes a new international system based on the multi-polar world order

iv. Sets out how Chinese modernisation complements and reinforces globalisation with Chinese characteristics

v. Presents Chinese modernisation framed as 'Security-Development-Peace' nexus

vi. Chinese modernisation that supports climate change mitigation and environmental protection

vii. Chinese modernisation based on Chinese characteristics and international relevance.

The above outline points to the three core dimensions of the new Chinese modernisation model: common prosperity, sound ecology, and peaceful development. Conceptually, the new Chinese modernisation strategic policy framework provides a lens through which China views and interacts with Sierra Leone, Africa, and the rest of the world based on cooperation rather than conflict or confrontation, based on amity and partnership rather than hostile competition. In effect, the new Chinese modernisation model challenges the dominant post-Second World War Western-centric international system and the post-Cold War Unipolar world order dominated and policed by the West. Implicit in this new development paradigm is a Chinese counter-hegemonic discourse and challenge to the Western geopolitical international system and the capitalist neo-liberal development model. The 20th Party Congress Report clearly states that "Chinese Modernisation offers humanity a new choice for achieving modernisation. The Communist Party of China and the Communist People have provided humanity with more Chinese insight, better input, and greater Chinese strength to help solve its common challenges and have made new and greater contributions to the noble cause of human peace and development"[15]. Based on this new Chinese political development model, China is offering itself as a clear alternative to the Western neo-liberal development model, and strategically positions itself to lead on the construction of a Community of Humanity with a shared future for global human security, peace, and development. Within this framework, China offers a 'path of peaceful development' that focuses on cooperation and partnership based on mutual 'win-win' engagements rather than conflict, confrontation, and hostile competition[16].

The new Chinese modernisation emanates from China's intrinsic understanding of its particular and context-specific history and development, and appreciation that the pathway to self-development is in recognising that there is 'No Development without Peace'[17]. So, for China, peace and development are two sides of the same coin. As such, the 'Peace-Security-Development' nexus has framed the understanding of China's interactions with Sierra Leone, Africa, and the rest of the world. This 'peace-security-development' nexus had become a significant anchor of China's foreign policy in maintaining world peace and promoting joint development. In essence, the new Chinese modernisation model originates from the age-old civilisational

---

[15] Ministry of Foreign Affairs of the People's Republic of China, The 20th national Congress of the Communist Party of China (CPC) on 22nd October 2022 approved the Report presented by Xi Jinping on behalf of the 19th CPC Central Committee
[16] Ibid
[17] Ibid

principle that if countries, peoples, societies, and communities strive to achieve common values of humanity, pursue common public goals and policies, strive to live in peace and harmony, and cooperate for win-win results, then humanity is guaranteed to enjoy sustainable security, development, and prosperity. This Chinese civilisational approach and practice is akin to the African proverb that says, "The elephant is too big for one person to eat", meaning cooperation, sharing for the common good, partnership, and win-win outcomes are far better than hostile competition, conflict, confrontation, and pursuit of parochial national interests.

The new Chinese modernisation frames China's diplomacy as focusing on promoting an independent, peaceful, open, green, and common development. Importantly, this new development model will learn from and embrace the positive achievements of other civilisations and, in the process, add to the choices for human development and progress, thereby creating a new form of human civilisation. Sceptical Western audiences and international media, often very critical of 'anything Chinese' and relatively intolerant of other non-Western values and civilisations, will outrightly dismiss the new Chinese modernisation model as mere propaganda without making the effort to constructively engage with what this new development paradigm is offering the world, a world faced by multiple and complex challenges. In the words of the 20th Party Congress Report, "China adheres to the Five Principles of peaceful coexistence in pursuing friendship and cooperation with other countries. It is committed to promoting a new kind of international relations, deepening and expanding global partnerships based on equality, openness, and cooperation, and broadening the convergence of interests with other countries"[18]. The Chinese government argues that its new modernisation model is not a framework to dominate and replace the dominant Western-centric international system, and hence, China advocates for multipolar world order and seeks to reform the existing Western hegemonic world order that is no longer capable of addressing and responding to the diverse, complex global problems and challenges. The 20th Party Congress

---

[18]Ministry of Foreign Affairs of the People's Republic of China, The 20th national Congress of the Communist Party of China (CPC) on 22nd October 2022 approved the Report presented by Xi Jinping on behalf of the 19th CPC Central Committee

Report states that "China plays an active part in the reform and development of the global governance system. It pursues a vision of global governance featuring shared growth through discussion and collaboration. China upholds true multilateralism, promotes greater democracy in international relations, and works to make global governance fairer and more equitable".[19]

Context of China's Emerging Global Leadership and Implications for Sino-Sierra Leone/Africa Relations

The Sino-Sierra Leone and Africa relations have emerged against the background of the emerging global leadership of China in the Global South. In fact, Sierra Leone's bilateral and international cooperation engagement with China is framed as part of China's engagement with the Global South. For a start, both China and Sierra Leone are members of the Global South, i.e., a geopolitical, geo-economic group of countries with ideological affinity that are geographically located in the Southern hemisphere and have been traditionally perceived or labelled in economic and development terms as Developing Countries and Least Developed Countries, that politically exposes anti-colonial, anti-imperial, and anti-hegemonic aspirations. These countries have traditionally belonged to the Non-Aligned Movement (NAM), Group of 77 (G77), South-South Cooperation, and Third World during the Cold War and are predominantly countries from Africa, the Pacific Islands, Asia, Latin America, and the Caribbean. In academic and policy discourse, the term Global South now transcends the narrow and traditional geopolitical conception. The Global South now describes the emerging role in world affairs of these traditionally marginalised and disposed group of countries in the international division of power and the international division of labour.

A demonstrable example is the Brazil, China, India, China, and South Africa (BRICS) geopolitical and geo-economic group led by China. In geoeconomic terms, the Global South is perceived as the collection of emerging economies that have a collective political

---

[19] Ditto

economy voice in world affairs with the capacity and power to influence the international system, in particular, the global financial system, such as the BRICS de-dollarisation agenda as well as the currency swap agreements to enable countries to trade, make international payments, and transact goods and services using local national currencies. By all indications, the Global South operates in geopolitical terms, in opposition to the Global North, led by America and the Western Alliance, which loosely describes the group of countries 'located' in the Northern Hemisphere, i.e., countries that make up 20% of the world's population but preside over 80% of the global wealth.

Understandably, China has modestly described itself as a 'Developing Country', which, by all indications, does not reflect the objective reality of China's growing superpower status on the global stage. Notwithstanding, President Xi stated that "as a member of the developing world and the Global South, China has always stood with other developing countries and firmly upheld their common interests... As a member of the Global South,... Africa should unite and call for raising the discourse and influence of developing countries in international affairs and enhancing the representation and voice of countries from the Global South in global governance".[20] China's emerging leadership of the Global South is borne out of the imperative that the current Unipolar world order dominated by the West and led by the United States is under attack and accused of creating tensions, hostile competition, instigating and fuelling wars and armed conflicts, monopolises global wealth and the international financial institutions, as well as being blamed for double standards in respect for international law, a rule-based world order, climate change, and environmental protection. What is clear is that in the second decade of the 21st century, we live in a fractured and turbulent world as manifested by the COVID-19 pandemic, the global economic depression and financial crises, the Russia-Ukraine war of February 2022 and the Hamas/Palestine-Israel war of October 2023, hostile rivalry between democracy and autocracy, protests of Gen Z, the

---

[20] P.W. NiuHaibin et al, 'The Rise of the Global South and China's Role. SIIS Report, Vol. 31, Nov 2023, p.10

resurgence of Cold War mentality, and confrontations. Across the world, there is growing resentment, especially in the Global South, that the Unipolar world order is no longer capable of policing the multiple global challenges and maintaining international peace and security. The general view is that to address the numerous global crises on a long-term and sustainable basis, we urgently need a new multipolar world order whereby more enormous regional powers can provide credible leadership to help resolve and respond to these multiple international problems and challenges.

Within this context, the Global South is now looking to China to play that leadership role in the emerging multipolar world order. The dominant Western world, understandably, does not take kindly to the emergence of China in the Global South and perceives China as a natural 'hegemonic challenger'. In effect, Global South countries such as Sierra Leone and other African countries will inevitably be caught up in the emerging great power rivalry between the West and China. Irrespective of these challenges, China offers specific distinctive opportunities for the Sino-Sierra Leone and China-Africa engagements. For a start, peaceful development is in China's DNA, which is responsible for China's spectacular rise and transformation from a developing country in just decades to a major contender as a world leader or superpower. Since its founding in 1949, the People's Republic of China has never invaded or gone to war with another country, never colonised or subjected another sovereign or independent country, never intervened in armed conflict in another country, politically interfered in the internal affairs of another country, or effected or orchestrated regime change in another country. Instead, China consistently advocated and promoted peaceful and friendly cooperation with countries based on its five core foreign policy principles. China has invested in global partnerships, which is crucial for its peaceful development.

The Chinese model of development is perceived as a very appealing model of development for Global South countries like Sierra Leone. The conduct of its foreign policy and international cooperation based on mutual respect, trust, and win-win outcomes are fundamental values that are highly appreciated by countries in the Global South.

They account for why most Global South countries prefer to 'do business' with China and their preference for China as an emerging global leader in politics, security, economics, and development. Like most African and Global South countries, Sierra Leone will use China's BRICS, the Belt and Road (BRI) leadership, and membership in the G20/21 and G77, to leverage strategic national interests, benefits, and opportunities. For Sierra Leone, like most of the Global South countries, development is the greatest and most urgent challenge. So, China provides an excellent working model and example of how to do 'development'. Sierra Leone and the rest of Africa understand that in China, development is a top priority for governing and rejuvenating China, and inclusive development is perceived as the 'golden key' to solve and unlock all the problems in the process of Chinese modernisation, hence the focus of the 'peace-security-development' nexus because inclusive and sustainable development guarantees peace and security.[21]

Why is Sierra Leone Important to China?

Sierra Leone, a rather small and relatively insignificant player in world affairs, has become an important friend, partner, and ally of China, a major superpower and the second-largest economy in geopolitical terms, for two reasons. Firstly, for political and diplomatic reasons and secondly, for economic reasons, mainly to access the vast natural resources and strategic mineral resources of Sierra Leone. To be clear, Sierra Leone today is firmly on the global stage and, though a small

---

[21]While serving as Chief Minister of the Government of Sierra Leone and part of the delegation accompanying President Bio at the September 2018 FOCAC Summit in Beijing, during a high-level bilateral meeting between the two presidents, President Xi explained that his government, in the past five years removed, 10 million people from abject poverty and that in the next 10 years, more than 20 million people will be removed from abject poverty. With these figures announced, President Bio suddenly turned and looked at me in astonishment, and both of us slowly shook our heads in utter shock and surprise that 10 million people can be taken out of poverty within five years, realising that Sierra Leone's population is just 7.5 million, more than the total population of Sierra Leone. This encounter and the impressive facts of the spectacular Chinese development, as explained by President Xi, left a lasting impression on me and the inspiration that it can be done!

country in terms of size and population, economically and developmentally classified as the least developed, is today a member of the UN Security Council for 2024/25, a member of the AU Peace and Security Council, a coordinator of the AU Committee of Ten (C-10) for Reform of the UN Security Council, and a member of the UNGA Special Committee on Decolonisation (C24). Under the New Direction administration of President Bio, Sierra Leone has received global acclaim and recognition for its liberal progressive governance policies, such as the abolition of the death penalty in 2021 after 223 years of its introduction under British colonial rule and the allocation of 22 per cent of its gross domestic product (GDP) to education, one of the highest in the world at that time.

How did Sierra Leone emerge as an important friend, partner, and ally of China? It started in 1971 after establishing bilateral diplomatic relations. Sierra Leone, while serving as an elected member of the UN Security Council for the first time in 1971[22] and also then serving as the unofficial leading spokesman for the powerful Third World grouping of G77 at the UNGA, championed the restoration of China's legitimate return to the United Nations and the UN Security Council as one of the Permanent Members (UNSC-P5).[23] As the unofficial spokesman for the G77 at the UNGA, the Sierra Leone Foreign Minister, Solomon A. J. Pratt, presented the main item for the session discussion, Resolution 2758, on the 'Restoration of the legitimate rights of the People's Republic of China' as the lawful representative of China at the United Nations. It is worth noting that the rather absurd political situation was that the United States of America and its Western allies actively supported the UN seat for China to be occupied

---

[22] Sierra Leone returned to the UNSC for the second time, in June 2023, for the tenure 2024/25. As Foreign Minister, I was privileged to lead the campaign and mobilised support for Sierra Leone and secured 188 votes at the UNGA on 6th June 2023.

[23] After the end of the Second World War in 1945, China was officially represented at the UN by the Western-backed breakaway Nationalist territory of Taiwan. With the military success of the People's Republic of China against the national forces led by Gen. Chang Kai Shek and their withdrawal to the island of Taiwan, the PRC Premier Zhou Enlai formally requested a seat in the UNSC in November 1949.

by the breakaway nationalist territory of Taiwan, the 'Free China" territory led by Gen. Chang Kai Shek, and not the mainland China of Peking/Beijing, led by the People's Republic of China under Chairman Mao Zedong. The President of the UNGA session was the Foreign Minister of Indonesia, and the G77 sponsored the motion for the 'Restoration of the legitimate United Nations Rights of Peking Communist China'. This motion was naturally challenged and countered by a counter-motion sponsored by the US and its Western allies to retain 'Free Taiwan, China'. The spokesman for this counter-motion was the US Ambassador and Permanent Representative to the UN, George Bush Sr. (who later became the 41st President of America).

In his autobiography, Solomon A. J. Pratt, the Foreign Minister of the Government of Sierra Leone, aptly described the high drama at the UNGA in mobilising support to restore China's legitimate rights and seat at the UNSC. Foreign Minister Solomon Pratt stated that "the UN debate soon developed almost into a feud between myself and Ambassador George Bush on US/Sino past relationships and policies. The UN debate went unimpeded until two o'clock the following morning. It was clear that our side, the Group of 77, was winning the day. Then Ambassador Bush moved that the session be adjourned. I counter moved that the question be now put, and the voting bells were sounded... As for myself and the Group of 77, we realised that any delay might prove catastrophic to our in-built majority, as we could not be sure about the length to which America would go during such a brief interval to intimidate some of our members... President Malik (Foreign Minister of Indonesia and President of the UNGA Session) now had no option but to put the motion by the Group of 77 that the legitimate rights of Peking China be restored without any further debate. The voting bells were again sounded.... the results of the voting were declared; we, the Group of 77, with majority members, had won, and Communist China had been admitted to her rightful place in the United Nations family of nations."[24]

---

[24]Solomon A. J. Pratt, (2010), Jolliboy: an Autobiography: From Street Starch Hawker to United Nations Debate Champion, Prince HywBull Publishers, North Carolina, p. 220-221

On 25 October 1971, the UNGA overwhelmingly adopted Resolution 2758 on the restoration of the lawful rights of the People's Republic of China in the United Nations. 'recognising that the representatives of the Government of the People's Republic of China are the only lawful representatives of China to the United Nations'. Sierra Leone was one of the 26 African countries that sponsored Resolution 2758. The UN Resolution 2758 firmly laid the fundamental principle of the 'One China' policy in international relations practice in that the resolution recognised and legitimised the People's Republic of China as the 'sole', legitimate, and lawful representative of the whole of China at the United Nations and UNSC.

Under the astute leadership and the skillful diplomatic maneuvering of the Foreign Minister of Sierra Leone, China secured the restoration of its legitimate rights in the UN family of nations. Foreign Minister Pratt modestly stated that "Beijing, China was obviously satisfied with the role Sierra Leone had played in helping to restore her rights in the UN, and we received an official invitation to visit that great country. I was still Foreign Minister, and I had many audiences with the Chinese Premier, Chou En Lai".[25] The people of China and successive governments of China have never forgotten the critical role that Sierra Leone played in restoring China's legitimate right at the UN and seat at the UNSC. This singular diplomatic feat, achieved by Sierra Leone for China, led to developing a long-standing political trust and catapulted small Sierra Leone into a significant player in China's geopolitics and Sino-Africa relations.

During the first State Visit of President Siaka Stevens to China in November 1973, he stated: "China and the great Chinese people are not strangers to me since I visited this great republic about a decade ago… We are indeed happy to have been one of the sponsors of the United Nations resolution to restore to the people of the People's Republic of China her rightful place in the world community of nations, and today we are proud… as we have this giant of Asia participating in the difficult process of restoring peace and tranquillity

---

[25]Ibid, p.20

in the troubled world".[26]   The Chinese Premier, Chau En Lai, stated during the State Visit of President Stevens that "His Excellency President Siaka Stevens is an old friend with whom we are well acquainted... He previously visited China in 1963 and made positive contributions to the enhancement of friendship between the peoples of China and Sierra Leone... I would like to take this opportunity to express our heartfelt thanks to the Government of Sierra Leone for supporting the restoration of China's legitimate rights in the United Nations". [27]

In justifying the reasons for firmly supporting United Nations Resolution 2758 on the restoration of China's legitimate rights at the United Nations family of nations, President Stevens unequivocally stated, "It is all very well for people in the West to say 'I'm a Communist' or 'I'm a Liberal', but in the Third World, we cannot afford that sort of luxury. We cannot sit in book-lined rooms and discuss with our friends whether Marx was right or wrong or whether Keynes's theories were of any practical use. We must roll up our sleeves and get down to the matter of raising living standards in Sierra Leone... For this reason, Sierra Leone pursued a policy of Non-Alignment. This sets us free from being pawns of one of the superpowers and allows us to voice our own individual opinion on world events... Sierra Leone earned a reputation for generating mature and sensible viewpoints and the voice of my country is a respected one in world affairs. It has always been a matter of great pride to me that my government was one of the first to recognise and establish diplomatic relations with the People's Republic of China... In turn, my government affirmed its recognition of the Government of the People's Republic of China as the sole legal government representing the entire Chinese people. It is difficult to realise now the courage that this decision demanded. The person who makes the first move, particularly when those around him are against it, must be brave. But my government and I thought that this was the right decision; we took

---

[26]'Chairman Mao meets President Stevens' Peking Review, Vol. 16, No. 46, 16 November 1973, p.9
[27] Ibid, p. 8-9

it, and we turned, out to be right".[28] Since this historic decision, Sierra Leone has emerged a vocal, trusted and committed supporter of the China 'One Country' principle, thereby making Since this historic decision, Sierra Leone has emerged as a vocal, trusted, and committed supporter of the China 'One Country' principle, thereby making Sierra Leone one of China's key bilateral trusted partners in Africa despite the country's size and politico-diplomatic relevance in world affairs.

The second reason why Sierra Leone is important to China is because the country creates the opportunity for China to access its abundant natural resources, strategic minerals, and access to its market. Evidently, Sierra Leone's importance to China is not for altruistic reasons. China knows that Sierra Leone is one of the most mineral-rich countries in Africa. Sierra Leone has vast and largely untapped natural resources and strategic mineral resources, with 24 known minerals, including diamond, gold, iron ore, rutile, bauxite, limonite, platinum, chromite, coltan, tantalite, columbite, zircon, real earth metals, and petroleum potential. Sierra Leone has one of the largest iron ore reserves in the world, with an estimated reserve of 12.8 billion tonnes of ore grading 64% iron metal. In perspective, China purchases more than 70% of its global seaborne iron ore volumes, with an estimated 294.34 million mt in the first three months of 2023 alone. China largely depends for its access to iron ore on imports from the following countries: Australia ($72.5 billion), Brazil ($18.2. billion), Canada ($1.67 billion), Peru ($1.47 billion), and South Africa ($1.36 billion)[29]. Therefore, Sierra Leone provides China access to a new and colossal iron ore deposit and de-risks its dependence on iron ore imports from Australia and Brazil, where China imports 80% of its iron ore.

In addition, Sierra Leone's strategic ports and harbours provide critical logistic networks and trade, commerce, and maritime gateways for China to Latin America. Therefore, it is not surprising that the largest mining company in Sierra Leone is a Chinese iron ore investment company. The Leone Rock Metal Group (LRMG) is an

---

[28] Siaka P. Stevens (2014), What Life has Taught Me: the Autobiography of Dr. Siaka P. Stevens – A Republication, Amazon, GB, pp.413-415

[29] OEC World Report, 'Iron Ore in China' www.oec.world reporter.cn

offshoot of the Shandon Steel Company and the China Kingho Group. In Sierra Leone, LRMG is the parent body of the Kingho Mining and Kingho Railway and Port Company. LRMG started in Sierra Leone as Kingho Investment Company Limited and has become one of the largest mining resource investment companies in West Africa. LRMG and Shandong Mining have invested an estimated $3 billion in iron ore mining in Sierra Leone, intending to transform iron ore mining into an in-country value-added industry. The objective is to transform Sierra Leone's iron ore mining into China's 6th largest iron ore/steel exporter. It becomes clear that Sierra Leone's importance to China is not necessarily for benevolent or charitable reasons but primarily for politico-diplomatic and economic reasons.

Benefits & Opportunities for Sino-Sierra Leone Relations: win-win strategic partnership

In Sierra Leone, as in much of Africa and the Global South countries, the conduct of foreign policy and international cooperation is often constructed and perceived by the citizens, and even among the ruling and governing elites in terms of tangible material benefits. Every external official's travel by the President, Vice president, and Ministers is expected to deliver concrete benefits for using public funds. As such, the Sino-Sierra Leone engagement since 1971 is expected to provide tangible and quantifiable benefits for the people and the country. In Sierra Leone, this is the raison d'etre for establishing bilateral relations with member states and international cooperation with multilateral institutions.

The Sino-Sierra Leone partnership has emerged as one of the most important bilateral relations in post-independence Sierra Leone. It has delivered multiple tangible, quantifiable, and intangible benefits for Sierra Leone. In conveying the emerging relevance and complexity of the China-Sierra Leone relations, Simone Datzbeger argued that "On the contrary, in impoverished Sierra Leone, the Red Dragon not only has emerged as a serious bilateral trade partner but also continues to invest in several urgently needed areas of development. By exploring the Sino-Sierra Leonean relationship in a conflict-shattered country's current acute development phase,… the conclusion is that China's activities are extremely important and may promote overall economic growth in Sierra Leone. However, in the long term, Chinese aid and investments may not necessarily lead to significant employment generation and effective poverty reduction".[30] In effect, the decades of China-Sierra Leone relations have delivered tangible benefits for Sierra Leone in the areas of infrastructure development, trade and economic development, education and scholarship programmes, medical aid and health capacity development, as well as cultural exchange and tourism.

By all indications, a significant benefit of China-Sierra Leone relations is in the area of infrastructural development in Sierra Leone. Before President Xi Jinping's Belt and Road Initiative was introduced in 2013, Chinese aid infrastructure projects had dotted the landscape of Sierra Leone, including iconic buildings, bridges, roads, hydropower dams, and power transmission stations. Today, China's infrastructure diplomacy has benefited Sierra Leone and led to the construction of the following significant projects: the Siaka Stevens National Stadium; Youyi Ministerial Building Complex; RSLAF HQs in the 1970s and 1980s; the China Friendship Roads; Friendship Hospital at Jui in Freetown; Magbass Sugar Complex; Kenema /Dodo Hydropower dam; Charlotte Hydropower dam; Bo mini Stadium; the China-Sierra Leone Friendship Middle School & Primary Schools; MoFAIC HQs Building; the MoFAIC – Foreign Service Academy Building; the Lumley / Juba Sengeh Pieh Bridge; the Limkokwing-Regent Road; Myohaug Officers' Mess and Single Officers Quarters; the National Optical Fiber Backbone Network, Maisaika Road and Tollgate.

The past 53 years of Sino-Sierra Leone relations have seen significant expansion in economic, trade, and commercial engagements and tangible benefits. The bilateral trade volume between Sierra Leone and China reached USD 530 million (2021), and China's foreign direct investment (FDI) to Sierra Leone in 2023 was USD 3.5 billion[31]. Several bilateral trade, economic, development, and technical

---

[30]S. Datzberger (2013), China's Silent Storm in Sierra Leone' SAIIA Policy Briefing, 71, p.9

[31] Government of China, Ministry of Foreign Affairs Embassy of the Peoples Republic of China to the Republic of Sierra Leone www.sl.china-embassy.gov.cn.eng

cooperation agreements have been signed between the two countries, leading to the establishment of Chinese companies and China-funded ventures in the agricultural and fishery sectors and the importation of Chinese mechanical, electrical, chemical, and textile products. China's main imports from Sierra Leone include minerals, coffee, cocoa, timber, and fisheries. To date, there are many registered Chinese companies in Sierra Leone, most of which are in the mining and construction business.

In the health and medical sector, since 1973, more than 550 Chinese medical staff have been dispatched to Sierra Leone under the Chinese Medical and Health Assistance programme. The Government of China provided significant medical and health assistance to Sierra Leone during the Ebola epidemic in 2014/15 and the COVID-19 pandemic in 2020. In addition, China has exercised soft power in Sierra Leone by significantly contributing to human capital development by offering Chinese scholarships and training programmes for Sierra Leoneans to study in China. In fact, some of the key government heads of Ministries, Departments, and Agencies (MDAs) have been trained in China. This significantly increased the people-to-people interactions and helped to strengthen the idea of a Sino-Sierra Leone shared future.

Chinese education and cultural agreements have been signed with the Government of Sierra Leone, and the implementation of the technical assistance projects has hugely benefitted Sierra Leoneans, especially the Chinese Scholarship programme and the agriculture and medical technical training programmes. A spin-off of this Sino-Sierra Leone cultural diplomacy is the signing of City-Twin Relations between Freetown and Chinese cities such as the Hefei (capital of East China Anhui province) with Freetown as well as the visit of several Chinese cultural delegations to Sierra Leone.

Uncordial Relations in the Sino-Sierra Leone Engagements

Despite the strong, cordial, friendly, and trusted relations between China and Sierra Leone, there are instances where relations between the two countries have been strained, but never to the point of fractious diplomatic ties that would demand the recall of ambassadors. In all bilateral relations, friendly and cooperating states sometimes have difficult periods of tense and confrontational relationships. A case in point is that despite the long-standing, strong, and cordial relations between the United States of America and Sierra Leone, there was a time in the early 1970s when relations between both America and Sierra Leone completely broke down, leading to the storming of the walls of the US Embassy in Freetown and the burning of the American flag by irate APC party supporters and youth on alleged complicity of America in 'encouraging' local dissidents and coup plotters against the APC government of President Stevens. Today, and given the cordial and long-standing relationship between Sierra Leone and America, it will be unfathomable that Sierra Leoneans, albeit a limited group of angry APC supporters and youth, could storm the American Embassy and desecrate the American flag. The point buttressed here is that these tense and hostile incidents occur in all bilateral political-economic relations between states, though they may not permanently undermine or destroy the long-standing engagements between the countries and their peoples.

The civil war in Sierra Leone between 1991 and 2001 led to a significant reduction in the country's Chinese political, economic, and commercial presence. Effective politico-diplomatic, financial, and development assistance engagements commenced after the formal end of the war and the visit of the Foreign Minister of Sierra Leone to Beijing in 2006. The political class, i.e., the ruling and governing elites, often describe this period as 'Chinese Abandonment' at a critical time when Sierra Leone needed all its friends, partners, and allies.

However, the most recent uncordial relations commenced in the run-up to the 2018 general elections. Before the election campaign, the governing APC party, under the leadership of President Ernest Bai Koroma, had fallen out with the Western diplomatic community and development partners, which led to the suspension of the IMF and World Bank credit facility to the Government of Sierra Leone. Understandably, the Ernest Koroma APC government accused the Western partners of a 'regime change' agenda. Therefore, it was not surprising that during the general elections campaign, the APC government presented itself as Beijing's favourite to continue in governance in Sierra Leone to demonstrate that it still had international support and credibility. Samura Kamara, the APC Presidential Candidate for the 2018 elections, used every opportunity to hype Beijing's support of the APC and his candidacy. Things became worse when, on the eve of the general election, APC supporters at campaign rallies chanted 'We are Chinese!', 'We are Chinese!'. To further aggravate the problem, social media footage showed Chinese men dressed in APC party regalia and T-shirts, openly campaigning for the APC party. Based on these election campaign incidents, the opposition SLPP party strongly condemned the 'dominance' of China's influence in the political economy of Sierra Leone during the 11-year rule of the APC-led Koroma administration. On the part of the SLPP Presidential Candidate, Julius Maada Bio, he strongly criticised what he described as the blatant interference in the internal politics of Sierra Leone, accusing China of election interference, stating that this is "the first sign of overt political interference of China or by any foreign power in Sierra Leone's elections since independence". The opposition SLPP presidential candidate even criticised the newly signed multi-million Chinese-funded agreement for a new international airport to be constructed by a Chinese firm, describing it as a "sham with no economic and development benefits to the people".

China's increasing concern became apparent when the newly elected President Bio cancelled the USD 420 million Chinese-funded new international airport project contract. This act by President Bio did not go down well with the Chinese leadership in Beijing. The recent attempt by the Bio administration to terminate in 2023 the Port and Rail infrastructure contract agreement held by the largest mining company in Sierra Leone, the Chinese LRMG, which has invested billions into the Tonkolili iron ore mining, was treated with deep concern by the Beijing leadership and was interpreted as an 'unfriendly act' by a trusted political ally. Beijing cannot understand why the LRMG port and rail infrastructure can be taken away and attempts to contract this critical mining infrastructure to a private company, ARISE IIP Africa.

The salient point that it made here is that relations between China and Sierra Leone have not always been cordial. It is important to note that there is no official or unofficial evidence to suggest that China/Beijing supported the APC party in the run-up to the 2018 general and presidential elections in Sierra Leone. What is more,

Beijing has a fundamental principle of non-interference in the internal affairs of member states, so any putative support or perceived support for the ruling APC party in the run-up to the general elections would have been in breach of the core tenets of China's foreign policy, especially in a friendly state like Sierra Leone, despite its avowed policy of support for the 'Government of the Day'. It is clear that China became caught up in the local election politics and was used by both parties, i.e., the governing APC government and the opposition SLPP. On the part of the SLPP presidential candidate and opposition party leader, it was clear to him that the Western partners in Freetown/Sierra Leone wanted 'regime change' but did not particularly like the presence of China in Sierra Leone and Africa. Realising that he would possibly be the next President and would have to work with China, the opposition presidential candidate, Julius Maada Bio's criticisms of China were measured and constructive, if not bothering with the usual political soundbites. In effect, the criticisms and condemnations of China were nothing more than political soundbites to satisfy the perceived 'anti-China' popular sentiment within some sections of the opposition SLPP and the Western audience. To be clear, the SLPP presidential candidate, Bio, having served as former Head of State of the NPRC military regime between January and March 1996, was aware of the political importance and economic might of China as a superpower and, thus, the imperative not to be on the wrong side of Beijing. The presidential candidate and senior advisers did not believe in making an enemy of China. Notwithstanding, the cancellation of the Chinese-funded new international airport was done in the name of protecting Sierra Leone's national interest, as this high-interest rate concessionary loan would have increased the debt burden and the debt service obligation of the new Bio-led SLPP Government. In political terms, the cancellation of the Chinese international airport loan, which pleased the Western partners and the IFIs such as the IMF and World Bank, their dazzling civilisations and formed distinct systems became a positive public relations scoop for the new Bio administration, as the predominantly Western media and anti-China lobbying groups used this to cast President Bio and his New Direction Government as 'champions of African independence'. However, faced with the harsh realities of governance delivery in a poor and underdeveloped country, the Bio administration wasted no time in recalibrating and prioritising cordial relations with China. For his part, President Bio had to immediately 'makeup' with Beijing, regain the Chinese government's trust and confidence, and encourage Chinese political, economic, and development influence to grow in Sierra Leone. To date, President Bio has visited China twice, and as Foreign Minister, I was 'mandated' to cultivate and develop strong, trusted, and cordial relations with China. Today, China is one of the most important bilateral partners and allies of Sierra Leone. Undoubtedly, Sino-Sierra Leone relations are marked by deepening and positive political, diplomatic, and economic influence in Sierra Leone.

Conclusion

The Sino-Sierra Leone engagement for the past 53 years is part of the broader China-Africa relations within the context of the reform and opening up of China in the 1970s that set the political, ideological, economic, and development pathway and trajectory based on Socialism with Chinese characteristics and under the leadership of the Communist Party of China. The rather impressive rapid development trajectory of contemporary China as a modern political, economic, and military power with the second largest economy in the world has been described as the 'Chinese Development Model'; 'Chinese Miracle'; 'Chinese Experience'; 'Chinese Path'; 'Chinese Phenomenon'. Most African countries like Sierra Leone, are now desperately trying to copy, replicate, and implement the Chinese development model. What is more, Sierra Leone and the rest of Africa perceive the 'Chinese Path' as an alternative and a departure from the colonial and post-independence Western-capitalist development model. Hongwu Liu and Jianbo Luo aptly state that "Both China and Africa have been, over different historical periods and in many areas, at the forefront of human civilisation... the peoples of Africa and China have created their dazzling civilisations and formed distinct systems of knowledge and ideas. The rich legacies of the two civilisations, including their unique knowledge and mindset, still manifest their impact today. When we try to probe deeper into the nature and roots of modernity and reassess the values of older civilisations by adopting a broad historical perspective, we will see that at once, ancient and modern, the civilisations of the China and Africa are set to unleash hitherto unseen creative powers and help reshape modernity. A global perspective is needed if we are to fully understand the historical significance and global implications of China-Africa partnership today'.[32] Within the context of the Global South and Africa, in particular, there is the increasing positive acknowledgement that China's win-win engagements with and influence on Africa will potentially lead to the overwhelming change and transformation in the development trajectory of the continent.

With this historical overview, what is the strategic value of Sierra Leone and Africa to China, and why does China see it as imperative and necessary to develop strategic Sino-African diplomatic, political, economic, and development partnerships with Africa? As this chapter has shown, Sierra Leone-China relations and the broader Sino-Africa engagements create an opportunity and framework for China to advance, promote, and implement the strategy of its global development model. China demonstrates to Africa that it is possible to emerge and transform a poor and developing country into a developed and industrialised people-centred developed country. This chapter has demonstrated that for Sierra Leone and the rest of post-independent Africa, 'development, development, development' has become the most important and pressing challenge for the country and its peoples. The Chinese development model therefore offers an attractive alternative to Western-capitalist development with its Brenton Woods institutions as represented by the IMF and World Bank, now generally perceived across Africa as a failed development paradigm. Liu and Luo, therefore, argue that:

> Like China, Africa –the continent with the largest number of developing countries- has tremendous and sustainable developmental needs with its vast territory, rich resources, diverse and age-old histories and culture and underdeveloped societies and cultures.

---

[32] Hongwu Liu & Jianbo Luo (2021), Sino-Africa Development Cooperation: Studies on the Theories, Strategies & Policies, Springer, Singapore, p. ix.

Therefore, the establishment of long-term strategic development relations between the world's largest developing country and the world's largest developing continent and the establishment of the world's largest organic development entity through combined creative energies of two major civilisation groups based on the principles of equality, mutual support and mutually beneficial initiatives, and with continued joint efforts, will realise joint development for these two significant civilisations.[33]

Therefore, it is not surprising that since the establishment of its first diplomatic relations in Africa in 1956, successive Chinese leaders have been consistent about the importance of Africa to China and its Sino-Africa engagements. Africa leaders have also stressed and, in some cases, prioritised the importance of China to Africa, as the President of Zambia, Kenneth Kaunda, once famously described China as an 'all-weather friend' to Africa. For China, relations with Africa provide a 'pivoting point' to link with other regions of the world, such as Europe and Latin America. As Liu and Lou succinctly put it, "When we examine the evolution of China-Africa relations, we see that since the founding of the People's Republic of China in the mid-twentieth century, China-Africa relations have served as a 'pivoting point' for China's relations with the external world. Hence, China-Africa relations are a special factor that can affect the structure of China's relations with Western countries and change China's strategic position in the international arena".[34] As such, Africa has emerged as an important political and diplomatic ally for China, especially in the conduct of its multilateral diplomacy. The overwhelming support of African countries for China invariably helps to project and promote China's global image, power, and influence that is different from the generally perceived predatory capitalist Western engagements.

With the rollout of the Chinese infrastructure diplomacy in the 1970s and 1980s, which saw the construction of the TARAZA Friendship Railway between Tanzania and Zambia, the construction of Sierra Leone's national stadium, and, more recently, the construction of the African Union headquarters and conference centre in Addis

---

[33] Liu & Luo, 2021, p. xv-xvi
[34] Ibid, p. 1.

Ababa, Ethiopia, have all helped to change the wrong impression given by the international western media that China has suddenly 'appeared' in Africa, in desperate search for and to exploit Africa's natural resources. This is far from the truth, as these, generally Western media, neglect the rich history of ancient, modern, and contemporary China-Africa engagements based on mutual trust, respect, and win-win outcomes. There is no denying that the China-Africa engagements have been influenced by the strategic economic and trading national interests to access Africa's abundant natural resources and strategic mineral resources, as well as its vast market and cheap labour. It is vital to point out that China's Africa engagements, if simply described as exploitative, are not different from the West's scramble for Africa and its predatory exploitation of the continent's natural resources.

Worthy of note is that the Chinese approach to its bilateral relations and development aid to Sierra Leone and other countries in the world is historically guided by the core fundamental principles of Chinese Foreign Policy and its 'One-China' policy as well as President Xi Jinping's dictum of the exercise of 'soft power with Chinese characteristics'. Sierra Leone, now with its global stage presence at the UNSC, the AU-PSC, and the AU C-10, has merged as a vocal, trusted, and committed supporter of the 'One-China' principle. The Chinese foreign policy and development aid approach within the context of its modernisation model has never been based on neo-liberal markets and economic development as in the case of the Western capitalist neo-liberal development model, nor have the Chinese foreign policy and development aid engagements been based on altruism. As a matter of pragmatic politics in international cooperation, China is strictly committed to observing its principle of non-interference in countries' internal affairs and respecting the political sovereignty and territorial integrity of all states, big or small. As such, China makes strenuous efforts not to interfere in internal politics but only to support the 'Government of the Day'.

To be clear, China's importance to Sierra Leone in terms of the overwhelming perception amongst the ruling and governing elites as well as the ordinary people is that China will fund and bankroll, through mineral wealth guarantee agreements, the construction of much-needed infrastructure deficits, which the country urgently needs to overhaul, economic diversification, economic growth, and enhance connectivity across the country to support its middle-income status aspirations, including the construction of the 10-kilometre major Lungi Bridge project that will connect the international airport in Lungi to the capital city, Freetown. It is fair to conclude that China's relationship with Sierra Leone has benefitted the country and its people. Over 50 years of engagements have produced win-win outcomes for both China and Sierra Leone, tangible, quantifiable material, intangible and non-material benefits for both countries. The future of the China-Sierra Leone relation is promising, and it is set to significantly increase to maximise the win-win results for both countries and peoples if the leadership in both countries remains committed to consolidating and building on their solid political trust in the pursuit of their strategic national interests.

References

Bruce Larkin (1971), China-Africa: 1949-1970: the Foreign Policy of the People's Republic of China, University of California Press.

Hongwu Liu (2024), Seventy Years of China-Africa Relations, Zhejiang University Press, Jinhun

Hongwu Liu (2007); 'The historical value and global significance of the new China-Africa strategic partnership' Foreign Affairs Review, Vol. 1

Hongwu Liu & Jianbo Luo (2021), Sino-Africa Development Cooperation: Studies on the Theories, Strategies & Policies, Springer, Singapore,

Julius Nyerere (1979), South-South Dialogue & Development in Africa, Dar Es Salam.

Solomon A. J. Pratt, (2010), Jolliboy: an Autobiography: From Street Starch Hawker to United Nations Debate Champion, Prince HywBull Publishers, North Carolina, p. 220-221

CHAPTER TWO

History of China-Sierra Leone Relations

Joe A. D. Alie

Introduction

Sierra Leone, a country on the West Coast of Africa, has been politically independent for sixty-three years. At its independence in 1961, the world was ideologically divided between the Capitalist West, led by the USA and its Allies, and the Soviet Bloc (the Soviet Union and its Allies). African and Asian countries were entangled in what was then called the Cold War. African countries had three clear choices: to remain tightly connected to the apron strings of their erstwhile colonial overlords (and in the case of Sierra Leone, Britain), to make new friends, or to forge new alliances. The third option gave birth to the Non-Aligned Movement (NAM).[1]

Sierra Leone's political leaders at independence were largely conservative, with Prime Minister Sir Milton Margai adopting a gradualist approach to national politics and foreign policy initiatives. Put differently, the Prime Minister was not prepared to rock the boat; instead, he was happy to remain with his old friends, the British and other Western Allies, unrealistically believing that he would obtain all the assistance he needed from them to develop his country. During Sierra Leone's Independence Talks in Britain, Sir Milton boldly stated

---

[1]The Non-Aligned Movement (NAM) was founded in Belgrade, Serbia, in 1961 with the view to advancing the interests of developing countries in the context of Cold War confrontation. The founding fathers were Jawaharlal Nehru (India), Josip Broz Tito (Yugoslavia), Rukmini Sukarno (Indonesia), Gamal Abdel Nasser (Egypt), and Kwame Nkrumah (Ghana). NAM was founded on five main principles: mutual respect for each other's territorial integrity and sovereignty; mutual non-aggression; mutual non-interference in domestic affairs; equality and mutual benefit; and peaceful co-existence.

that he was not prepared to exploit new sources of aid or investment as long as his British friends were willing to assist.

> We need help in various ways to develop... our natural resources, and for this help we would like to look first to our old friends (the British). There are all too many offers from other sources, which we would prefer not to encourage, as long as our old and proved friends are prepared to stand by us and help us.[2]

Considering the poor state of the British economy in the post-World War II era, it seemed highly unlikely that Sierra Leoneans would expect much development aid from the West[3]. Nevertheless, Sierra Leone established diplomatic relations with the USA and other Western countries in 1961. The following year, diplomatic relations were established with the Soviet Union.[4]

Genesis of informal China-Sierra Leone Relations

Sierra Leone's foreign policy objectives began to undergo major changes during the premiership of Sir Milton's successor, Albert Margai, in 1964. An avowed nationalist and a radical, Sir Albert Margai desired to move away from the conservative approaches of his elder brother and explore new directions without cutting himself off entirely from the West. Consequently, Sierra Leone then became a member of the Non-Aligned Movement.[5]

In his desire to make the country self-sufficient in rice production, he made friends with the Republic of China (ROC). Taiwanese agricultural teams subsequently came to Sierra Leone, where they successfully demonstrated a multiple cropping system whereby it was

---

[2]"Text of the Speech of Sir Milton Margai", The Lancaster House Conference, Command Papers 1029/1960, pp.13-15. Report of the Sierra Leone Constitutional Conference Held in London in April and May 1960. Cited in Christopher Fyfe, *Sierra Leone Inheritance*, Oxford: Oxford University Press, 1964, pp.338-341.
[3](Alie 2015, p36)
[4] George Ginsberg, Robert M. Slusser (1981). A Calendar of Soviet Treaties: 1958-1973. Springer: The Netherlands. p. 165
[5] By 1964, the Non-Aligned Movement was beginning to play a crucial role in decolonisation, the formation of new independent states, and the democratisation of international relations.

possible to grow two or even three rice crops a year in the inland valley swamps with yields averaging 1.5 to 2.5 tonnes per acre[6]. The team established demonstration farms in many towns upcountry, and these are still fondly referred to as "China Farms".[7]

Establishment of formal diplomatic ties with the People's Republic of China (PRC)

Formal diplomatic relations with mainland China (PRC) began in 1971 when Siaka Stevens was Prime Minister (later President) of Sierra Leone. Stevens was the leader of the All People's Congress (APC) party. An astute politician, Stevens had carefully calculated that he stood to gain much if he affiliated with the Communist world. It is believed that Stevens and his APC associates received seed money for their party from East Germany and China. When he became Prime Minister in 1968, Stevens continued to reach out to more communist countries, including North Korea and Cuba. While Cuba was a member of the NAM, it, at the same time, stoutly opposed American imperialist tendencies by aligning itself with the Soviet Union.

However, not wanting to alarm the West, Stevens took a staunchly pro-British/Western stance at the United Nations and other international forums. One of the most contentious issues in the United Nations at the time was the two China (ROC and PRC) questions.[8]

Since 1949, China's foreign policy has been anchored on mutual respect and non-interference in the domestic policies of other

---

[6]Alie, 2015, p.48

[7] See Eddie Momoh (Critique of the Siaka Stevens regime (*West Africa*, 9 December 1985).

[8] Following the defeat of the Nationalist forces under the command of Chiang Kai-shek by Mao Zedong's Communist forces, the former had retreated to an island south of the mainland with his troops and supporters and established the Republic of China (ROC), commonly referred to as Taiwan, with stout western backing. Meanwhile, Mao had exercised absolute control over the entire mainland of China and consequently created the People's Republic of China (PRC) on October 1, 1949. Office of the Historian, US Department of State. "The Chinese Revolution of 1949" (history@state.gov)

countries, which, incidentally, was in line with Sierra Leone's foreign policy trajectory. To further these goals, the Governments of the People's Republic of China and the Republic of Sierra Leone signed a Joint Communiqué in Peking on 29 July 1971 to establish full diplomatic relations. The full text of the communiqué read as follows:

> The Governments of the People's Republic of China and Sierra Leone, following the interests and wishes of the people of the two countries, decided to establish diplomatic relations at the ambassadorial level as of today.
>
> The Chinese Government and people firmly support the Government and people of the Republic of Sierra Leone in their struggle against imperialism, colonialism and neo-colonialism and in their efforts to safeguard national independence and state sovereignty.
>
> The Government of Sierra Leone recognizes the Government of the People's Republic of China as the sole legitimate government representing the entire China.
>
> The two Governments agree to develop diplomatic relations, friendship and cooperation between the two countries on the basis of the principles of mutual respect for sovereignty and territorial integrity, mutual non-aggression, non-interference in each other's internal affairs, equality and mutual benefit, and peaceful coexistence.[9]

Referring to this historic agreement several years later, President Siaka Stevens wrote in his Memoir:

> It is difficult to realise now the courage that this decision demanded. The person who makes the first move, particularly when all those around him are against it, must be brave. But my Government and I thought that this was the right decision; we took it, and we turned out to be right. Of course, none of this would have been possible if we had not been firmly non-aligned[10]

---

[9]Chinese Foreign Ministry October 10, 2006
[10]Stevens, 1984, p.368.

Up to 1971, Taiwan (ROC), ostensibly with America's strong influence and backing, had been the de jure representative of the whole of China at the United Nations instead of the People's Republic of China. This was a monumental historic wrong, and righting it required the total commitment and support of most members of the United Nations[11]. The People's Republic of China (PRC) had always argued with justification that China was one country represented by the PRC, and since Taiwan was an integral part of mainland China, it should not be regarded as a separate entity. This conformed with the PRC's "One China" policy.

Sierra Leone, then a non-permanent member of the United Nations Security Council, serving a two-year mandate from 1970-71, fully supported the PRC's position. Not surprisingly, Sierra Leone was one of the 26 co-sponsor countries of Resolution 2758[12]. On October 25, 1971, the 26th session of the U.N. General Assembly passed United Nations Resolution 2758 (XXVI), which stated that the People's Republic of China is the only legitimate government of China. The resolution replaced the ROC with the PRC as a permanent member of the Security Council in the United Nations. [13] Thus, the PRC's "One China Policy" had been realised.

Among the 76 delegates that voted "yes" to support the motion, 26 were African countries. President Mao was thankful for the African solidarity. He said, among others, "It was our fellow developing countries (including those from Africa) that carried the People's Republic of China into the United Nations."[14]

On 26 October, President Stevens sent a message of congratulations to Chairman Mao Zedong. President Stevens said that he had taken a keen interest in the United Nations debate, culminating in China's admission to the UN as legal representative of the Chinese people, and he was delighted that the People's Republic of China had

[11]Winkler Sigrid (2012

[12]Alieu Badara Kabia 2015

[13]UNGA Resolution 2758 Brooks No Challenge, and the One-China Principle Is Unshakable. Consulate General of the PRC in Los Angeles, 2024-05-17)

[14] Hu Yuwei and Lin Xiaoyi "How African representatives 'carried' PRC into the UN", (*Global Times* Oct 26, 2021)

now taken its rightful place in the world community of nations. He concluded by remarking that the Sierra Leone government was confident that China would continue to contribute to world peace and security.[15]

The UN decision to readmit China was taken when China was still considered a developing country and grappling with the effects of the Cultural Revolution. This was a period of "ideological, social, and political ferment that lasted from 1966 to1976, during which Chairman Mao purged his enemies and sought to eradicate capitalism from China.[16]

Two years later, in 1978, Chinese leader Deng Xiaoping began his "reform and opening up" phase, a process marked by far-reaching economic liberalisation, political reforms, and a gradual opening of its domestic market to the outside world.[17] Sierra Leone too underwent a major political transformation in 1978, when the APC political leadership, following a flawed referendum, declared Sierra Leone a one-party state to be run ostensibly along socialist principles[18]. This so-called anti-capitalist posture by the Stevens regime may have provided some ideological glue to the Sino-Sierra Leone relations in the late 1970s and early 1980s. Sierra Leone then became one of the larger recipients of Chinese aid in Africa. Visible signs of such aid included the construction of the Youyi (Friendship) Building, which houses many of the government ministries; the National Stadium; the Mange and Kambia bridges in north-western Sierra Leone; the headquarters of the military and police establishments; and the hydroelectric project at Dodo in the eastern region of Sierra Leone.

The focus of Chinese aid to Sierra Leone in the 1980s and 1990s was to promote or facilitate economic cooperation based on reciprocity rather than ideological diplomacy. Thus, China emphasised that economic and technological cooperation should come in both ways, and the goal of such collaboration was to boost the economic and social development of both sides and improve their capacity for

---

[15]Sierra Leone – 12 Years of Economic Achievement and Political Consolidation under the APC and Dr. Siaka Stevens 1968-1980. Freetown: Office of the President, pp.116

[16]Muktar Usman Muktari-Janguza, "Maada Bio's China Dilemma, 2018"

[17]Ibid.

[18]Alie 2015

development. China should not only give fish to Africa but should also teach them how to fish[19].

Sino-Sierra Leone cooperation for mutual benefit started in 1984 when the Fujian-Africa Fishing Company of China signed fishing cooperation contracts with the Okeky Agent Company of Sierra Leone. The Company of International Cooperation on Agriculture, Husbandry, and Fishery of China also signed some contracts of mutual benefit with Sierra Leone.[20] It is important to note that Chinese relations with Sierra Leone were part of a broader Sino-African relationship based on eight core principles since 1963[21]

Sino-Sierra Leone's diplomatic relations were kept in cold storage during the latter's civil war (1991-2002) but were revived immediately after the war, thanks to the exertions of the Tejan Kabbah administration (1996-2007). His Foreign Minister, Momodu Koroma, travelled to China and had fruitful discussions with his Chinese counterpart, Li Zhaoxing. The result was increased Chinese engagement in the agricultural and hospitality industries. However, the future of Sino-Sierra Leone relations lay in trade, commerce, and infrastructure, not aid. A Sierra Leone government official put it this way:

---

[19]Liu 2021, pp.13-14

[20]Chinese Foreign Ministry October 10, 2006

[21]Liu 2021, p.10.
These eight core principles were outlined by Premier Zhou Enlai: 1. The Chinese government would provide aid to Africa based on equality and reciprocity. 2. China would not attach any strings to its aid to Africa, and national sovereignty would be respected. 3. The Chinese government would provide favourable aid to African countries and would ensure that the aid would not add up to the burden of the recipients. 4. Chinese aid was aimed not to create dependency but to improve African countries' ability of development. 5. The Chinese government focused on effective investment and intended to increase the income of recipient countries. 6. The Chinese government would provide good-quality equipment at prices common in the international market. 7. The Chinese government would ensure that personnel in the recipient countries have the technological knowhow of the projects built with Chinese aid. 8. Chinese experts sent to Africa would enjoy no privileges but the same treatment as the local experts.

The Chinese ambassador was the most active of all the ambassadors. He kept insisting that aid is not what the country needs, but commercial ties. The ambassador and the economic counsellor are always looking for commercial potentials, and they look to see how they can work with the government to realise it. The other donors might do a good job at their big projects – microfinance and livelihood programmes. They last for three years, and then everybody sits down and waits until another programme comes in. The programme does not last beyond those three years. So we are standing still[22]

Foreign Minister Momodu Koroma was to remark that unlike the aid given by Western countries, Chinese aid was tailored to the needs of the recipient country:

There is a difference, and it is huge. What they [i.e. the Chinese] want to help you with, is what you have identified as your need. With Britain, America, *they* identify your needs. They say: 'Look, we think there is a need *here*.' The German President visited. They promised €12.5 million assistance. President Kabbah said we will use this for rural electrification. But a few months later, GTZ [the German aid agency] said it would be used for their human security project[23]

During the Kabbah era, Magbass Sugar Company in Tonkolili District and Chinese investors rehabilitated and ran the Bintumani Hotel. At the official re-opening of the hotel in January 2003, President Kabbah remarked

I am therefore delighted to be here today, not only to formally re-open this hotel, but also to personally applaud the effort of the Beijing Urban Construction Group and its local co-workers for transforming what unfortunately had become an eyesore, into a beautiful, decent and top-class hotel.

Of course, today's event would not have been possible without the assistance of one of our most reliable and sympathetic development partners, the People's Republic of China. By undertaking this project,

---

[22]Muktari-Janguza, 2018.
[23] Ibid

the Chinese Government has demonstrated confidence in our national reconstruction effort. Its contribution to the refurbishing and re-opening of this hotel will undoubtedly encourage other partners and potential partners to invest in Sierra Leone. For this we are exceedingly grateful.[24]

Based on the cooperative agreement reached by Henan Guoji Investment and Development Company Limited and the Ministry of Trade and Industry of Sierra Leone, the Henan Guoji Trade and Industrial Zone was established at Cline town in the east end of Freetown and opened for business in April 2005. On November 22, President Kabbah, together with Cabinet Ministers, Chinese Ambassador Cheng Wenju, and the respective Presidents of the Sierra Leone and Chinese Chambers of Commerce, graced the official opening of the Sierra Leone International Commodities Exhibition and Trade Fair at the zone.[25]

At the same time, cultural ties between the two countries were cemented. A delegation from the Chinese People's Association for Friendship with Foreign Countries (CPAFFC) visited Sierra Leone at the invitation of the Sierra Leone - China Friendship Society from December 8 to 12, 2005. Vice President Solomon Berewa, the Speaker of the Sierra Leone Parliament- Edmond Cowan, and Minister of Lands- Bobson Sesay, who was also Chairman of the Sierra Leone China Friendship Society, received the delegation headed by Mr. Wang Daoyu, Vice Chairman of the Standing Committee of the Shandong Provincial People's Congress. Vice President Berewa, on behalf of President Kabbah, expressed his warm welcome to the Chinese team, saying that under the efforts of the government and people of the two countries, the Sino-Sierra Leone friendship and bilateral relations were being constantly strengthened, and Sierra Leone was highly

---

[24]Speech by the President Alhaji Dr. Ahmad Tejan Kabbah at the Official Opening of the Bintumani Hotel Aberdeen, Friday, 31 January 2003. Sierra Leone Web. https://www.sierra-leone.org › Ahmad_Tejan_Kabbah

[25] Embassy of the People's Republic of China in the Republic of Sierra Leone. "The 2005 Sierra Leone International Commodities Exhibition and Trade Fair launched" http://sl.china-embassy.gov.cn/eng/

appreciative and grateful for China's support and assistance before, during, and after the civil war. Mr. Wang, on behalf of the visiting team, thanked Vice President Berewa and pointed out that China and Sierra Leone were developing countries with similar historical experience and common development tasks, and the bilateral cooperation between the two countries enjoyed a solid foundation and broad prospect.[26]

President Kabbah continued to be held in high esteem by the Chinese leadership even after he had left office. On March 8, 2011, Chinese Ambassador Kuang Weilin visited the former president and praised President Kabbah for his relentless efforts in promoting China-Sierra Leone relations. President Kabbah, for his part, spoke highly of the tremendous contributions China had made to the economic development, peace restoration, and reconstruction of Sierra Leone and firmly believed that both countries would continue to work closely together to further enhance bilateral relations and cooperation.

When President Kabbah passed away, the Chinese Vice Foreign Minister Zhang Ming visited the Sierra Leone Embassy in Beijing to sign the Book of Condolence on March 19, 2014. Sierra Leoneans also mourned the passing of former President Jiang Zemin, whom one Sierra Leonean journalist described as "an avid promoter of China-Sierra Leone relations"[27].

China-Sierra Leone relations received a big boost, if sometimes controversial, during the presidency of Ernest Bai Koroma (2007-2018). President Koroma made a state visit to China from November 30 to December 6, 2016. The purpose of the visit was fourfold.

- To thank the government and people of China for their unprecedented humanitarian and technical assistance to Sierra Leone during the Ebola epidemic (2014-16).
- To scale up Sino-Sierra Leone relations, especially in trade and infrastructural development.
- To continue to solicit China's support for an African seat in the UNSC.
- To concretise APC ties with the Chinese communist party.

---

[26]Embassy of the People's Republic of China in the Republic of Sierra Leone (2005). "Chinese delegation pays a friendly visit to Sierra Leone"
[27]Kef Sesay 2022

Months before the visit, President Koroma had conferred on Chinese President Xi Jinping and the Chinese Ambassador to Sierra Leone, Zhao Yanbo, the honorary titles of Grand Commander of the Republic of Sierra Leone (GCRSL) and Commander of the Order of the Republic of Sierra Leone (CRSL), respectively, in recognition of their continuous support to Sierra Leone, particularly during the Ebola epidemic. This was the first time that top Chinese leaders had been honoured in Sierra Leone.

President Koroma met with President Xi during the state visit, and both leaders agreed to elevate their bilateral relations to a Comprehensive Strategic Cooperative Partnership (CSCP). A CSCP is considered the highest level of bilateral relations for China, a position only 14 African countries held with China. They are in addition to Sierra Leone, the Republic of Congo, the Democratic Republic of Congo, Ethiopia, Gabon, Guinea, Mozambique, Kenya, Namibia, Senegal, South Africa, Tanzania, Zambia, and Zimbabwe.[28]

The two leaders then signed the following six agreements:

- Creation of a new West Africa Tropical Disease Research and Treatment Centre (representing a 300 million RMB Economic and Technical Cooperation Agreement);
- Freetown Ring Road (Limkokwing University to Regent Village);
- Debt relief of 20 million RMB (of a previous interest-free loan);
- The establishment of a consultation mechanism between the two foreign ministries;
- A Cooperation Agreement for Hospital Partner Assistance;

---

[28]A comprehensive strategic partnership is a high-level relationship between two countries that involves a wide range of cooperation across various areas such as politics, economics, security, culture, and more. It signifies a deep and multifaceted commitment between the two nations to collaborate closely on a broad spectrum of issues of mutual interest and concern. Such partnerships typically involve regular high-level dialogues, exchanges, and joint initiatives aimed at strengthening ties and achieving shared objectives. By establishing a comprehensive strategic partnership, countries aim to deepen their relationship beyond traditional diplomatic ties and work together more closely to address common challenges, promote mutual prosperity, and enhance regional and global stability. These partnerships are often seen as a significant step towards building a long-term and sustainable relationship between nations.

- An agreement on mutual visa exemption of diplomatic and service (official) passport holders.[29]

President Xi also pledged 100 million Yuan to support the capacity building of Sierra Leone's Naval Wing and 100 million Yuan in rice aid. He further pledged a 300 million Yuan grant to boost Sierra Leone's health sector.[30] President Koroma later met with Chinese business executives in the mining industry.

One important political outcome of President Koroma's 2016 state visit to China was the strengthening of ties between his APC party (which had always professed a vague socialism) and the Chinese communist party. In the run-up to the 2018 elections in Sierra Leone, ethnic Chinese were seen on social media campaigning for the APC. Overzealous APC supporters were heard singing, "We are Chinese." The SLPP leadership viewed these happenings with disfavour and interpreted them as gross interference in the domestic politics of another sovereign nation. The Communist Party in China had in early 2017 funded the construction of a multi-story APC Western Area Regional Party office in Freetown, which was a visible expression of the historically close ties between the APC and their counterparts in Beijing[31].

Although the SLPP, led by President Julius Maada Bio, was highly critical of China during the 2018 elections in Sierra Leone, the anger soon dissipated. As soon as Bio was sworn in as President, his Foreign Minister Professor David Francis visited Beijing from May 15 to 18 and met with his Chinese counterpart Qin Gang and other Chinese officials to further enhance China-Sierra Leone ties, particularly in such areas as trade and investment, agriculture, and infrastructure development to benefit the two peoples. In addition, he applauded China's important role in safeguarding world peace and stability.[32]

Foreign Minister Francis's visit was followed by a state visit to Beijing by President Bio from August 30 to September 7, 2018. While in Beijing, President Bio attended the Forum on China-Africa

---

[29]The Worldfolio.https://www.theworldfolio.com-news,sierraleone
[30] Ibid.
[31]Muktari-Januza, 2018
[32]Embassy of the People's Republic of China in the United Kingdom of Great Britain and Northern Ireland (2018).

Cooperation (FOCAC). In his meeting with President Xi, Bio stressed the need to expand Sino-Sierra Leone relations:

> As the newly elected President (of Sierra Leone), I am committed to strengthening our long-standing friendship by focusing on strategic and cooperative partnership. Attracting foreign direct investment from China; fixing the volume of trade imbalance between our two countries, and leveraging opportunities in development aid from China would be key in this strategic and cooperative partnership.[33]

New agreements were signed, which included a deal for China to send a team of nine experts to conduct a feasibility study on the fish harbour project, an agreement for the Chinese Government to provide emergency humanitarian assistance for a batch of rice valued at 50 million RMB Yuan; a Memorandum of Understanding on cooperation within the framework of the Belt and Road Initiative; and an agreement on economic and technical cooperation with gratuitous assistance from the Chinese Government of 250 million RMB Yuan.[34]

Looking back

The year 2021 marked the 50th anniversary of Sino-Sierra Leone relations, coinciding with the centenary of the Communist Party of China. Since 1971, the diplomatic relations established by the two countries, despite their varying degrees of size, distance, economic development, and political ideologies, have mainly worked to the mutual benefit of both countries. Chinese assistance to Sierra Leone has been more profound in the following sectors.

1. *Medical aid* through the provision of Chinese medical personnel, equipment, and drugs, particularly during the Ebola epidemic and Covid-19 pandemic.

---

[33] Sierra Leone State House (2018). Chinese President Xi Jinping praises President Bio on State Visit.
[34] Ibid.

2. *Human resource development.* Chinese higher institutions of learning have trained hundreds of Sierra Leonean students and workers who are contributing immensely to the development of the country. Chinese students have also been trained in Sierra Leone.

3. *Agriculture:* providing tractors and other agricultural equipment, popularising rice cultivation techniques

4. *Cultural ties:* Sierra Leonean artists have popularised their country's rich cultural heritage in China and vice versa. The Confucius Institute, established at Fourah Bay College (University of Sierra Leone), offers Chinese language courses and a diverse array of activities such as martial arts and tai chi. The Chinese education ministry funded the Confucius Institute with the aim of promoting Chinese language and culture and supporting academic exchanges.

5. *Infrastructural development,* particularly the construction of government office buildings, road and bridge construction, and sporting complexes.

6. *Trade and commerce:* The Chinese are heavily involved in mining. Chinese factories and products are found all over the country. Sierra Leonean merchants and traders also regularly visit China for trade. There are joint enterprises run by Chinese and Sierra Leonean entrepreneurs.

China and Sierra Leone regard each other as strategic international relations and bilateral trade partners. Sierra Leone has significant mineral resources required by China's growing industries. 2021 Sierra Leone exported $341 million worth of goods to China. These were primarily raw materials such as titanium, iron, and aluminium ores, followed by wood and diamonds. [35]

China is also Sierra Leone's most significant source of foreign direct investment (FDI). For instance, in 2021, China invested $106 million in the country, compared to the United Kingdom's $66 million and the United States $1 million. China's lending for infrastructure development as well as aid for other sectors such as livelihoods,

---

[35] The Diplomat (2024). President Bio's visit charts a more holistic path for China-Sierra Leone relations. https://thediplomat.com 2024/03

healthcare, education, and agriculture has been a key area for collaboration.[36]

Moreover, Sierra Leone has been the Chair of the African Union's Committee of Ten (C10) on reform of the United Nations Security Council (UNSC), of which China is a permanent member. Thus, Sierra Leone's leadership within the African Union and on UNSC reform makes it crucial to engage with and explain Chinese positions and views and understand African perspectives.

However, China-Sierra Leone relations, especially in the area of commerce, have attracted some severe criticism. A survey by the Institute of Governance Reform (IGR, 2021) in Freetown among local fishing and road construction communities in the Western Area of Sierra Leone concluded that the operations of Chinese companies have not resulted in a "win-win" situation and that Chinese companies have been the greatest beneficiaries. A spokesperson from the Chinese Embassy in Freetown challenged some of the views expressed in the IGR Report.[37]

The future of Sino-Sierra Leone relations

China's growing ability to advance its strategic interests through co-option, cooperation, and inducements, which President Xi Jinping has called "soft power with Chinese characteristics", seems to be working well for China and African countries.[38] The next fifty years of Sino-Sierra Leone cooperation promise to be even more productive. During President Bio's second state visit to China, from February 28 to March 2, 2024, he and his key ministers met with a wide range of Chinese entrepreneurs and potential investors at a Roundtable Investment Forum. At the forum that President Bio chaired, Sierra Leonean ministers made detailed presentations "on bankable projects to

---

[36]Ibid.

[37]Interview by Calabash (Newspaper) with the Spokesperson of the Chinese Embassy in Sierra Leone on a China-Related Report by the Institute for Governance Reform (2021-03-06).

[38] Africa Centre for Strategic Studies (2018). "Grand strategy and China soft power push in Africa."

Chinese attendees from diverse sectors, including infrastructure, mining, ICT, manufacturing, and education." Furthermore, the presentations "called for investments in infrastructure and mining and agriculture and agro-processing of palm oil, rice, sugar, cocoa, oil palm, poultry, and seafood, all to provide new jobs in Sierra Leone and cut poverty. Accordingly, the forum also called for investments in education, training, and skill transfers."[39] If the Chinese investors could help President Bio realise these dreams for his people, history would be very kind to him.

References

Alie, Joe A D (2015). Sierra Leone Since Independence: History of a postcolonial state. Freetown: SLWS.

Bräutigam Deborah (2010), China, Africa and the International Aid Architecture, Working Papers Series N° 107, African Development Bank, Tunis, Tunisia.

Bräutigam Deborah (2011) China in Africa: Seven Myths (ARI)

Centre for Chinese Studies (2006). China's Interest and Activity in Africa's Construction and Infrastructure Sectors. Stellenbosch University

Clifford, Sarah and S. N. Romanuk (2020). Cuban Cold War Internationalism and the Non-Aligned Movement (E-International Relations).

Consulate General of the PRC in Los Angeles (2024). "UNGA Resolution 2758 Brooks No Challenge, and the One-China Principle Is Unshakable"

Department of State, USA (1949). The Chinese Revolution of 1949. history@state.gov.

Dotzberger, Simone (2013). "China's Silent Storm in Sierra Leone". South African Institute of International Affairs. https://www.jstor.org/stable/resrep32541

---

[39] The Diplomat (2018). President Bio's visit charts a more holistic path for China-Sierra Leone relations.

Embassy of the People's Republic of China in the United Kingdom of Great Britain and Northern Ireland 2024

Fyfe, Christopher (1964). Sierra Leone Inheritance, Oxford: Oxford University Press.

Ginsberg, George and Robert M. Slusser (1981). A Calendar of Soviet Treaties: 1958-1973. Springer: The Netherlands.

Hu Yuwei and Lin Xiaoyi (2021) "How African representatives 'carried' PRC into the UN", (*Global Times* Oct 26, 2021)

IGR (2021) China's Emerging Influence in Sierra Leone: Voices & Views of Local Fishing and Road Construction Communities, February 2021.

Kabia, Alieu Badara ( ). "The Evolution of China-Sierra Leone Cooperation ". China Daily. http://blog.chinadaily.com.cn

Liu, Hongwu (2021). Seventy Years of China-Africa Relations. Jinhua: Zhejiang University Press.

Momoh, Eddie (1985). "Critique of the Siaka Stevens regime" (*West Africa*, 9 December 1985).

Muktari-Janguza Muktar Usman (2018)., "Maada Bio's China Dilemma" email: janguza.arewa@gmail.com

Office of the President, Freetown (1980). Sierra Leone – 12 Years of Economic Achievement and Political Consolidation under the APC and Dr Siaka Stevens 1968-1980

Sarah Clifford and Scott N. Romaniuk, (2020) Cuban Cold War Internationalism and the Nonaligned Movementhttps://www.e-ir.info/2020/12/19/cuban-cold-war-internationalism-and-the-nonaligned-movement/

Speech by President Alhaji Dr. Ahmad Tejan Kabbah at the Official Opening of The Bintumani Hotel Aberdeen, Friday 31 January 2003. Sierra Leone Web. https://www.sierra-leone.org › Ahmad_Tejan_Kabbah

Stevens, Siaka (1984). What Life Has Taught Me. Abbotsbrook: The Kensal Press.

Winkler Sigrid (2012). "Taiwan's UN Dilemma: To Be or Not To Be". http://www.brookings.edu

CHAPTER THREE

China-Sierra Leone Political, Economic, and Development Engagements

Abraham John

Conceptual Framework for the Engagements

The China-Sierra Leone political, economic, and development engagements date back to 1971. Fifty-three years later, this relationship crystalised in many ways, including tangible political and economic outcomes that resulted in mutual benefits for both countries. These include mutual support for reforming the United Nations Security Council (UNSC) and Sierra Leone's all-time bilateral and multilateral support for the "One China" policy. On the other hand, large Chinese investments in several sectors have contributed to Sierra Leone's economic growth and development trajectory, which will be analysed further in this chapter. The political, financial, and development engagements between China and Sierra Leone continue to be guided by the principles of mutual respect for sovereignty and non-interference in the internal affairs of each other's country, commitment to multilateralism, partnership, sustainable development, and dispassionate commitment to promote global peace and security within the broader framework of the United Nations Charter, South-South Cooperation (SSC), Non-Alignment Movement (NAM), and the Group of 77 (G-77) States.

A nuanced understanding of the political, economic, and development engagements between China and Sierra Leone for fifty-three years can be better appreciated within a conceptual framework. Furthermore, it may help to change the sense of suspicion and negative allegations that China's relationship with African countries is driven by exploitative tendencies over other considerations[1]. The alternative views proffered from a Sierra Leonean or African perspective may help to inspire a re-write of the Sin-Africa relationship by Africans rather than by non-Africans. This aligns to an African proverb that states that "until the lions have their own historians, tales of the hunt shall always glorify the hunter"[2]. This African proverb can be interpreted to mean that dominant narratives on Sino-African relationships will never change if Africans do not take the challenge to present a true account based on realities and experiences gained in the relationship. This work seeks to initiate a conversation in that direction.

The literature on engagements or cooperation between states has been dominated by Western discourse, especially in the pre-and post-Cold War era. The leading proponents were the realist scholars in the field of international relations. They argued that the engagements or cooperation between states were power-driven, wherein the more robust and more powerful states used their power advantage to coerce weaker states into cooperation or engagements[3]. The basis of the realist arguments was underscored by Morgenthau. He endorsed that "...regardless of social, economic, and political conditions, states have met each other in the contest of power"[4]. The veracity of the realist arguments has not been sustained beyond the post-Cold War era. In this period, there has been an avalanche of cooperation and engagement between states based on economic, political, and social win-win situations, not for the contest of power. The relationship between China and Sierra Leone, on the one hand, and China and other states on the continent of Africa is a testament to cooperation and engagements based on win-win interests.

In tandem with the Realist school of thought, the Classical Realists school of thought has posited that human nature is inherently selfish, and therefore, state actors negotiating on behalf of their states are motivated by self-interest, and therefore, conflict is inevitable in the engagement with other states[5]. These narratives, like the realist school of thought, have proven to be flawed in the context of states

---

[1]Xia, 2020

[2]Achebe, Chinua

[3]K. Waltz, 1979, p. 256; Donnely, Jack, 2000; Mearsheimer, 2013, 77-93

[4] Morgenthau, 1965, p. 33

[5]Schuett, 2010, pp. 23-26

interaction in the post-Cold War era. In this era, states now engage not on power considerations but on the genuine desire to cooperate in pursuance of their national interests, mainly focusing on political, economic, and other interests of mutual benefit to the cooperating states.

The rise of liberal ideas, including liberal peace theory and liberal democracy in the post-Cold War era, was not driven by the contest of power. They argued that human nature has the propensity to hold back the desire for aggression and that security dilemma can be resolved through mutual and positive engagements between states.[6] Others argued that states cooperate in pursuing mutual economic benefits beyond the "contest of power"[7]. This strand of the liberal argument is arguably in line with the rationale for engagements between states at the bilateral and multilateral levels.

Commonalities in Ideological Commitment and Colonial Experience

It is crucial to interrogate fifty-three years of sustained and unbroken political and economic engagements between China and Sierra Leone. This will help to unearth why China and Sierra Leone present a contemporary and successful case study of political and economic engagements between states on the African continent. It is, therefore, pertinent to delve briefly into the background of the Sino-Africa relationship.

The foundation for the Sino-African relationship was partly laid by the theory of 'Intermediate Zones,' espoused by Mao Zedong, founder of the People's Republic of China. His theory was inspired by the conditions and sufferings of exploitation, division, and rule meted out by the respective colonialists. In this context, Mao Zedong was determined to help African countries free themselves from the shackles of colonialism and post-colonialism[8]. Mao Zedong's theory of "intermediate zones" in later years formed a solid basis for China-

---

[6]Jervis, R., 1999, p. 43.
[7]Lewis, K. 2016; Doyle, 2005; Rasmussen, 2003
[8]Charles Mutasa, 2018

Africa bilateral relations. Over time, the theory has metamorphosed into the largest of Africa's bilateral trade. It is counter-intuitive to suggest that China's support for anti-colonialism in Africa would, in later years, engage in activities with a semblance of colonialism. The China-Sierra Leone political, economic, and development engagements for fifty-three years have been guided by mutual bilateral consent as sovereign states with the application of country-specific laws, rules, and regulations relating to political and economic engagements. It is, therefore, flawed to suggest that the political and economic engagements between China and Sierra Leone are exploitative or based on the "contest of power" as advanced by the realist and classical realist schools of thought.

In addition to the above, the political cooperation between the two countries was cemented by the ideological commitment to the South-South Cooperation (*SSC*) framework. This provided for mutual support and the transfer of skills and knowledge between and among developing countries. However, the ideological underpinnings of the SSC subsequently gravitated beyond theoretical circles to more hands-on and practical engagements between cooperating states in 1980[9]. This was exemplified in the successful and cordial bilateral relationship between China and Sierra Leone.

Sierra Leone and China are members of the Non-Aligned Movement (NAM). The NAM was established to represent and advocate the interests and aspirations of developing countries to which both countries are members[10]. The NAM developed within the context of two of the most important global developments of decolonisation and the Cold War. The movement was initially concerned with the interests of Asian and African countries, particularly relating to the resistance and influence of the major powers in the affairs of their countries. These ideological underpinnings of the NAM provided the platform where China and Sierra Leone shared a common vision for their countries.

The Group of 77 (G-77), like the NAM, was also formed in the 1960s after the decolonisation of many countries. The common problems relating to the post-colonial states in the global south served

---

[9] Jönn Altmann:pp. 143 – 147
[10] (Munro, André, 2024)

to mobilise them into the G-77 to amplify collective and stronger voices in international negotiations. By 1945, several Member States in the UN General Assembly were from the global south, mainly from Latin America and Africa. Thus, by the end of 1960, their simple majority had grown to two-thirds after many Asian and African nations became UN Member States.

Sierra Leone and China have common alignments and membership in the SSC, NAM, and G-77. The commonalities in their alignment helped to strengthen the bond, which also progressed to the bilateral and multilateral levels. Therefore, it is easy for both countries to cooperate and/or engage in matters of mutual political interest.

Contextualising Political Engagements between China and Sierra Leone

China and Sierra Leone have mutually supported each other's political interests at the bilateral and multilateral levels. Sierra Leone has always supported China's interest to isolate Taiwan in the pursuance of the 'One China' policy within the context of the United Nations Charter and International Law. On the 25th October 1971, the Government of Sierra Leone was among the 21 African countries that co-sponsored and voted in favour of UNSC Resolution 2758 for the recognition of the People's Republic of China as the sole legitimate representative of China in the United Nations. This was a fundamental political decision by the Government of Sierra Leone to reinstate the People's Republic of China to the UNSC with full veto powers. This episode laid a solid diplomatic foundation, which continues to crystalise in a several ways, including political and economic engagements between the two countries.

During the fifty-three years of committed bilateral engagements, China and Sierra Leone have cooperated based on their respective foreign policy and economic interests within the framework of the United Nations Charter. This underscores the argument that cooperating states with similar political objectives are more likely to deepen their engagements sustainably. Justifiably, Sierra Leone continues to cooperate with China in supporting international norms concerning multilateralism and the principle of equality among all countries[11]. In this regard, Sierra Leone hardly objects to China's interest in the pursuit of security and economic and political ties with friendly countries[12].

China and Sierra Leone have supported each other's political interests on a reciprocal basis. There is nothing wrong with this practice. In the engagements between states, this principle is often invoked for purposes of trade and other cooperating interests[13]. In line with the principle of reciprocity, China has supported Sierra Leone political interests on the global stage. For instance, China was one of the P-5 members of the UNSC that supported Sierra Leone's bid to secure a seat in UNSC in the non-permanent category for the period 2024-2025. In the election held in June 2023, Sierra Leone secured 188 votes to secure a seat in the UNSC. Arguably, this was a vote of confidence in Sierra Leone's ability and increasing respectability on the global stage. In this regard, China's diplomatic support for Sierra Leone's return to the UNSC was phenomenal.

In addition, China supports Sierra Leone's coordination role and Chair of the African Union Committee of Ten (C-10) for the reform of the UNSC. In this context, China continues to play a significant role by amplifying the voices of Africa for increased representation in the UNSC to redress the historical injustices done to Africa. To this end, China has supported Sierra Leone and the rest of the C-10 members by reiterating the African Common Position as enunciated in the Ezulwini Consensus and the Sirte Declaration as the only viable option to address the historical injustices done to Africa. This political support is worthy of note as part of the positive political engagements between the two countries.

Contextualising Economic Engagements between China and Sierra Leone

Sierra Leone and China present a successful case study of countries with strong and viable economic cooperation that has existed for fifty-three years. The economic cooperation between both countries is

---

[11](Wang, H.; 2011 pp 37-56

[12](Hartmann & Noesselt, 2019; Korvig, 2018

[13]Zoller, E. 1984. p. 15

based on a solid bilateral and diplomatic foundation. Within ten years of diplomatic relations, Sierra Leone became the largest recipient of Chinese aid in Africa[14]. This was a positive indication that the economic engagement between both countries would be promising in later years between two developing countries. Fifty-three years later, China remains the largest trade and investment partner with Sierra Leone[15]. Trade and investment are in several key sectors, including mining, health, agriculture, infrastructure, and marine resources.

Economic cooperation engagements between both countries have been guided by bilateral or multilateral framework agreements, including SSC, FOCAC, Joint Economic and Technical Cooperation Agreements, the Belt and Road Initiative, and Trade Partnership, among others. Therefore, the economic cooperation frameworks represent the needs and aspirations of both countries and are not influenced by power dominance or exploitative tendencies. Economic cooperation at the bilateral or intergovernmental levels is aimed at enhancing positive economic relations, trade and investment, and economic development[16]. Such cooperation may take the form of aid assistance, industrial collaboration, research, agriculture, and economic commissions, among others[17]. This resonates with the economic cooperation between Sierra Leone and China.

Some Tangible Outcomes of Economic Cooperation

The key outcomes of fifty-three years of economic cooperation between Sierra Leone and China can be argued to be impressive. A quick tally of economic cooperation between Sierra Leone and China dating back to the 1970s will reveal tangible evidence that the Chinese have invested in Sierra Leone more than any other friendly country. Sierra Leone has established diplomatic relations in the last fifty-three years. The outcomes of some of the key economic cooperation projects are presented in the succeeding subheadings and paragraphs.

---

[14](Brautigam, 2010. pp. 324–348)
[15]The OEC, 2022
[16]Caraiani and Georgescu, 2013, p. 9
[17]Barston, 2014, p. 391

a. Investment in the Magbass Sugar Complex

The Magbass sugar complex is an outcome of the China-Sierra Leone economic engagements in the 1970s. The Magbass plantation and sugar complex, located in the Tonkolili District, was the first large-scale sugar plantation in West Africa and had a land area of 1,280 hectares[18]. The company provided jobs for young people, paid statutory taxes to the government, and paid an annual rent of US$150,000 to land-owning families. This helped to improve their livelihoods and social conditions. In addition, the contract stipulated that the yearly rent to land-owning families would increase each year depending on the expected production rates until it levelled off to the whole development level. The huge investment signalled a promising relationship based on win-win cooperation and true friendship between Sierra Leone and China.

The complex operated from 1982 to 1996, when, unfortunately, the rebel war broke out in Sierra Leone, and the company was forced to close down its operations due to security threats to life and property. However, in 2005, the Magbass sugar plantation recommenced operation and provided job opportunities for approximately 1,500 workers. This helped to provide livelihood opportunities for the employees and their families and contributed to the economy of Sierra Leone.

b. Investment in bridges and road infrastructure

One of the tangible outcomes of economic cooperation between Sierra Leone and China is bridges and road infrastructure. During the fifty-three years of economic cooperation, key roads and bridges, as well as infrastructure supported by China, included the Mange Bureh Bridge, which provides a strategic economic link between Port Loko and Kambia District, which borders the Republic of Guinea. This is linked to the Economic Community of West African States (ECOWAS) regional priority Freetown-Conakry road corridor for facilitating the movement of people and goods. Other bridge infrastructures constructed by Chinese include the Lumely-Juba Sengbe Pieh Bridge,

---

[18]Davies, N. 2003

Savage Street Bridge, and many more, either constructed or refurbished in major road construction nationwide.

Roads constructed through China-Sierra Leone economic cooperation include the Lungi-Port Loko Road. The route also connects the Freetown-Conakry road corridor, contributing to regional trade and investment between Sierra Leone and the Republic of Guinea. Before its reconstruction, the poor state of the road impeded the movement of people, goods and services around the Lungi-Port Loko Road axis. With the completion of the reconstruction work, there is increased access to markets and agricultural produce and enhanced movement of goods and services between Freetown and the rest of the Northern region.

The Wellington-Masiaka highway is one of the iconic road infrastructure projects. The road is the first toll road in Sierra Leone operated under a twenty-seven-year Finance, Design, Build, Operate, and Transfer (FDBOT) Agreement signed in April 2016 between the CRSG and the Government of Sierra Leone. The safety and economic importance of this road include a reduction in very high accident rates and a reduction in high travel time due to traffic congestion between the Waterloo-Freetown Highway. The economic importance of the road includes increased income generated by commercial vehicles due to the number of trips generated. It has also created employment opportunities for Sierra Leoneans working in the toll gate facilities and road maintenance activities. What is more, the government's contractual arrangements with the CRSG took off the financial burden from investing in the much-needed reconstruction venture. This enabled the government to focus on other equally critical developmental priorities.

The Grafton-Regent Road constructed by the CRSG is another outcome of economic cooperation project. The 11.26-kilometre road, worth US $30 million, was financed through the Chinese bilateral development funds[19]. These funds help developing countries build small and medium-sized social welfare and other projects, including technical cooperation, material assistance, and to construct public

---

[19](Xinhua, April 27, 2014)

facilities. The traffic congestion was significantly reduced, and Freetown was linked to other suburban cities like Grafton, Jui, and Kossoh Town.

The roads and bridges infrastructure built through the China-Sierra Leone economic engagements have immensely contributed to trade and investment, facilitated the movement of goods and people, and connected communities, opening new networks and opportunities. This intervention has a cumulative benefit to Sierra Leone's economic growth and development.

c. Initial investment in agro-technical stations stop

In the last 53 years, China has made commendable efforts to boost rice production in Sierra Leone. These efforts include transferring knowledge and appropriate technology to boost large-scale rice production in Sierra Leone. This can be argued in accordance with the tenets of the SSC, wherein developing countries made commitments to support each other by transferring appropriate technology and knowledge in line with country-specific needs. The Chinese agro-technical support included the construction of agricultural extension stations and farms[20]. Between 1971 and 1977, the Chinese constructed five agrotechnical stations in Rolako, Makali (Northern Region), Lambayama (Eastern Region), Njagboima Station (Southern Region), and Ogoo Farm (Western Area). The agrotechnical stations were measured into several hectares of irrigated plots and targeted 900 local farmers. The technical assistance introduces intensive Chinese technology to increase rice production and inspires individual small farmers and beneficiaries to replicate the knowledge acquired to boost rice production in their communities. Furthermore, the project offered seasonal credit for production inputs, ploughing services, and free pesticide spraying to enhance high yield. Unfortunately, Sierra Leone has continued to grapple with rice cultivation for fifty years.

Agriculture and food security are priority sectors for economic growth in Sierra Leone. In recognition of this, the China-Aid Agricultural Technical Cooperation Team, under a Chinese government grant, has steadily promoted the increase in rice and maize

---

[20]Wang 2008

production for local farmers in Ogoo Farm (Western Urban), Lumley (Western Rural), Newton (Western Rural), Bo District (Southern Region), and other places across the country. The technical cooperation focuses on imparting modern agricultural science and technology to agricultural technicians and local farmers to improve grain output in Sierra Leone.

d. Investment in hydroelectric power generation

The government and people of Sierra Leone have benefitted from Chinese aid and loan facilities for the construction of several hydroelectric power stations, including one in Kenema District (Goma) and another in Port Loko District (Bankasoka). These technical cooperation projects can be appreciated against the backdrop that Sierra Leone has one of the world's lowest rates of electricity access, with electrification at 27.5 per cent. Energy accessibility and use contribute to sustainable socio-economic and agricultural development, trade, investment, and production.[21]

In November 1973, the Government of Sierra Leone and the Government of the PRC signed the supplementary protocol to the Agreement on Economic and Technical Cooperation. Between 1976 and 1985, the Goma hydroelectricity power plant project was designed and constructed using mostly Chinese technical expertise. The project had the capacity to produce 4 megawatts and became fully operational in 1986[22]. To boost and expand electricity supply to residents of Kenema and Bo, the Government of Sierra Leone in 2004 secured a credit facility in the tune of USD 3 million to China National Electric Engineering Co. Ltd. (CNEEC), for the upgrade of the Goma hydroelectric power plant from 4 to 6 megawatts. The plant connects thermal power plants in Bo and Kenema to a regional grid.

In the Port Loko District, the Chinese constructed a three-megawatt capacity plant on the Bankasoka River. The Government of China-funded this work through the United Nations Industrial

---

[21]Pearce and Webb, 1987.
[22]Davidson, D.R., 1988. p.64

Development Organisation (UNIDO). The project's objective was to promote industrial development, alleviate poverty, and enhance inclusive government for the people of Port Loko.

e. Joint Economic and Technical Cooperation Agreements

Sierra Leone and China have established a system of signing Joint Economic and Technical Cooperation (JETC) Agreements over the years. These agreements are a means of concretising economic cooperation projects through which necessary arrangements, guarantees, and incentives are agreed upon for transferring capital and investments for the mutual benefit of both countries. These agreements are aligned with Sierra Leone's national development plans and conform to the laws and regulations in force in the cooperating states. Two key JETC agreements relate to the construction of an industrial fishing harbour in Freetown and support for the Government of Sierra Leone's priority plans for four years, effective.

f. Construction of an industrial fishing harbour in Freetown

In 2019, the Government of Sierra Leone and China signed a JECT Agreement worth USD 29 million to construct an industrial fishing harbour in Freetown. Investment in the fishing sector is in line with Sierra Leone's National Development Plan, which prioritises the development of fisheries to diversify the economy. The industry will bring substantial social and economic benefits, including job creation and contribution to the country's Gross Domestic Product (GDP).

The industrial fishing harbour, yet to be completed, will have cold storage facilities, bonded stores, ice sales, systems for the purchase of fish and fishery products for export, and the maintenance of fishing and patrol vessels in the territorial waters of Sierra Leone. In addition, a USD 3.2 million partnership agreement to improve fish smoke ovens and water, sanitation, and hygiene was also signed to complement investment in the industrial fishing harbour[23].

---

[23]Sierra Leone Country Commercial Guide; 2021

g. Support for the government's five priority areas

In 2023, the Government of Sierra Leone and the Government of China signed a JECT agreement worth USD 13 million in Freetown. After the signing of the Agreement, the Minister of Foreign Affairs of the Republic of Sierra Leone confirmed that the grant would be utilised to support the government of Sierra Leone's five priorities in the areas of agricultural productivity, human capital development (HCD), youth empowerment, revamping the public service architecture, and lastly, investment in infrastructure, technology, and digitilisation.

Economic Cooperation through FOCAC

Sierra Leone was part of the founding states of FOCAC in 2000. This was another epoch-making event for Africa in general and for the Sino-Sierra Leone relationship in particular. The Forum was partly established to enhance 'a just and equitable new international political and economic order and promote 'collective dialogue', 'solidarity', and 'equality and mutual benefit'[24]. This Declaration resonates with the colonial experiences of China and Africa and the collective aspiration to support each other[25]. In much the same vein, the FOCAC Declaration is also in tandem with the principles of SSC, NAM, and G-77, to which both countries are members.

One of the outcomes of successive FOCAC summits since 2000 was the imperative to broaden and deepen Sino-African trade and economic relations on a win-win cooperation basis. This has demonstrably resulted in increased levels of Chinese investment in infrastructural development, trade, and investment, among other areas[26]. Sierra Leone is no different from other African countries.

Within ten years of establishing FOCAC, bilateral trade between China and Sierra Leone increased from over US $8.6 million in 2000 to US $510 million in 2019. In percentage terms, trade volumes between

---

[24]FOCAC I Declaration
[25]Taylor. I. 2011
[26]Alden & Jiang, 2019

both countries increased by 193.37 per cent. The increase in trade also resulted in job creation for about 4,500 Sierra Leoneans. At the height of the COVID-19 pandemic, trade volume between China and Sierra Leone impressively reached US $320 million in the first eight months of 2020[27].

Between 2021 and 2024, the trade volume between China and Sierra Leone increased at an appreciable level. In 2021 alone, the export value from Sierra Leone to China was $341 million. In 2022, again, the export value from China to Sierra Leone was US $573.14 million. In February 2024, the volume of goods exported from China was valued at $81.4 million. Conversely, goods imported from Sierra Leone to China were valued at $92.6 million. Between February 2023 and February 2024, goods exported from China increased by $63.4 million. In percentage terms, there was an increase in exports to China by 352 per cent. The volume rose from $18 million to $81.4 million. On the other hand, imports increased by $15.3 million (19.8%) from $77.3 million to $92.6 million[28]. The trajectory in trade between China and Sierra Leone is impressive, and the attendant results may include an increase in gross domestic product (GDP) and the government's revenue base. These were part of the consolidated fund utilised for national development programmes like Human Capital Development (HCD). Other FOCAC project initiatives include constructing the ultra-modern Foreign Service Academy, which is worth millions of dollars.

Conclusion

The China-Sierra Leone political, economic, and development cooperation has existed on a positive trajectory for over fifty-three years. In the context of their relationship, China and Sierra Leone have demonstrated that political and economic engagements between states for win-win cooperation are possible. China is the second economic power after the United States and has superior technology in the military, information, communication, and technology and other sectors more than Sierra Leone. However, there is no evidence that

---

[27] Government of Sierra Leone Ministry of Trade & Industry Trade Statistics 2023
[28] United Nations COMTRADE database on international trade: 2020-2024

China has ever used its military prowess to coerce Sierra Leone into either political or economic engagements. Rather, China has engaged Sierra Leone as equal sovereign states at the bilateral and multilateral levels for fifty-three years. This shows respect and true friendship.

As a developing country, Sierra Leone has limited infrastructure facilities, including roads and bridges. In support of this, scientific evidence shows that investment in paved roads, especially in developing countries with limited road infrastructure, has been proven to provide an impressive return on the economy[29]. In recognition of this crucial national need, the Chinese have supported Sierra Leone to construct several roads and bridges, including the Waterloo-Masiaka Highway and the Mange Bridge that links Port Loko to Kambia, which borders with the Republic of Guinea. These have in turn facilitated the efficient movements of people, goods, and services, improved access to markets by farmers, social services, and employment by reducing the overall transportation times and costs.

China has contributed immensely to the agriculture growth of Sierra Leone, which is in turn crucial to the economic growth of the country. In the last fifty-three years, the Chinese have considerably contributed to the agricultural development of Sierra Leone. These include the transfer of Chinese technology for rice production and assistance with farming implements. In 2022, the Chinese government donated 400 mobile rice threshers, 400 winnowers, 60 rice whiteners, 400 brush cutters, 500 rice transplanters, 100 chain saws, 400 knapsack manual sprayers, 200 repair tool kits, 100 hand drills, 5 diesel generator sets, 200 grease guns, and 10 diesel welder sets. These agricultural implements will contribute to the agricultural flagship program of the Government of Sierra Leone.

---

[29]Canning & Bennathan. 2000

List of Political, Economic, and Development Technical Cooperation Agreements between Sierra Leone and the PRC

No	Agreement(s)	Year
1	Magbass Sugar Complex Investment Agreement	1970
2	Agro-technical Cooperation on the Establishment of Agro-Technical Stations	1971
3	Supplementary Protocol to the Agreement on Economic Technical Cooperation	1973
4	Joint Economic and Technical Cooperation Agreements: This Agreement is signed on an annual basis depending on the technical needs of Sierra Leone	
5	Bilateral Cooperation Agreement under the Belt and Road Initiative	2013
6	China-Sierra Leone Strategic Cooperative partnership	2016
7	Finance, Design, Build, Operate and Transfer (FDBOT) Agreement	2016
8	Technical Cooperation Agreement for the Freetown Ring Road	2016
9	Forum on China-Africa Cooperation	2018
10	Global Development Initiatives	2021

References

Alden, C., & Jiang, L. (2019). Brave new world: Debt, industrialisation and security in China–Africa relations. International Affairs, 95(3), 641–657.

Barston, R. P. (2014), Modern Diplomacy, Routledge, New York.

Brautigam D, 'Foreign assistance and the export of ideas: Chinese development aid in The Gambia and Sierra Leone', Journal of Commonwealth & Comparative Politics, 31, 3, pp. 22–42.

Brautigam D, The Dragon's Gift, The Real Story of China in Africa. Oxford: Oxford University Press, 2011, pp. 38–39;

C. Wang, 2001, *China's Strategies from Higher Level: Diplomacy*. Shaanxi Normal University General Publishing House Co., LTD.

Canning, D. and Bennathan, E (2000). The social rate of return on infrastructure investments, Development Research Group, Public Economics and Private Sector Development and Infrastructure Group, World Bank

Caraiani, G. and Georgescu, C. (2013), Cooperare economica internationala, Pro Universitaria, Bucuresti.

Charles Mutasa, (Cham: Palgrave Macmillan, 2018).

Charles Mutasa, "Introduction: Inspirations and Hesitations in Africa's Relations with External Actors," in Africa and the World: Bilateral and Multilateral Diplomacy, ed. Dawn Nagar and

Davidson, D.R. (1988): Energy Decisions in Developing Countries in Africa. A Case Study of Sierra Leone. International Development Research Center, Ottawa, Canada

Davies, N. (2023). "Sweet Mother": The Neoliberal Plantation in Sierra Leone. In: Le Petitcorps, C., Macedo, M., Peano, I. (eds) Global Plantations in the Modern World. Cambridge Imperial and Post-Colonial Studies. Palgrave Macmillan, Cham.

Donnelly, Jack. (2000). Realism and International Relations. Cambridge University Press.

Elizabeth Zoller, Peacetime Unilateral Remedies (Dobbs Ferry, N.Y.: Transnational, 1984.

Goldstein, J. S. (1991). Reciprocity in superpower relations: An empirical analysis. *International Studies Quarterly, 35*(2), 195–209.

Hartmann, C., & Noesselt, N. (2019). China's new role in African Politics: From non-intervention towards stabilization?. In China's New Role in African Politics (pp. 1-14). Routledge.

Jervis, R. (1999). Realism, Neoliberalism, and Cooperation: Understanding the Debate. International Security, 24(1),

Jönn Altmann: «South-South Cooperation and Economic Order», Intereconomics, vol. 17, issue 3, (May- June 1982), pp. 143-147;

Kovrig, M. (2018). China expands its peace and security footprint in Africa. International Crisis Group, 24.

Lewis, K. (2016). What has the European Union ever done for us? [Online] The Independent. Available at: https://www.independent.co.uk/news/uk/politics/eu-what-has-european-union-done-for-us-david-cameron-brexit-a6850626.html[Accessed 17/03/2024].

Mearsheimer, J. (2013). "Structural Realism," in Dunne, T., Kurki, M., & Smith, S., eds., International Relations Theories: Discipline and Diversity, 3rd Edition. Oxford: Oxford University Press;

Meng, Wenting (2004). Developmental Peace: Theorizing China's Approach to International Peacebuilding. Ibidem. Colombus University Press.

Morgenthau, H. J. (1965). Politics among nations: the struggle for power and peace. New York: Knopf

Munro, André. "Non-Aligned Movement". *Encyclopedia Britannica*, 28 Mar. 2024, https://www.britannica.com/topic/Non-Aligned-Movement. Accessed 10 April 2024.

Murphy, Daen C. (2002). China's Rise in the Global South: the Middle East, Africa, and Beijing's Alternative World Order. Stanford, California: Stanford University Press.

Pearce D, Webb M (1987). 'Rural electrification in developing countries' a reappraisal. Energy Policy 15(8): 329-38

Rasmussen, M.V., 2003. The West, Civil Society, and the Construction of Peace. Palgrave, London.

Schelling, T. C. (1980). *The strategy of conflict* (2d ed.). Cambridge, MA: Harvard University Press.

Schuett, R. (2010). Classical realism, Freud and human nature in international relations. History of the Human Sciences, 23(2), pp.23-26.

Shinn, David H.; Eisenman, Joshua (2023). China's Relations with Africa: A New Era of Strategic Engagement. New York: Columbia University Press.

Sierra Leone – Country Commercial Guide - https://www.trade.gov/country-commercial-guides/sierra-leone-agriculture-sector   - (Accessed 3rd April, 2024);

Taylor, I. (2011). The Forum on China–Africa Cooperation (FOCAC). Routledge

The Observatory of Economic Complexity – Https://oec.world /en/profile/bilateral-country/chn/partner/sle Waltz Kenneth N. Theory of International Politics - Addison-Wesley Publishing, 1979. — 256 p.

Wang, H. (2011). China's Image Projection and Its Impact. In: Wang, J. (eds) Soft Power in China. Palgrave Macmillan Series in Global Public Diplomacy. Palgrave Macmillan, New York.

Xia, Y. (2020). Chinese Investment in Africa: An Empirical Investigation of Trends, Dynamics, and Regulatory Challenges. In:

Chaisse, J., Choukroune, L., Jusoh, S. (eds) Handbook of International Investment Law and Policy. Springer, Singapore

Xinhua, April 27, 2014 - http://news.xinhuanet.com/2014-04/27/c_1110430819.htm (Accessed 3rd April, 2024)

Yan, Zhou (28 May 2010). "CAD Fund to boost footprint in Africa." China Daily. Retrieved 24th March 2024.

CHAPTER FOUR

China's Development and Financial Assistance to Sierra Leone

Sahr L. Jusu

Introduction

The chapter discusses China's development cooperation and financial assistance to Sierra Leone since establishing a formal diplomatic relationship in 1971. The data on financial flows are based on published international and domestic sources. It is analysed based on the objective of the assistance and the social and economic impact of the flow. The data reveal that China's financial aid to Sierra Leone includes grants, interest-free loans, concessional loans, debt relief, investments in human and physical capital, and public administration, transport, and the health sector. China's development assistance to Sierra Leone is estimated at US$ 3 billion in the 53 years of bilateral cooperation[103]. The hardcore implication is that, continued China support for Sierra Leone in terms of infrastructure can reduce the public investment resource gap with multiplier effects that support inclusive and sustainable growth. Despite the increased financial flow, there is a dire need for more concessional resources to support economic transformation, especially in the energy and agricultural sectors in Sierra Leone.

Economic development remains a critical want by all governments around the world. While the quality of institutions remains important to economic development, the inputs into the process, such as the quality and quantity of labour and capital, are also crucial. However, to shift the amount and quality of labour and capital, governments need

---

[103] Government of Sierra Leone Ministry of Trade & Industry Trade & Investment Statistics 2023

to spend the resources raised domestically in the form of tax and non-tax revenue. Where resources are not enough, governments must leverage other sources, including external ones. This has been long expressed in the two-gap model[104]. This can take the form of building physical or human capital or the transfer of capital. This has been emphasised in[105].From the external front, borrowing and grants are the sources of such financing. Among others, key areas where other countries support domestic governments to build the quality and quantity of production inputs, which has virtuous effects on inclusive and sustainable growth and poverty reduction, are building the quality of institutions, which can take the following, namely health and education—to build the quality of labour; physical infrastructure—to facilitate service delivery and production in various sectors; military—to build security; and debt cancellation or rescheduling—to provide more space for government budgetary operation.

China has been a major bilateral player in the development process of Africa, especially in the 2000s. China's financial assistance to Africa has included loans for various development projects. For example, as observed in the China-Africa Bulletin (2024), data from the Chinese Loans to Africa Database (2023) indicates that in 2022, African countries received US$ 999.5 million from China as loans, down from US$ 15.93 billion in 2017 and US$ 8.50 billion in 2019. Also, during the period 2000-2022, 1,243 loans were made to African countries who received a total loan amount of US$170.08 billion from China, with 78.8% of it coming from the Export-Import Bank of China (CHEXIM) and China Development Bank (CDB), which are the two primary development finance institutions in China. The highest was in 2016, with about US $28 billion, followed by 2013 with about US $17.5 billion, 2017 with about US $16 billion, and 2018 with about US $14.9 billion, while the least was in 2000 with less than US $1 billion; followed by 2001 with about US$1 billion, and 2002 with about US $2 billion. Based on the same source, during this period (2000 to 2022), Sierra Leone received US $751.17 million in concessional loans. However, a declining trend was observed during 2016 to 2022. The declining trend could be due to increased debt burdens, which lead to

---

[104]Griffin, 1970 and Griffin and Enos, 1970
[105]Radelet (2006) and Chowdhury and Garona (2007)

reduced room for borrowing. According to[106], through the China Inter national Development Cooperation (CIDCA), which was established in 2018, China has strengthened its diplomatic means through foreign aid.

According to the China-Africa Bulletin (2024), about 34% of these loans were for the energy sector, which amounted to US$ 52.38 billion, with about half of this amount dedicated to fossil fuel projects with oil, gas, and coal energy sources, though with little for renewables, including solar (with about 2 percent). In addition, China accounted for 13% of the total external debt of Africa in 2022, and this amount was almost the same as what was owed to the World Bank, though lower than what was owed to bondholders (28%), with the largest debtors being Angola, with US $20.98 billion in 2022; Ethiopia with US $6.82 billion; Kenya with US $6.69 billion Zambia with US $5.73 billion; and Egypt with US $5.21 billion.

At the 6th Ministerial Conference of the Forum on China-Africa held in South Africa in December 2015, President Xi Jinping announced a US $60.0 billion package to "upgrade the new type of China-Africa strategic partnership". The development cooperation financing assistance covers US $5.0 billion of grant and interest-free loans, US $35.0 billion of the preferential line of credits, US $5.0 billion to the China-Africa Development Fund, and US $10.0 billion for the development of production capacity in Africa. Sierra Leone has already received its fair share in development financing, technical and economic cooperation support, and private sector investment under the Chinese Belt and Road Initiative.

In a recent state visit to China on February 28, 2024, the Chinese President, President Xi Jinping, and the President of the Republic of Sierra Leone, President Julius Maada Bio, signed a bilateral cooperation agreement with growth implications for agriculture, which is Sierra Leone's most prominent labour force employer and contributor to economic activities. It also has implications for other economic development fronts. Specifically, China's debt cancellation of US$ 2.78 million and technical assistance to Sierra Leone worth US $ 6.9 and food assistance worth 1,500 tonnes are elements of Sierra Leones' direct benefit in the cooperation component. This is consistent with

---

[106]Kitano and Miyabayashi (2023)

the Big Five Initiative of the Government of Sierra Leone, with agriculture at the centre of having food security.

Despite the increased China-Sierra Leone cooperation for economic welfare enhancement in Sierra Leone for over half a century, we are not aware of any study that comprehensively identifies the developmental role of China's financial assistance. The chapter's objective is to discuss China's development cooperation and financial aid to Sierra Leone. Driven by the data availability issue, the chapter focuses on identifying projects with dynamic social and economic impacts on Sierra Leone.

The rest of the chapter is organised as follows: Section 2 covers the sectoral spread and role of China's financial assistance to Sierra Leone. Section 3 discusses China's Financial Assistance Relative to Sierra Leone's Official Development Assistance and Government Gross Fixed Capital Formation, and Section 4 concludes.

The Sectoral Spread and Role of China's Development Assistance to Sierra Leone

China's aid to Sierra Leone started in the early 1970s, focusing on physical infrastructural projects. However, during this time, China also assisted similar African countries. Sierra Leone was among Africa's largest recipients of Chinese aid in the 1970s and 1980s. Sierra Leone has had a long-standing bilateral development cooperation relationship with China, with about 53 years of a sound relationship; however, the period of the eleven-year civil war experienced a slowdown.

Bilateral development cooperation and financial flows have been mainly in terms of supporting infrastructure projects, concessional loans, debt relief, technical and economic cooperation assistance covering infrastructure projects of energy, roads, sports, education, health, agriculture, security, gender and women's empowerment, and cultural affairs, as well as other spheres of the development landscape, including agriculture.

In celebrating 51 years of China-Sierra Leone diplomatic relations in July 2022, the Chargés d'affaires of the Chinese Embassy to Sierra Leone remarked as follows:

> The past 51 years have witnessed the notable results of cooperation between China and Sierra Leone, including: the construction of the

Youyi Building, the National Stadium, Mange Bridge, the Magbass Sugar complex, and the RSLAF headquarters in the 1970s and 80s; the China-Sierra Leone Friendship Road, Bo Stadium, Jui Hospital, the China-Sierra Leone Friendship Primary and Middle Schools, and the
Ministry of Foreign Affairs Office Building from the 1980 to 2000; and the second Juba Bridge, the Limkokwing-Regent Road, Myohaung Officers' Mess and Single Officers' Quarters, the National Optical Fiber Backbone Network Phase Two, as well as the Foreign Service Academy etc. up to 2018.[107]

He also stated as follows:

...our bilateral trade volume has now reached over US$ 500 million, and the accumulated direct investment from China to Sierra Leone has reached US$3 billion. Since 1973, the Chinese government has dispatched more than 500 Chinese medical personnel to Sierra Leone under the health assistance programme, and since 1976, China has provided government scholarships for over 1000 Sierra Leonean students to study in China. China has also dispatched about 100 agricultural experts to Sierra Leone since 1991 to provide technical training[108].

In addition, the Chinese aid has also funded the office block for the Sierra Leone Parliament, the West Africa Tropical Disease Research and Prevention Centre and the ongoing reconstruction and rehabilitation of the National Stadium. Despite the total cost of China's financial aid to Sierra Leone, it has contributed significantly to the state's functioning as the Youyi building constructed by China. It hosts a large number of ministries, thus supporting public service provision. The Youyi building hosts several government ministries, departments and agencies. The Ministry of Foreign Affairs and International Cooperation building plays a similar role to the Youyi building, though the former hosts multiple ministries. The National

---

[107] Embassy of the People's Republic of China to the Republic of Sierra Leone, Freetown, Sierra Leone
[108] Ibid

Stadium also hosts the ministries of sports, youth and the National Youth Commission.

In addition, China's support during the deadly Ebola virus disease and the COVID-19 pandemic is a quintessence of its contribution to the health sector resilience in Sierra Leone. China's financial assistance to Sierra Leone has also included sports, education, and agricultural interventions.

Table 1 presents a summary of development assistance to Sierra Leone. The key observation is that China has supported Sierra Leone in a wide range of sectors, including infrastructure to host government ministries, infrastructure to support the movement of people and goods, infrastructure to support energy, human capital building, agriculture, sport, and security.

Another important observation from the table is that, given the long-term use of the financial assistance outcomes, China's financial assistance has not been for short-term purposes but for the long-term growth and development of Sierra Leone. For example, while the National Stadium was one of the earliest Chinese assistance to Sierra Leone, it has also been renovated to maintain its quality. For example, for over a year, it has been under renovation by China.

Table 1: A Summary of Selected Development Assistance to Sierra Leone

No.	Assistance	Sector	Role of Assistance	Years in Use
1.	Youyi Building and Miatta Conference Hall	Public Administration	It was among the earliest Chinese assistance to Sierra Leone. The building hosts some ministries, and the conference hall has been used for a number of meetings to coordinate government activities as well as regional integration efforts.	>40
2.	Construction of the National Stadium,	Sport	This was among the earliest Chinese assistance to Sierra Leone. The stadium is the only one that has been hosting international matches, until recently when the Bo stadium contributed in this respect. Major domestic matches, including the matches in the national Premier League, take place there.	>40
3.	Reconstruction and Rehabilitation of the New National Stadium	Sport		
4.	Bo Football Stadium in Bo	Sport	Major national matches are hosted at the stadium, including the national premier league matches.	>7
5.	Ministry of Foreign Affairs and International Cooperation New Building	Public Administration	The building hosts the Ministry of Foreign Affairs and International Cooperation. A ministry that coordinates international cooperation activities for the Government of Sierra Leone, among others.	>10
6.	Ministry of Foreign Affairs and International Cooperation Diplomatic Academy Complex	Public Administration	It hosts meetings involving the Ministry of International Cooperation and Foreign Affairs and other stakeholders, including Sierra Leone's Development Partner Committee (DEPAC) meetings.	>5

Source: Ministry of Foreign Affairs and International Cooperation

Table 1: A Summary of Development Assistance to Sierra Leone Continued

No.	Assistance	Sector	Role of Assistance	Years in Use
7.	Dodo Hydro Dam in Kenema District	Electricity	This dam provides electricity to Kenema, a district that accounts for about 10% of the population of Sierra Leone.	>30
8.	Charlotte Hydro Dam in Gloucester	Electricity	The dam provides electricity for a significant size of the Western Rural population, which accounts for about 52% of the population of the capital city (Freetown) and about 8.8% of the population of Sierra Leone.	>5
9.	Bankasoka Hydro Dam in Port Loko Town	Electricity	The dam provides electricity for a significant size of the North-Western population, with Port Loko accounting for about 7% of the total national population.	>7
10.	Wellington- Masiaka Road Widening (67 Km)	Transport	This road is the only one that links the city, Freetown, to the provinces. Before it was widened, there used to be heavy traffic in the first few kilometres starting from Wellington, especially Wellington, to Calaba Town and Jui. In its current form, there is a lower chance of an opposite traffic accident as two vehicles moving in opposite directions are now far apart than they used to be. This is the case especially with big vehicles transporting goods in opposite directions with others or with passenger vehicles. Therefore, is more efficiency in transporting goods to the city and provinces with little delay, traffic, and/or road accident.	>10
10.	The Regent-Jui Road Project	Transport	Since this road was completed, movement of vehicles to the west end of Freetown from the east end at Jui and beyond has been easier. This includes those who move for work and other businesses, as well as children that attend schools at the west end of Freetown. This has also reduced the transport cost in real terms and brought increased flow of commercial vehicles, leading to more competition and lower transport costs from Jui to Wiberforce and Lumly in real terms.	>10

Source: Ministry of Foreign Affairs and International Cooperation

Table1: A Summary of Development Assistance to Sierra Leone Continued

No.	Assistance	Sector	Role of Assistance	Years in Use
11.	The Cockrill Military Complex	Security	This complex hosts a military facility, thus contributing significantly to state security.	>30
12.	The construction of military officers' accommodation block-Wilberforce	Security	This facility hosts military officers, making them comfortable to take up their state role, thus contributing to state security.	>5
13.	Construction of an ultramodern medical lab at 34 Military Hospital, Wilberforce	Health	The facility contributes to building the health sector and is accessed by the military population and family, as well as the non-military population, on a low-cost basis. It does contribute to health service delivery by the state.	>3
14	Limkokwe University to Regent (3.1 Km) paved road including high retaining walls		The road is very useful in shaping smooth transportation, bringing convenience and more commercial vehicles that transport goods and people.	>10
15.	Medical support particularly during Ebola and COVID-19 pandemics.	Health	The Ebola virus disease was deadly and capital-hostile. The same held for the COVID-19. Due to COVID-19's impact, Sierra Leone experienced a negative growth of -20.5% in 2015 following the outbreak of the disease in the second quarter of 2014. Growth was -2.0% in 2020, driven by disruptions in supply-chains and a weak investment hospitable environment. During this trying time, Chinese government supported Sierra Leone in its health shock response. For example, Chinese government donates 200,000 sinopharm COVID-19 vaccine doses in February 2021. Also, in March 2021, the Chinese government. donated 200,000 Sinopharm COVID-19 vaccine doses.	>7 (Ebola) >3 (COVID-19)

Source: Ministry of Foreign Affairs and International Cooperation

Table 1: A Summary of Development Assistance to Sierra Leone Continued

No.	Assistance	Sector	Role of Assistance	Years in Use
16.	Educational Training in Various sectors	Education	The role of human capital in development is important. This involves training in a wider area to support various sectors and service provision, including research and development (R&D). China has supported the training of a large number of Sierra Leonean students in higher-level education in universities in China. This makes the government of Sierra Leone saving such funding costs to be used on other projects and government services and also simultaneously building the human capital of its people.	>30
17.	Mange & Kambia Bridges	Construction	The bridge supports physical infrastructure and hence the transport sector, making it easier to move agricultural products from one end to the other and thus building the value chain through rural transportation and trade.	>10
18.	West Africa Tropical Disease Research and Prevention Centre	Health Research and Development (R&D)	Given that health shocks have shown to be destructive from a labour and capital perspective, the centre is a robust medical research facility for the prevention of epidemic. It does contribute to having a resilient health sector.	>5
19.	Magbass Sugarcaine Project	Agriculture	This is a key agricultural project. Thus, China's assistance in Sierra Leone extends to agriculture as well.	>20
20.	Office Block for Parliament	Public Administration	The building hosts members of parliament, which is a key contribution to legislation in Sierra Leone, as the right working environment is conducive to performance and productivity.	>10
21	Wilberforce Official Accommodation Complex	Security	This facility accommodates military officers, making them comfortable to take up their state role, thus contributing to state security.	>3

Source: Ministry of Foreign Affairs and International Cooperation

China's Financial Assistance Relative to Sierra Leone's Official Development Assistance and Government Fixed Capital Formation

1.1 China's Debt Relief and Loans in the Post-War Era to the Global Financial Crisis

While we do not have available data on financial inflow in the form of financial assistance from China to Sierra Leone during the war (1991 to 2002), the decade after the war saw continued financial assistance to Sierra Leone in an effort to have a strong fiscal space to address the post-war development agenda. For example, there was debt relief from China in 2007, coupled with grants, non-interest loans, and concessional loans from China from 2004 to 2008. Thus, even during the global financial crisis, China's assistance to Sierra Leone continued.

Table 2 shows the flow of financial resources to Sierra Leone and the incentive in the form of debt relief to build fiscal space for economic development and efficient public service delivery. The table shows that during the period 2004 to 2008, financial resources Sierra Leone benefitted from China in the form of debt relief, grants, non-interest loans and concessional loans amounted to US$ 22 million, US$ 22.5 million, US$ 43.5 million, and US$ 19.722 million, respectively. In addition, the size of non-interest loans was not only higher than that of concessional loans, but more than twice that.

Total financial assistance to Sierra Leone in the form of debt relief, grants, non-interest loans, and concessional loans from 2004 to 2008 amounted to US$107.7 million, which was equivalent to 5.6% of Official Development Assistance (ODA) to Sierra Leone, 11.7% of gross capital formation during 2004 to 2008, 26.3% of public sector gross capital formation during 2004 to 2008, and 17.0% of total external debt of 2008.

Excluding debt relief from China, which was in 2007, total financial assistance to Sierra Leone in the form of grants, non-interest loans, and concessional loans from 2004 to 2008 amounted to US$85.7 million, which was equivalent to 4.4% of official development assistance (ODA) to Sierra Leone, 9.3 % of gross capital formation during 2004 to 2008, 20.9 % of public sector gross capital formation during 2004 to 2008 and 13.5 per cent of external debt in 2008.

Table 2: China's Debt Relief, Grants, and Loans during 2004 to 2008

Financial Flow	Period	Millions of US$	% Official Development Assistance	% of Total Gross Capital Formation	% of Government Gross Fixed Capital Formation	% of External Debt of 2008
Debt Relief	2007	22	1.1	2.4	5.4	3.5
Grant	2004-2008	22.5	1.2	2.4	5.5	3.5
Non-Interest Loans	2004-2008	43.5	2.2	4.7	10.6	6.9
Concessional Loans	2004-2008	19.7	1.0	2.1	4.8	3.1
Total	2004-2008	107.7	5.6	11.7	26.3	17.0
Total, excluding debt relief	2004-2008	85.7	4.4	9.3	20.9	13.5

Source: Ministry of Finance and World Development Indicators

1.2 China's Loans in the Post-War to the Pre-COVID-19 Pandemic Period

Table 3 shows China's loans to Sierra Leone from 2004 to 2019 by sector and lender Type, which reveals that, at least from a lending perspective, China has been a strong development partner for Sierra Leone, as in the case of other African countries such as Angola, Ethiopia, Kenya, Zambia, and Egypt, which were top on loans from China during 2004 to 2020. A total of US$ 121.27 million in concessional loans came to Sierra Leone for energy, public administration, information, communication technology, as well as transport. This is equivalent to 9.06% of Official Development Assistance (ODA) during this period, 8.81% of gross fixed capital formation, and 24.41% of public gross fixed capital formation during this period, implying that China's development assistance to Sierra Leone in the post-War era to the COVID-19 pandemic era was significant.

Table 3: China's Loans to Sierra Leone: 2004 to 2020

Year	Project Name	Millions of US$	Borrower	Lender	Lender Type	Sector
2004	Goma Hydropower Project Repairs in Dodo chiefdom Kenema District, Gorata Village 4X1.5MW	3.00	National Government	China National Electric Engineering Co. Ltd. (CNEEC)	Construction	Energy
2005	GOSL/China Gov debt clearing account (2005281/SL GOSL	3.0	National Government	China	China	Finance
2006	GOSL/China Gov debt clearing account (2006281/SL GOSL	3.0	National Government	China	China	Finance
2006	Sierra Leone Rural and Sub-urban Telecommunication CDMA Network Project	16.69	Sierra Leone Telecommunications (Sierratel) (SOE)	CHEXIM	Development Finance Institutions	Information and Communication Technology (ICT)
2007	SIERATEL wireless local Cr No(2007)011918	16.0	Sierra Leone Telecommunications (Sierratel) (SOE)	CHEXIM	Development Finance Institutions	Information and Communication Technology (ICT)
2011	Dedicated Security info. systemCr.No. GC1018	11.0	National Government	CHEXIM	Development Finance Institutions	Public Administration
2011	Sierra Leone's National Security Network	15.48	National Government	CHEXIM	Development Finance Institutions	Public Administration
2012	National Optic Fiber Backbone Project Phase 1	15.00	National Government	CHEXIM	Development Finance Institutions	Information and Communication Technology (ICT)
2019	National Fiber Optic Backbone Project, Phase 2	30.00	National Government	CHEXIM	Development Finance Institutions	Information and Communication Technology (ICT)
2020	Agreement on debt suspension with China EXIM Bank(1st May to 31st Dec 2020)	2.0	National Government	CHEXIM	Development Finance Institutions	Public Administration
2020	Agreement on debt suspension with China EXIM Bank(1st Jan to 30th June 2021)	1.9	National Government	CHEXIM	Development Finance Institutions	Public Administration
2020	Agreement on debt suspension with China EXIM Bank(1st July to 31st Dec 2021)	1.1	National Government	CHEXIM	Development Finance Institutions	Public Administration
	Total	121.27				

Source: Boston University Global Development Policy (GDP) Centre's Chinese Loans to Africa Database (2023) a and GOSL, 2023: Statement of Economic and Financial Policies Exchange rate of US$ 1= CNY 7.26 www.bing.com/exchange rate

1.3 China's Capital Grant to Sierra Leone

China has made significant capital investment grants to Sierra Leone. For example, from 1993-2020, China made substantial investment grants to governance, energy and power, agriculture, health and sanitation, and entertainment sectors. This includes the sum of US $ 2,000,000,000,000, which was channelled for industrialisation, US

$45,000,000 for education, US $40,000,000 for sport, US $11,946,970 for health and sanitation, US $5,437,879 for governance, US $2,719,697 entertainment, US $2,106,061 for agriculture, and the sum of US $287,879 for energy and power. Table 4 shows these identified sectoral financial inflows to Sierra Leone from 1993 to 2020 in current prices (exchange rate).

Table 4: Identified Sectoral Financial Flow to Sierra Leone (2004-2023)

Sector	US$
Governance	5,437,879
Energy and Power	287,879
Agriculture	2,106,061
Health and Sanitation	11,946,970
Entertainment	2,719,697
Industry &Manufacturing	2,000,000,000
Food Aid	2,000,000
Sport	40,000,000
Education	45,000,000
Grand Total (US$)	**2, 120,298,486**

Source: Ministry of Finance, Sierra Leone

1.4 China's Recent Official Financial Flows to Sierra Leone

China continues to provide financial assistance to Sierra Leone even after the early years of the postwar period in Sierra Leone, and this support remains significant. This was also the case during the COVID-19 pandemic. For example, China Development Bank provided a loan of US$ 2 billion for Phase 2 of the Tonkolili Iron Ore project. It also provided US$3.6 million worth of COVID-19 vaccine. Table 5 provides a list of selected recent financial assistance to Sierra Leone.

Table 5: Recent China's Financial Assistance to Sierra Leone: 2021 to 2023

No	Description	Project Cost (in US$)	Sector	Flow Type	Direct receiving Agencies
1	Chinese Government donated 200,000 sinopharm COVID-19 vaccine dose in February 2021	3,600,000	Health	Grant	GOSL
2	China Development Bank provided a loan for Phase 2 of the Tonkolili Iron Ore Project (linked to Project ID No. 30068)	2,000,000,000	Industry, Mining	Loan	Kingho Railway/Port Company
3	The Chinese Government provided food aid to Sierra Leone for the Food Aid Tripartite Corporation Project.	2,000,000	Developmental Food Aid	Grant	Ministry of Social Welfare
4	The Chinese Embassy in Sierra Leone provided the Chinese Ambassador Scholarship to 147 students	US$ 45,000	Education	Grant	GOSL
5	The Chinese Government donated 200,000 Sino pharm COVID-19 vaccine doses in March 2021.	3,600,000	Health	Grant	GOSL
6	Chinese Government donated 200,000 Sino pharm COVID-19 vaccine doses and other supplies in August 2021	3,600,000	Health	Grant	GOSL
7	Rehabilitation, Reconstruction and Expansion of the National Sport Stadium Project	US$40,000,000.	Sport	Grant	GOSL

In a recent State visit to China on February 28, 2024, the Chinese President, President Xi Jinping and the President of the Republic of Sierra Leone, President Julius Maada Bio, signed a bilateral cooperation agreement with growth implications for agriculture, which is Sierra Leone's largest labour force employer and contributor to economic activities. It also has implications for other economic development fronts. Specifically, China's debt cancellation of US$ 2.78 million and technical assistance to Sierra Leone that is worth US$ 6.9 and food assistance worthy of 1,500 tonnes are elements of Sierra Leone's direct benefit in the cooperation component. This is consistent with the Big Five Initiative of the Government of Sierra Leone, with agriculture at the centre of having food security.

Conclusion

China's outstanding partnership, cooperation, and financial assistance have funded numerous development policies and projects in Sierra Leone, greatly impacting the country's infrastructure, human capital development, technology, and knowledge transfer positively. The various supports have been directed towards various sectors, including infrastructure, agriculture, education, mineral and metals, trade, investment, health and sanitation, waste management, mining, marine, and sport.

Going forward, as agriculture takes the largest share of labour force employment and economic activities and economic transformation remains important to Sierra Leone for inclusive and sustainable growth as well as poverty reduction, in addition to the importance of energy in economic transformation, the reduction of the reliance on food imports and building solar energy are important directions for harnessing China's assistance to Sierra Leone going forward. The Chinese government's goodwill, gestures, and humanitarian efforts are important aspects for appreciation by the people of Sierra Leone.

References

China-Africa Economic Bulletin (2024), https://www.bu.edu/gdp-/2024/04/01/china-africa-economic-bulletin-2024-edition/

Chowdhury, A and Garona, P (2007), "Effective Foreign Aid, Economic Integration and Subsidiarity: Lessons from Europe" United Nations Economic Commission for Europe Discussion, Paper Series N0 2007.2

Griffin, K. (1970),"Foreign Capital, Domestic Savings and Economic Development". Bulletin of the Oxford University Institute of Economics and Statistics, 32 (2): 99-112.

Griffin, K. and J. L. Enos (1970), "Foreign Capital, Domestic Savings and Economic Development," Oxford Bulletin of Economics and Statistics, vol. 32, pp. 99-112.

Kitano, N., and Miyabayashi, Y. (2023), "China's foreign aid as a proxy of ODA: preliminary estimate 2001-2022", Journal of

Contemporary East Asia Studies, Vol.12 (1), pp. 264–293. https://doi.org/10.1080/24761028.2024.2316532

Radelet, S (2006), "A Primer on Foreign Aid," Center for Global Development. Working Paper, No. 92, July 2006.

CHAPTER FIVE

Sierra Leone–China Relations: Cooperation at the UN Human Rights Council

Lansana Gberie[109]

The China-Africa traditional friendship is what we value dearly. Unity and cooperation with African countries have always been an important foundation of China's foreign policy. This will never change, even should China grow stronger and enjoy a higher international standing. China believes in equality among all countries, big or small, strong or weak, rich or poor. China upholds justice and opposes the practice of the big bullying the small, the strong lording over the weak, and the rich oppressing the poor, just as it opposes interference in others' internal affairs

President Xi Jinping[110]

It is an orthodoxy within the global human rights community that China actively works to make irrelevant the UN Human Rights Council and that, in pursuit of this policy, cajoles or coerces African and other developing countries to do the same. In a 2017 report, Human Rights Watch, perhaps the world's foremost human rights organisation, cited a European diplomat as saying that there are African countries "who are heavily dependent on Chinese assistance and who would not dare to say one word of criticism against China." The report claimed that, indeed, in recent years, China's economic clout has been such that even some European countries are vulnerable to its manipulation, including its "threats of punitive action, such as shutting out a country from the Chinese market or subjecting it to a diplomatic freeze." Such pressures, it claimed, "result in some

[109] I am grateful to Essate Woldemichael, Abdul Tejan-Cole, and Kingsley Lington for very helpful comments on the initial draft of this paper.
[110]Xi Jinping, *The Governance of China* (Beijing: Foreign Languages Press, 2014), 337.

delegations on the Council, even from Western countries, choosing to tone down or dispense with criticism rather than face China's ire."[111]

Where African states are concerned, this perspective, as will become apparent from these pages, which focus on China's relationship with small and economically vulnerable Sierra Leone at the Human Rights Council in Geneva, simplifies a complex and mutually supportive relationship rooted in remarkably consistent foundational commitments that have become more and more relevant with China's rise to global economic dominance.

It is important to note from the outset, however, that this chapter does not pretend to evaluate the entire human rights situation in China; still less does it pretend to dissect the complex interplay of principles and self-interests that underpin the foreign relations of such a dominant global power. Its purpose is chiefly to evaluate the mutually supportive relationship between China and Sierra Leone at the Human Rights Council, putting in context Sierra Leone's support for China on issues of extensive and powerful interests.

A Fundamental Commitment

Diplomacy tends to produce mountains of platitudes. Yet what is remarkable about China's relations with African countries, however small and economically negligible, is that the sentiments expressed at the establishment of formal diplomatic ties between them have remained essentially the guiding principles of that relationship.

On 29 July 1971, China and Sierra Leone signed a Joint Communiqué establishing diplomatic relations in Beijing. The Chinese government and people, it stated, "support categorically the government and people of Sierra Leone in its struggles against imperialism, colonialism, and neo-colonialism, in its efforts to safeguard national independence and sovereignty." Sierra Leone, for its part, "recognised that the Government of the People's Republic of China is the sole legal government representing the whole of China." Diplomatic relations and friendly cooperation between the two profoundly unequal countries, it was agreed, were to "develop based

---

[111] Human Rights Watch, *The Costs of International Advocacy* (New York, 2017) https://www.hrw.org/report/2017/09/05/costs-international-advocacy/chinas-interference-united-nations-human-rights

on mutual respect for sovereignty and territorial integrity, of mutual non-aggression and non-interference in each other's internal affairs, and of equality and mutually beneficial peaceful co-existence."[112]

High words. Yet, though the language is period, the underlying sentiments and anxieties have never been seriously compromised or betrayed. China provided important support to liberation movements in Africa and is the biggest foreign investor in Africa. Chinese investments in Africa, particularly in road and rail infrastructure construction, are of a scale that has never been seen before in some parts of Africa. On its part, Africa has provided staunch diplomatic support to China and was probably the most consistent and influential voice in support of the People's Republic of China's reclamation of its membership as the sole legal China at the UN (UNGA and UNSC) in 1971. Sierra Leone's commitment to the One China policy—the recognition that "the Government of the People's Republic of China is the sole legal government representing the whole of China", including Hong Kong and Taiwan—is the primary commitment that governs the different facets of its relations with China, including at the Human Rights Council. China's core anxiety about the integrity of its natural territory–which is expressed in various ways, now as respect for state sovereignty, equality and mutual respect, and now as non-interference or intervention into the internal affairs of sovereign states—and multilateralism, dialogue, and cooperation, which is glibly derided by Western commentators[113]—is shared often in visceral and profound ways by African and developing countries. Many of these countries (like China) were themselves violated and despoiled by the countries to which those commentators belong. Against this background, Sierra Leone's (and Africa's) close cooperation with China at the UN Human Rights Council must be primarily understood.

---

[112] These developments were carefully monitored by American intelligence. See: United States Central Intelligence Agency, *Daily Report, Foreign Radio Broadcasts*, Issues 141-150, (1971), pp. 43-44.

[113]Ted Piconne, *China's Long Game on Human Rights at the United Nations* (Washington DC:

Brookings Foreign Policy Paper Series on International Conference, September 2018) : https://www.brookings.edu/wp content/uploads/2018/09/FP_20181009_china_h uman_rights.pdf

The UN Human Rights Commission

The UNHRC is one of the world's most politically potent and contentious UN organisations. It is based in Geneva, Switzerland. The Council was established on 15 March 2006 by the UN General Assembly in resolution 60/251, replacing the Commission on Human Rights, the governing body for human rights at the U.N. from 1946 to 2006 and was widely criticised as being ineffective. To make the new Council substantively different, the resolution creating the HRC mandated it to "undertake a universal periodic review, based on objective and reliable information, of the fulfilment by each state of its human rights obligations and commitments in a manner that ensures universality of coverage and equal treatment with respect to all states".[114] Around 193 UN member states are subjected to this review: China has undertaken the universal periodic review of its human rights four times since the mechanism started (in 2009, 2013, 2018, and 2024); Sierra Leone three times. Both countries have been active at the HRC since it was established in 2006 China, which has long maintained a large Permanent Mission in Geneva, far more so than Sierra Leone, which only established a Permanent Mission in Geneva in 2012.

The UPR is a mechanism unique to the HRC, and it is safe to say that it cannot be dismissed as perfunctory; it certainly cannot be seriously manipulated or rigged. The review is based upon information provided by the country under review, often in the form of a "national report"; the reports of independent Special Procedures mandate holders, who are human rights experts; and national human rights institutions and non-governmental organisations, which are often at variance with the positions of the national government. Though the process is optional, China has submitted itself to this rigorous peer review four times since it was established, more than many other countries.

The Council has 47 governing members, selected (or elected) from the five UN-designated regional groupings: Africa (13 seats), Asia-Pacific (13 seats), Latin American and Caribbean (8 seats), Western Europe and others (7 seats), and Eastern Europe (6 seats). China has

---

[114] See: https://www.ohchr.org/en/hr-bodies/upr/basic-facts (accessed 5 July 2024.)

served in the 47-member Council four times, Sierra Leone only once (elected in November 2012). The regional groupings take turns nominating a candidate for chair, who often gets unanimously endorsed by the Council. The current chair of the Council is held by Morocco on behalf of the African Group. The Council is far more active than most UN bodies, with the notable exception of the UN Security Council: it holds at least three regular sessions a year for at least ten weeks: in February-March, June-July, and September-October. According to the work programme, some sessions can run for up to five or six weeks, which seems to get overpiled each year. The Council can decide at any time to hold a special session to address human rights violations and emergencies if a third of the Member States votes for it. Such special sessions, however, always rare, have become especially difficult to hold given the Council's polarisation: efforts by the Organisation of Islamic States, many African and developing countries to hold such a session on the atrocities in Gaza since Hamas' terror attacks in Israel have not been successful.[115]

Cooperation at the Council

Because rival powers have aggressively sought to portray China's diplomatic success in Africa and much of the developing world as malign and discreditable, it is important to begin with a clear and unambiguous statement: Unlike some of its critics, who have suspended their cooperation with the Council when decisions not to their liking have been made, China has engaged, with unfailing commitment and seriousness, with the HRC since its establishment. It has not taken anything for granted. Like other developing countries, China understands that the principles and practices that underpin institutions like the HRC, not to mention the personnel that drive and implement its policies, are Western-led and dominated. Still, it has not rejected them. China has instead calibrated its engagement with creative energy and resourcefulness to ensure that its views and principles are not ignored.

---

[115]However, prior to those attacks, the UN Human Rights Council held two special sessions on "The grave human rights situation in the Occupied Palestinian Territory, including East Jerusalem" – at the 28th session in 2018 and the 30th session in 2021.

Ambassador Chen Xu, China's Permanent Representative to the UN in Geneva, articulated China's attitude towards the HRC in a circular, canvassing other countries to support China's bid to be elected to the Council – which Sierra Leone supported – in October 2022 thus:

> The Chinese government attaches great importance to the promotion and protection of human rights. China has made historic achievements in its human rights cause, takes an active part in global human rights governance, earnestly fulfils international human rights obligations, acts in the spirit of the Charter of the United Nations and the Universal Declaration of Human Rights. China has actively participated in the work of the Human Rights Council, upholding the principle of impartiality, objectivity, non-selectivity and non-politicisation of the Council, advocating objective dialogue and cooperation on the basis of equality and mutual respect, staying committed to promoting all kinds of human rights in a balanced and systematic way.[116]

No doubt many other countries agreed with this self-assessment– China was overwhelmingly elected by the UN General Assembly to the Council in that election, for the sixth time. Those countries clearly appreciate in China's approach the very essence of multilateralism. China's enemies or geopolitical rivals, however, see something baneful: in the words of a paper published by the Washington DC-based Brookings Institution, China "has shifted from its traditionally more defensive posture to a more activist role, particularly on the U.N. Human Rights Council. This stems from a two-part strategy that seeks to 1) block international criticism of its repressive human rights record, and 2) promote orthodox interpretations of national sovereignty and noninterference in internal affairs that weaken international norms of human rights, transparency, and accountability."[117] It is this sort of framing, the reductive tendency to consign countries siding with China—on any number of issues upon which votes are taken and statements made—as suppliant clients, that has merely served to expand and entrench support for China at the HRC. The point is that allegations in respect of China's repressive policies are often

---

[116] A copy of the circular was sent to the present; it is in his possession.
[117] Ted Piconne, *China's Long Game on Human Rights at the United Nations;* op.cit.

exaggerated and sometimes downright fabricated, as many less jaundiced observers, including this writer, invariably find out from, say, a visit to Xinjiang, a province in China that is portrayed by Western countries, the Human Rights Watch, and corporate media as the scene of genocide and crimes against humanity. I will return to this important case shortly.

Since October 2018, I have served as Sierra Leone's Permanent Representative to the UN and other international organisations in Geneva. The HRC has been one of the key institutions that I have worked on; indeed, it takes up more than a quarter of all our engagements in Geneva. I write this chapter from the perspective I have gained from this engagement, including from my interactions with counterparts at the Permanent Mission of China in Geneva and missions of other countries. I have had close working relationships with the Permanent Representatives of China, of African countries and developing countries, and of several key Western countries and organisations, particularly the United Kingdom and European Union. My interactions with all of them have been invariably courteous and constructive, though we have not always agreed on key issues, mostly in respect of China.

Sierra Leone's relations with China, as with the European Union, the United States, and the United Kingdom, are of primary importance. The framework of our relations with China is our commitment to the One China policy. This commitment has extensive implications, and where the HRC is concerned, it implies support for China on some core issues that are most persistently raised at the HRC by China's critics: Xinjiang, Hong Kong, and Tibet. All the basic elements defining China's policy towards or within the HRC,— including the studied insistence that China's internal affairs "brook no external interference", the objection to "groundless accusations against China out of political purposes and based on disinformation", and the rejection of "the political manipulation by some countries out of their anti-China strategy and their attempt to initiate anti-China actions at the Human Rights Council, which will only aggravate confrontation and politicisation at the Human Rights Council"[118]–derive from these three core anxieties.

There is a far less defensive perspective from which Sierra Leone, like other African and developing countries, supports China at the HRC, however: it is a genuine admiration for China's remarkable achievements, particularly its eradication of absolute poverty and its transformation, within a generation, into a technological powerhouse. China frames the issue in a way that captures its approach to governance, including human rights and democracy: as a "people-centred philosophy" that has lifted "nearly 100 million people out of poverty, eradicated absolute poverty once and for all, and achieved moderate prosperity in all respects. It had also built the world's largest education, social security, and healthcare systems."[119] No one can doubt that this unprecedented achievement provides the soundest basis for the enhancement of wider freedoms and opening up of the liberal space and the effort by some Western commentators to denigrate these achievements in order to criticise China's human rights records has been singularly counterproductive. The fact is that Chinese citizens enjoy far greater freedoms than many others in the developing world, and most developing countries support China in genuine admiration of its enormous achievements in respect of human dignity and standards of happiness and living that their own citizens can only envy.

Sierra Leone is a free, democratic society that commits to the advancement of fundamental human rights, including the right to religion, a free press, free and transparent elections, and the rule of law. We find in China's emphasis on economic and social rights nothing that contradicts our values and aspirations; indeed, they represent, in important ways, their apotheosis.

In a speech that is collected into a book, *The Governance of China*, published in 2014, China's President Xi Jinping declared: "We should make safeguarding social stability our basic task, promote social

---

[118] The quotes are from a circular distributed as talking points to other Permanent Missions in Geneva by the Permanent Mission of China in 2022 as "key elements" in the affirmation of support for the One China policy (in author's possession.)

[119] See: Human Rights Council, Fifty-sixth session 18 June–12 July 2024 Agenda item 6 Universal periodic review Report of the Working Group on the Universal Periodic Review, China: https://documents.un.org/doc/undoc/gen/g24/034/58/pdf/g2403 458.pdf?token=uBFHtXiYbO48HtClvX&fe=true

fairness and justice as core values, and ensure a happy life for the people as a fundamental target.[120] President Xi also said:

We must ensure that all citizens enjoy extensive rights in accordance with the law, that their right of the person and property and basic political rights are inviolable, and that their economic, cultural and social rights are exercised. We must safeguard the fundamental interests of the overwhelming majority of the people, and fulfil their aspirations for and pursuit of a better life.[121]

These statements encapsulate, in a most fundamental way, China's approach to governance, human rights, and democratic freedoms: with its massive land mass and very large and heterogenous population, it focuses on the stability of state and society as the primary consideration and insists that the exercise of individual rights and freedoms must always be in sync with the "fundamental interests of the majority of the people." This alone, China's leaders contend, is what can support the enhancement of all the core values of a free and democratic society. In Sierra Leone, a country that endured years of violent civil disorder, these sentiments hold great value and attraction. Less easy has been the issue of religious freedom and tolerance, values for which Sierra Leone is justly celebrated—embraced, indeed, as a defining identity issue.

The concern in this respect arose from the case of Xinjiang at the HRC. In July 2019, a group of 22 countries–including Australia, Belgium, Canada, Germany, France, Japan, and the United Kingdom–wrote to the UN High Commissioner for Human Rights, drawing her attention to "credible reports of arbitrary detention in large-scale places of detention, as well as widespread surveillance and restrictions, particularly targeting Uighurs and other minorities in Xinjiang, China." The letter stated that China's repressive policies in the province particularly targeted "Muslim and minority communities" and called upon China's government to "uphold its national laws and international obligations and to respect human rights and fundamental freedoms, including freedom of religion or belief."[122] A few days later, a group of 37, mainly African and other developing, countries

---

[120] Ibid., 163.

[121] Ibid., 156.

[122] The letter can be found at: https://www.hrw.org/sites/default/files/supporting_r esources/190708_joint_statement_xinjiang.pdf (accessed on 10 August 2024).

submitted a spirited defence of China, in which they opposed "politicising human rights". The signatories defended China's policies in Xinjiang as effective and necessary measures to combat "the grave challenge of terrorism and extremism" and hailed the "deradicalisation measures in Xinjiang, including setting up vocational education and training centres," which the 22 countries had described as vast detention camps.[123] In a sort of follow-up to this, in February 2020, Croatia, acting on behalf of the European Union and other governments, circulated a draft resolution entitled "Freedom of religion or belief", initiated under agenda item 3, and opened it for sponsorship. The original draft of this resolution called for an independent investigation into the situation in Xinjiang, but, facing opposition, references to China or Xinjiang were removed, and it was adopted as a thematic resolution focused on the "promotion and protection of all human rights, civil, political, economic, social, and cultural rights, including the right to development."[124]

A few weeks later, the UK circulated a statement accusing China of "large-scale arbitrary detention, widespread surveillance, restrictions on freedom of movement, forced labour, as well as restrictions on cultural and religious practices, including prayer and reading the Qur'an, particularly targeting the Uighurs and other minorities."[125] Both the European Union and the UK appeared to have gotten information about the situation in Xinjiang from Human Rights Watch, which had published a dire report on China alleging that "Thirteen million Uyghur and other Turkic Muslims in Xinjiang are suffering particularly harsh repression." This includes the confinement of over one million Turkic Muslims in "political education camps" by the Chinese

---

[123] For a fairly balanced, and entertaining, review of these diplomatic manoeuvrings, see Catherine Putz, "Which Countries are for and against China's Xinjiang Policies," in *The Diplomat*, 15 August 2019; found at: https://thediplomat.com/201 9/07/which-countries-are-for-or-against-chinas-xinjiang-policies/ (accessed on 10 July 2024).

[124] See: https://documents.un.org/doc/undoc/ltd/g20/070/12/pdf/g2007012.pdf (accessed on 10 August 2024). The reference to the "right to development" doubtless indicates the length to which China and many African and other developing countries had to be placated in order for this resolution to be adopted.

[125] Undated draft statement, circulated in March 2020 by the UK Permanent Mission in Geneva (in author's possession).

authorities, where, according to HRW, "they are forced to disavow their identity" and "some have received lengthy and even death sentences" because of the practice of their religion.[126] Shortly after this, China, in obvious reaction at these attacks, circulated a "joint statement" for cosponsorship rejecting the allegations in totality, and describing the measures it had undertaken in Xinjian as "a series of counter-terrorism and deradicalisation measures in accordance with the law to address both the symptoms and root causes of terrorism and extremism, including setting up vocational education and training centres to free people of all ethnic groups in Xinjiang from threats of terrorism and extremism." It claimed that the measures "have effectively protected people's human rights. There was no single terrorist attack in Xinjiang in the last three years."[127] Urged to sign on to the China statement, I wrote a memo to the Minister of Foreign Affairs and International Cooperation, dated 09 March 2020, advising against cosponsoring any of the statements, China's and the EU's. The issue, I wrote, "is of fundamental interest to us. China is a very important partner of ours; it has come to our support in critical moments, and it is one of our most important and consistent economic and diplomatic supporters. We must always strive to support its core aspirations, like indeed we do over Taiwan and Hong Kong, and not act in defiance of its requests. However, we must also be mindful that we are respected globally for our commitment to democracy, to religious diversity and tolerance, and to all fundamental human rights. This is a major asset and represents a core national interest." Sierra Leone abstained from the conversation at the HRC.

Xinjing: A Defining Case

There the matter rested, until July 2022. On 18 July of that year, perhaps because of Sierra Leone's curious abstention from the Xinjiang debate—we had tended to cosponsor all of China's joint statements—and perhaps because my views had become known to the Permanent Mission of China, I received an invitation from Ambassador Chen Xu to visit Xinjiang, at China's expense. The invitation read in part: "To enhance a better understanding of China's

---

[126]Human Rights Watch, *World Report 2020*, 130-141.
[127] The statement is in the author's possession.

development and promote mutual exchanges in human rights, the Chinese Government will invite a group of Geneva Ambassadors from friendly countries to visit China in August. The program will include a trip to Xinjiang and other places. I look forward to the participation of you…" China organises such visits to parts of the country as a routine aspect of its diplomatic outreach. The invitation was accepted.

The background to this invitation was a very loud campaign by China's critics pressuring the UN High Commissioner for Human Rights, Michele Bachelet, to release a report entitled "OHCHR Assessment of human rights concerns in the Xinjiang Uyghur Autonomous Region, People's Republic of China," which had been written months earlier. China opposed the release of the report on grounds that it was ill-motivated, sloppy, and lacked basic objectivity —in other words, that it was politicised and constituted an assault on China's sovereignty. It then extended an invitation to Ms. Bachelet to visit China, including the Xinjiang Uyghur Autonomous Region, to make her own assessment before making a decision about releasing the OHCHR report. The government of China first extended the invitation to the High Commissioner in September 2018 when it was notified that an assessment of the human rights situation in Xinjiang was being undertaken. However, partly on account of the COVID-19 situation and partly because of enormous pressure from the US, UK, and EU, an agreement for the visit was only reached in March 2022. In May 2022, Ms. Bachelet made the trip. The Government of China made arrangements, upon the request of the OHCHR, for the High Commissioner to visit many areas and facilities in Xinjiang, including prisons, hospitals, experimental or education centres, mosques, and Uighur homes and cultural centres in May 2022. She also met virtually with President Xi Jinping, as well as with State Councillor Wang Yi, the Chief Justice of the Supreme People's Court, and with senior officials on public security, justice, ethnic affairs, and human resources, the State Procuratorate, and the Governor of Guangdong Province. In her report after the trip, issued on 28 May 2022, she also reported meeting with the "All China Women's Federation, the Secretary of the Chinese Communist Party of the Xinjiang Uyghur Autonomous Region (XUAR), the Governor and the Vice-Governor in charge of public security, and interacting with civil society organisations, academics, community and religious leaders, and others inside and outside the country."[128]

Many of us in Geneva found Bachelet's report on the trip to be painstakingly fair and balanced. She noted acts of terrorism committed by extremist groups, which have had "a terrible, serious impact on the lives of victims, including those tasked to protect the community," but urged that in its counter-terrorism measures, China avoids "human rights violations" of its own. Ms. Bachelet praised China's poverty alleviation and the eradication of extreme poverty, which "are tremendous achievements." She also praised the "introduction of universal health care and almost universal unemployment insurance schemes, which go a long way in ensuring protection of the right to health and broader social and economic rights."[129]

The High Commissioner found no evidence of concentration camps, genocide, or crimes against humanity, as widely reported by Western corporate media and human rights organisations like Human Rights Watch. For this factual and objective report, the High Commissioner was heavily criticised by the US, UK, and European governments, which forced her to abandon her planned re-election bid. Amidst the venomous backlash, China drafted a joint statement for circulation at the HRC opposing the release of the report without authorisation by the Council; on that ground, Sierra Leone, along with dozens of member states, cosponsored the statement.

Our—a group of Ambassadors and representatives of Permanent Missions in Geneva—visit to Xinjiang and other parts of the country happened two months after Ms. Bachelet's—in early August 2022 for three weeks. Like hers, our visit was guided, but we were shown all the relevant sites where genocide was allegedly taking place. As important, we visited mosques and Islamic centres and spoke with revered religious leaders. I can testify to the accuracy of Ms. Bachelet's basic observations. We found that the practice of Islam was not only respected by the state but was actively supported, and we found no

---

[128] Office of the High Commissioner for Human Rights, *Statement of UN High Commissioner of Human Rights Michele Bachelet after Official Visit to China, 28 May 2022*; found at: https://www.ohchr.org/en/statements/2022/05/statement-un-high-commissioner-human-rights-michelle-bachelet-after-official
[129] Ibid.

evidence of homicidal or genocidal intent, let alone activities, of the state against any group in the Xinjiang region or elsewhere. Instead, we saw evidence of remarkable economic and social investments in the formerly impoverished, remote region.[130]

We learnt during the visit that the Xinjing region, an integral part of China for centuries, suffered a series of terrorist attacks from around 2014 through 2019 and occasionally beyond. The attacks were perpetrated by radical Islamist elements, clearly influenced by Jihadists in Afghanistan and Iraq. The region has a large population of Muslims, whose religious freedom has never been abridged. Theirs was a cosmopolitan brand of Islam, relaxed and shorn of the fanaticism common in the Wahhabi variety. The extremist attacks and propaganda, therefore, shocked the Chinese government, which, though committed to its communist brand, had never tried to suppress Islam in the region; in fact, the religion has thrived there, with thousands of well-attended mosques that are subsidised by the state. The problem for the government was that, twisted up with the religious extremist propaganda and violence, there was a strong separatist tendency: the ideology being preached by the Jihadists from Afghanistan and Iraq is that the Uighur of Xinjiang are Turkic people who properly belonged to a wider Islamic Emirate, not China, which is dominated by the Han. The religious extremism, in other words, is fuelled by a corrosive separatist tendency stemming from abroad and that the Chinese government was naturally determined to stamp out.[131]

On 31 August 2022, under enormous pressure, Ms. Bachelet had the report released an hour before her one-term mandate ended on 31 August 2022, and quietly exited the scene.

The 45-page "OHCHR Assessment of human rights concerns in the Xinjiang Uyghur Autonomous Region, People's Republic of China", its authors said, was compiled from a desk review of "publicly

---

[130] Upon the suggestion of a British friend, I kept a diary; I'll be publishing my impression in due course.

[131] My knowledge of the Xinjiang was entirely derived from Western newspaper reports (particularly *The New York Times* and the UK's *Guardian*) and the reports of Human Rights Watch. On the trip there, however, I carried as reading material Fitzroy Maclean's *Eastern Approaches* (first published in 1949 and reprinted and issued by Penguin Global; (September 1, 2004) and James A. Milward's *Eurasian Crossroads: A History of Xinjiang* (Columbia University Press, 2021). Both proved enormously useful as background material.

available official documentation, as well as research material, satellite imagery, and other open-source information, examining their origin, credibility, weight, and reliability in line with standard OHCHR methodology." In fact, the methodology was skewed, and all the substantive allegations–of torture, sterilisation, mass detentions, and other serious violations–are based on the testimonies of 40 unnamed individuals said to have originated from the Xinjiang region who had sought asylum abroad, mainly in the West. None of the authors visited China.[132]

Following its release of the report despite this opposition, the European Union introduced a draft resolution in the Human Rights Council in September 2022 calling for the Council to "hold a debate on the situation of human rights in the Xinjiang Uyghur Autonomous Region at its fifty-second session under agenda item 2." On 13 September 2022, China circulated a draft Joint Statement for co-sponsorship condemning the release of the report in defiance of the Council and concerned government; the report, it said, depicted the "opposite to the realities of Xinjiang" and was based on "disinformation and draws erroneous conclusions." It noted: "We are deeply worried that it will undermine dialogue and cooperation in the field of human rights and exaggerate the existing trend of politicisation and polarisation at the Human Rights Council."[133] Dozens of countries, including Sierra Leone, cosponsored the statement, and the European draft resolution was soundly defeated in the Council, following which there was wide applause— unprecedented in the history of the Council. All African members of the Council, except Libya and Somalia, voted against the resolution. The Gambia, Namibia, Senegal, Gabon, Benin, and Cameroon all voted against the resolution.

---

[132]OHCHR Assessment of human rights concerns in the Xinjiang Uyghur Autonomous
Region, People's Republic of China, 31 August 2022, found at: https://www.ohchr.o rg/sites/default/files/documents/countries/2022-08-31/22-08-31-final-assesment.pdf
[133] The statement is in this author's possession.

Conclusion

I have discussed the Xinjiang case at length because it brings together many of the anxieties that underpin China's approach to the HRC and explains why many countries in Africa and other parts of the developing world tend to China at the Council's proceedings. It certainly was a defining moment for me.

Our cooperation with China at the Human Rights Council, however, goes beyond that important issue as I have tried to demonstrate. In order to expand the parameters of the conversation and policy options at the HRC, China has routinely introduced joint statements on the right to development and has co-sponsored major events on violence against women, one of the most important issues of great interest to Sierra Leone. While writing this paper, I reached out to the Permanent Mission of China in Geneva to get its views on the relationship between China and Sierra Leone at the HRC. In response, I got this note:

> Sierra Leone and China, both as members of the Like-minded Group, Group of Friends of Dialogue and Cooperation, and Group of Friends in Defense of the United Nations Charter, have delivered our common call on various of human rights issues. In terms of thematic issues, Sierra Leone and China have delivered joint statements on safeguarding rights of indigenous children and opposing unilateral coercive measures. During 26th Session of Human Rights Council, Sierra Leone and China, as members of Group of Friends of Family, have put forward the resolution on the Protection of family. In terms of country-specific issues, Sierra Leone has always co-sponsored China's joint statements on respect for sovereignty, independence and territorial integrity of states and non-interference in internal affairs of sovereign states.[134]

In the spirit of multilateralism, and in the interest of a mutually beneficial relationship, may this cooperation long endure.

---

[134]*Communication from the Permanent Mission of China to the Permanent Representative of Sierra Leone in Geneva*, 14 May 2024.

CHAPTER SIX

The China's Belt and Road Initiative: Infrastructure Diplomacy and Impact on Trade and Investment between Sierra Leone and China

Edward Hinga Sandy

Introduction

Sierra Leone, situated along the West African coastline, has embarked on a journey towards economic revitalisation through its participation in the Belt and Road Initiative (BRI). This ambitious global development strategy, spearheaded and launched by the People's Republic of China (PRC) in 2013, is a monumental infrastructure and economic development project aimed at enhancing global trade and stimulating economic growth across Asia, Europe, and Africa[135]. In the context of Sierra Leone, a country with a rich tapestry of natural and mineral resources, the BRI presents both opportunities and challenges. This chapter delves into the intricate dynamics of the BRI within Sierra Leone, exploring its implications for the nation's socio-economic landscape, infrastructure development, and international relations.

Historical and Geopolitical Context

Sierra Leone and the PRC have cultivated a robust and multifaceted relationship spanning several decades, characterised by cooperation, economic partnerships, and diplomatic solidarity. This relationship has evolved through various phases, reflecting both countries' strategic interests and geopolitical dynamics[136]. Sierra Leone established diplomatic relations with the PRC on July 29, 1971, during a period

---

[135]Alden et al., 2008; Brautigam, 2009; Corkin, 2011
[136]Zhang, 2020

marked by the Cold War and decolonisation efforts across Africa. This move was part of a broader trend among African nations recognising China as a key player in the international arena and an ally in the struggle against colonialism and imperialism. Since the establishment of diplomatic ties, Sierra Leone and China have engaged in high-level political exchanges and mutual support on international platforms[137]. China has consistently backed Sierra Leone in its efforts to maintain sovereignty and stability, while Sierra Leone has supported China's core interests, including the One-China policy and China's candidacy for international positions.

Economic cooperation forms a cornerstone of the Sino-Sierra Leone bilateral relationship. China has invested significantly in Sierra Leone's infrastructure, agriculture, health, and education sectors. Key projects include the construction of roads, bridges, hospitals, and schools, which have contributed to Sierra Leone's socio-economic development.

Bilateral Cooperation in Infrastructure Development

The strong bilateral ties between the two countries have translated into cooperation in infrastructural development in Sierra Leone. One of the early interventions was the construction of a multi-story building to house government offices, "the Youyi Building," as a symbol of friendship between the two countries. This three-winged building now houses more than half of government offices, including the Ministries of Health, Lands, Trade, and Industry etc. This bilateral support to Sierra Leone was done alongside the construction of a thirty-thousand-seat sporting and recreational complex now dubbed the National Stadium. Subsequent rehabilitation and/or expansion over the years have been fully supported by the Government of China through the ever-growing bilateral cooperation between the two countries. Other interventions separate from the "Belt and Road" initiative include the construction of the Head Quarters of the Ministry of Foreign Affairs and International Cooperation, the Foreign Service Academy, the Sierra Leone China Friendship Hospital in Jui, the China-Sierra Leone Friendship House, etc. All these interventions have helped in

---

[137]Moyo, 2019

institutional strengthening but have also improved the people-to-people relationship between the two countries.

Under the Belt and Road Initiative, China sees Sierra Leone as a strategic partner, particularly in the Mano River sub-region. China's efforts to have a competitive advantage for natural resources have seen the need to strengthen ties with the entire African continent for mutual win-win cooperation (Shen, 2015). Consequently, the country has intensified efforts to cooperate with African countries in investing in key infrastructural initiatives to bolster trade cooperation. In Sierra Leone, China's interest in pursuing this initiative has been demonstrated in both bilateral cooperation and investment in roads, railways, bridges, and ports.

Through bilateral cooperation, China has supported Sierra Leone in the construction of the Hill Station-Jui Hill-side By-pass, the Sengbeh Pieh Bridge in Juba Hills, the Savage Street Bridge, and commercial investment initiatives have seen investments by the China Railway Seventh Group in reconstruction and expansion of the Wellington-Masiaka dual-carriage highway funded through a "Build, Operate, and Transfer" (BOT) financing model. This intervention has immensely improved connectivity between the capital, Freetown, and the rest of the country, with a huge impact on economic growth.

Trade and Investment

Trade between Sierra Leone and China has grown substantially over the years. China is one of Sierra Leone's major trading partners, with significant exchanges in minerals, timber, and agricultural products. Chinese companies have also invested in Sierra Leone's mining sector, particularly in iron ore and bauxite extraction, contributing to the country's economic diversification. Sierra Leone can now boast of hosting over ten Chinese mining companies in various minerals ranging from gold, diamond, iron ore, coltan, ilmenite, etc. Iron ore is the key mineral exported to China from Sierra Leone, and several Chinese companies have footprints in the sector. Currently, Leone Rock Metal Group has launched over USD $153 million on the upgrade and reconstruction of the Tonkolili-Pepel Railway and Port infrastructure to handle an estimated haulage of $18.8 billion tonnes of iron ore[138]. This railway and port are also open to use for haulage of other companies' minerals. Other Chinese mining companies have expanded and improved a considerable amount of feeder roads linking rural areas to markets. Chinese companies in the timber industry have invested in timber processing factories that have created thousands of skilled jobs for youths and women. The construction of warehouses and other export processing facilities has contributed to the increase in valued-added exports, invariably contributing to GDP. In the manufacturing sector, Chinese companies have invested in the creation of manufacturing zones, which have contributed to the country's import substitution drive.

China has played a vital role in providing humanitarian aid and technical assistance to Sierra Leone, especially during health emergencies and natural disasters. During the Ebola outbreak in 2014-2016, China was one of the first countries to respond, sending medical teams, supplies, and financial aid to combat the epidemic. This timely assistance strengthened the country's healthcare system to respond to such emergencies. During the COVID-19 global outbreak, China supported Sierra Leone with both personnel and vaccines to strengthen the resilience of the National Response Strategy. China also responded with support during the natural disasters, like the Freetown mudslide that washed hundreds of people along disaster-prone areas. All of this support from China has resulted in the strengthening of people-to-people cooperation between the two countries.

Cultural and educational exchanges have also been a significant aspect of the bilateral relationship. China offers scholarships to Sierra Leonean students, fostering educational ties and mutual understanding. In the last ten years alone, China has trained over 1000 Sierra Leones in various fields of study ranging from science, engineering, medicine, leadership, public administration etc. The number of professionals trained in China is gradually dominating the public and civil services. Through short programs, China provides capacity building for civil servants and members of the security sector, including the military[139]. Additionally, cultural delegations and events have promoted people-to-people exchanges, enriching the cultural fabric of both nations.

---

[138]Leone Rock Metal Group – Sierra Leone www.leonerock.com
[139]Benabdallah, 2019

The relationship between Sierra Leone and China is poised to grow stronger, with continued cooperation in various fields. Future prospects include deepening economic ties, expanding infrastructure projects, and enhancing collaboration in areas such as technology, tourism, and renewable energy.

Geopolitical significance of Sierra Leone in the context of BRI

Sierra Leone's position along the Atlantic coast makes it a vital maritime hub within the BRI framework. The country's deep-water port in Freetown is one of the largest natural harbours in the world, providing an essential gateway for maritime trade routes linking Africa to Europe, the Americas, and Asia. This strategic location enables Sierra Leone to serve as a pivotal point for the Maritime Silk Road, facilitating the movement of goods and resources across continents.

Sierra Leone's abundant natural resources, including diamonds, iron ore, bauxite, rutile, and fisheries, present significant economic opportunities within the BRI context. Chinese investments in the mining sector, coupled with infrastructure development projects, have the potential to unlock these resources, driving economic growth and fostering trade[140].By integrating Sierra Leone into the BRI, China can secure access to critical raw materials, supporting its industrial and economic ambitions.

Infrastructure development is a core component of the BRI[141], and Sierra Leone stands to benefit substantially from Chinese investments in this area. Key projects, such as the construction of roads, bridges, and the Mamamah International Airport, aim to enhance connectivity within Sierra Leone and between the country and its regional neighbours. Improved infrastructure not only facilitates trade but also promotes regional integration, economic diversification, and social development (UNDP, 2021).

Sierra Leone's participation in the BRI strengthens its diplomatic and political ties with China, one of the world's leading economic and geopolitical powers. This relationship provides Sierra Leone with a reliable partner for development assistance, technological transfer, and capacity building. In return, China gains a supportive ally in West

---

[140]Renwick & Gu, 2016
[141]Vines, 2014

Africa, bolstering its influence and presence on the continent. This reciprocal relationship enhances China's ability to project its soft power and pursue its strategic interests in the region.

The stability and security of West Africa are crucial for the success of the BRI. Sierra Leone's role in regional peacekeeping and its commitment to political stability contribute to a favourable environment for BRI projects. China's engagement in Sierra Leone, through investments and developmental aid, helps promote stability, economic growth, and governance reforms, aligning with the broader objectives of the BRI.[142]

Integrating Sierra Leone into the BRI framework provides China with expanded access to West African markets, fostering increased trade and investment opportunities[143]. Sierra Leone can serve as a trade and logistics hub, connecting Chinese businesses with markets in the Economic Community of West African States (ECOWAS) and beyond. This expanded market access supports China's goal of diversifying its trade routes and reducing dependence on traditional markets.

The BRI also encompasses cultural and educational exchanges, enhancing people-to-people connectivity. Sierra Leone's inclusion in the BRI promotes cultural understanding, educational collaboration, and technological exchange between the two countries. Chinese scholarships, cultural delegations, and language programs contribute to building a foundation of mutual respect and cooperation.

Infrastructure Development under BRI:

The BRI has brought substantial infrastructure investments to Sierra Leone, focusing on enhancing connectivity, promoting economic growth, and fostering regional integration. Two notable BRI-funded projects in Sierra Leone are the road linking Hill Station to Jui Junction and the road connecting Freetown to Masiaka. These projects have had significant impacts on the country's socio-economic landscape.

The construction of the road linking Hill Station to Jui Junction is a critical infrastructure project designed to improve urban mobility and alleviate traffic congestion in Freetown. This highway serves as a key

---

[142]Zhang, 2020.
[143]World Bank, 2022

link between the city centre and its eastern suburbs, significantly enhancing the flow of people and goods. The improved road infrastructure has substantially reduced travel times between Hill Station and Jui Junction, providing a significant boost to local businesses by facilitating the efficient movement of goods and services[144]. This has stimulated economic activities in the region. The road improvements have also led to a notable rise in property values along the route, attracting both residential and commercial investments, which contribute to urban development and economic growth. Additionally, the construction and ongoing maintenance of the road have created numerous employment opportunities for local communities, thereby reducing unemployment rates in the area.

From a social perspective, reduced travel times and improved road conditions have significantly enhanced the quality of life for residents. Easy commutes mean less time spent in traffic, better access to essential services such as healthcare and education, and an overall increase in daily life efficiency. Furthermore, the new road infrastructure incorporates improved safety features, including clear signage and pedestrian crossings, which have reduced the risk of accidents and enhanced overall road safety for drivers and pedestrians.

Similarly, the road connecting Freetown to Masiaka is a pivotal BRI-funded project, serving as a major transportation corridor that links the capital city with the rest of the country. The upgraded road infrastructure has streamlined the transportation of goods between Freetown and other regions of Sierra Leone, boosting trade, reducing transportation costs, and increasing the efficiency of supply chains. This has provided significant benefits to the overall economy. Additionally, the road has spurred economic activities along its route, promoting the growth of towns and communities. Improved connectivity has attracted investments in various sectors, including agriculture, retail, and tourism, thereby driving regional development. By enhancing access to different parts of the country, the road has also enabled economic diversification, opening up new markets for local products and facilitating the movement of labour and resources, contributing to a more dynamic economy.

---

[144]Financial Times, 2019; The Economist 2020

The improved road infrastructure has significantly enhanced mobility for residents, providing easier access to employment opportunities, educational institutions, and healthcare services. This has promoted social inclusion and reduced regional disparities. The road project has included the development of ancillary infrastructure, such as bridges and drainage systems, which benefit local communities. These improvements have enhanced the resilience of these communities to environmental challenges, such as flooding, thereby improving their overall living conditions. The improved road network has also facilitated the delivery of public services, including emergency response and utility maintenance, thereby improving the overall quality of life for residents along the route and ensuring better access to essential services.

Challenges and Opportunities

The Belt and Road Initiative (BRI) has presented Sierra Leone with a unique blend of challenges and opportunities in the realm of infrastructure development. As Sierra Leone endeavours to leverage BRI investments for its economic and social advancement, it is essential to navigate the complex landscape of development effectively.

Opportunities

The infusion of BRI funds into Sierra Leone's infrastructure sector has the potential to catalyse significant economic growth. Improved infrastructure such as roads, bridges, and airports enhance connectivity, facilitating trade and commerce both within the country and with international partners. For instance, the construction of major roads linking key regions boosts the efficiency of supply chains, reduces transportation costs, and opens up new markets for local businesses.

Infrastructure projects funded by the BRI create numerous employment opportunities for the local population. The construction and maintenance of roads, bridges, and other facilities require a substantial workforce, providing jobs to thousands of Sierra

Leoneans[145]. Additionally, these projects offer opportunities for skill development and capacity building in sectors such as construction, engineering, and project management.

BRI projects often involve the introduction of advanced technologies and best practices in infrastructure development. Chinese firms, with their extensive experience and expertise, bring in modern construction techniques and management strategies. This transfer of technology and knowledge can significantly enhance the capabilities of local firms and professionals, fostering a more skilled and competitive workforce in Sierra Leone.

Improved infrastructure facilitates better regional integration, not only within Sierra Leone but also with neighbouring countries. Enhanced connectivity through road networks and ports can strengthen Sierra Leone's position as a regional trade hub, promoting economic cooperation and development across West Africa.

Challenges

One of the primary concerns associated with BRI projects is the issue of debt sustainability. The large-scale infrastructure projects often require significant financial investments, leading to increased borrowing by the host country. Sierra Leone must manage its debt levels prudently to avoid the risk of debt distress, which could undermine long-term economic stability and development.

Infrastructure development can have adverse environmental impacts, including deforestation, habitat destruction, and increased pollution. It is crucial to ensure that BRI projects in Sierra Leone adhere to stringent environmental standards and implement sustainable practices to minimise ecological damage and preserve natural resources.

Large infrastructure projects may lead to the displacement of local communities and the disruption of livelihoods. Addressing the social impact of these projects is essential to ensuring that affected populations are adequately compensated and resettled and that their socio-economic well-being is safeguarded.

---

[145]African Development Bank, 2020

The quality of construction and the transparency of project implementation are critical factors in the success of infrastructure development. Ensuring that BRI projects in Sierra Leone meet high standards of quality and are executed with transparency and accountability is vital to maximise their long-term benefits and mitigate potential risks of corruption and inefficiency.

Political instability and regulatory challenges can pose significant risks to infrastructure projects. Changes in government, policy shifts, and regulatory hurdles can delay or derail projects, leading to increased costs and uncertainties. Strengthening political stability and creating a conducive regulatory environment are essential to attract and sustain BRI investments.

Economic Implications

The BRI has had a significant influence on Sierra Leone's economy, particularly in terms of trade and investment opportunities. The BRI has enabled Sierra Leone to diversify its trade partnerships, moving beyond traditional trading partners and tapping into new markets. China's active engagement through the BRI has opened significant export opportunities
for Sierra Leonean products, particularly in the mining and agricultural sectors[146]. Minerals such as iron ore and bauxite, along with agricultural commodities, now find broader markets in China, boosting export revenues.

The development of critical infrastructure under the BRI, such as roads, railways, ports, and airports, has greatly improved Sierra Leone's trade logistics. The enhanced transportation network has reduced the cost and time associated with moving goods, making Sierra Leonean exports more competitive on the global market. For instance, the upgraded road network linking Freetown to key regions facilitates smoother and faster transit of goods to international markets.

With better infrastructure, Sierra Leone has increased its export capacity, particularly in sectors where it has a competitive advantage. Improved road networks and port facilities have enabled the efficient extraction and export of natural resources[147]. The country's enhanced

---

[146]AidData, 2020
[147]China Research Initiative, 2021

export capacity not only boosts its trade volumes but also attracts foreign direct investment (FDI) into these sectors, further stimulating economic growth.

The BRI has significantly increased FDI inflows into Sierra Leone, particularly from Chinese enterprises. These investments span various sectors, including mining, agriculture, infrastructure, and manufacturing. Chinese companies have invested heavily in the development of mining projects, bringing in capital, technology, and expertise. These investments have not only increased production capacities but have also created jobs and spurred local economic activities.

Social and Environmental Considerations

BRI projects in Sierra Leone have significant socio-cultural implications for local communities. The displacement of communities due to large-scale infrastructure developments is one of the most profound impacts. These projects often require extensive land acquisitions, which can displace people from their ancestral lands. This disruption affects traditional land use practices, such as subsistence agriculture and local resource management, leading to the loss of livelihoods and cultural heritage. The affected communities may face difficulties adapting to the economic changes introduced by these projects, which often come with a shift from traditional practices to new forms of employment and economic activities.

The cultural erosion resulting from BRI projects is another critical issue. The influx of external actors and the introduction of new economic activities can undermine local traditions, languages, and social structures. As new cultural influences permeate local areas, there can be a gradual erosion of traditional values and practices. The integration of foreign lifestyles and economic models may displace indigenous cultural practices, leading to a dilution of cultural identity.

Social inequality is often exacerbated by BRI projects. While such initiatives can provide economic benefits, the distribution of these benefits can be uneven. Those with connections to project stakeholders or who are able to leverage new economic opportunities may benefit disproportionately, while marginalised communities may find themselves excluded or inadequately compensated. This disparity can result in heightened social tensions and conflicts within affected communities, as those left out of the economic gains may feel neglected or exploited.

Despite these challenges, BRI projects can offer significant economic opportunities. Enhanced infrastructure, such as improved transportation, communication, and energy networks, can stimulate local economies by providing better access to markets, healthcare, and education. However, the key to maximising these benefits lies in ensuring that they are equitably distributed. Effective engagement with local communities during the planning and implementation phases of BRI projects is crucial. Involving local stakeholders in decision-making processes and ensuring their active participation can help mitigate negative socio-cultural impacts and foster a sense of ownership and inclusion.

The environmental sustainability of BRI projects is a pressing concern, particularly in regions like Sierra Leone where ecological balance is delicate. Large-scale infrastructure projects can lead to significant disruptions in local ecosystems. Changes in land use, such as deforestation and habitat destruction, can adversely affect biodiversity and disrupt ecological balance. To address these issues, it is essential to conduct comprehensive environmental impact assessments (EIAs) before project initiation. These assessments should identify potential environmental risks and outline mitigation strategies to protect natural habitats and wildlife.

Resource management is another critical aspect of environmental sustainability. BRI projects often involve the extraction and utilisation of natural resources, including minerals, timber, and water. Overexploitation of these resources can lead to long-term environmental degradation. Sustainable resource management practices, such as regulated harvesting and waste minimisation, are necessary to ensure that resource use does not compromise future availability and ecological health.

Pollution and waste generated from construction and operational activities are significant environmental concerns. Infrastructure projects can produce air and water pollution, as well as solid waste, which can harm local ecosystems and communities. To mitigate these impacts, it is important to implement robust waste management systems, adopt pollution control measures, and utilise green technologies that reduce environmental footprints.

Climate change considerations must be integrated into BRI project planning and execution. Infrastructure development can contribute to increased greenhouse gas emissions and alter local climate patterns. Therefore, incorporating climate resilience measures into project designs—such as using energy-efficient technologies and adapting to changing environmental conditions—is vital. By addressing potential climate impacts and promoting practices that reduce carbon footprints, BRI projects can contribute to overall climate sustainability.

Promoting sustainable development practices within BRI initiatives can further enhance their environmental sustainability. This includes adopting eco-friendly construction methods, improving energy efficiency, and supporting conservation efforts. Collaboration with environmental organisations and local communities is essential to ensure that projects align with conservation goals and contribute to long-term environmental stewardship.

Political Dimensions:

Sierra Leone's involvement in the BRI carries several significant political implications, shaping the country's domestic and international standing. One of the key political impacts is the enhancement of Sierra Leone's strategic importance in the global arena. By participating in the BRI, Sierra Leone positions itself as a key partner in China's extensive network of trade and investment. This alignment can increase the country's geopolitical leverage, attracting further investments and fostering a more prominent role in international trade routes. However, it also means that Sierra Leone's foreign policy and economic strategies may become increasingly intertwined with China's interests, potentially influencing its alignment in broader geopolitical conflicts or negotiations.

Sierra Leone's engagement with the BRI may also lead to shifts in its domestic political dynamics. The infusion of Chinese investment and the development of infrastructure projects can alter local power structures and economic dependencies. Political leaders may leverage the benefits of BRI projects to bolster their domestic support, but this could also lead to increased scrutiny and criticism, particularly if the projects are perceived as favouring certain political elites or if there are issues related to transparency and accountability.

Moreover, the influx of foreign investment and development projects can intensify local political dynamics and tensions. Communities affected by BRI projects might demand greater transparency, fair compensation, and adherence to environmental and social safeguards. These demands could lead to increased political activism and influence, potentially reshaping local governance and policy priorities.

Sierra Leone's participation in the BRI has significant implications for its diplomatic relationships and international partnerships. The initiative has facilitated a strengthening of ties between Sierra Leone and China, leading to deeper diplomatic and economic engagements[148]. This partnership extends beyond mere trade and investment, encompassing areas such as technology transfer, infrastructure development, and cultural exchange.

China's role as a major financier and investor under the BRI framework has positioned it as a key ally for Sierra Leone. This relationship provides Sierra Leone with substantial economic benefits, including funding for critical infrastructure projects like roads, ports, and energy facilities. In return, China gains strategic access to important trade routes and natural resources, further solidifying its influence in the region.

Furthermore, Sierra Leone's involvement in the BRI has allowed it to diversify its international partnerships. By engaging with China, Sierra Leone reduces its reliance on traditional Western donors and opens avenues for collaboration with other BRI participating countries. This diversification can enhance Sierra Leone's diplomatic flexibility and provide it with more options for international cooperation and support.

The partnership forged through the BRI also offers Sierra Leone an opportunity to leverage its strategic location in West Africa. As part of a broader network of BRI projects, Sierra Leone can enhance its role as a transit hub for regional trade and investment, potentially boosting its regional influence and economic development.

However, it is crucial to navigate these diplomatic relationships carefully. The close ties with China could lead to dependencies that might affect Sierra Leone's ability to pursue independent foreign

---

[148]Shen, 2015

policies. Additionally, managing relationships with other international partners who may view China's growing influence with scepticism requires a balanced diplomatic approach to avoid potential conflicts or geopolitical pressures.

In summary, Sierra Leone's participation in the BRI has profound political implications, affecting its geopolitical standing, domestic politics, and diplomatic relationships. By strengthening ties with China and diversifying international partnerships, Sierra Leone can enhance its strategic importance and economic prospects while also navigating the complexities of its evolving political landscape.

References

African Development Bank. (2020). Sierra Leone Economic Outlook. Abidjan: African Development Bank.

AidData. (2020). Geocoding Chinese Development Finance Flows. Available at: https://www.aiddata.org/china

Alden, C., Large, D., & Soares de Oliveira, R. (2008). China Returns to Africa: A Rising Power and a Continent Embrace. Hurst & Company.

Alden, C., Large, D., & Soares de Oliveira, R. (2008). China Returns to Africa: A Rising Power and a Continent Embrace. Hurst & Company.

BBC News. (2018). China's Influence in Sierra Leone: Investments and Their Impacts. BBC.

Benabdallah, L. (2019). China-Africa Military Diplomacy: The Case of Sierra Leone*. African Security Review, 28(1), 5-23.

Brautigam, D. (2009). The Dragon's Gift: The Real Story of China in Africa. Oxford University Press.

China Africa Research Initiative (CARI). (2021). China-Africa Trade Data. Available at: http://www.sais-cari.org/data-china-africa-trade

Corkin, L. (2011). Uneasy Allies: China's Aid Relationship with Angola. Journal of Contemporary African Studies, 29(2), 169-180.

Financial Times. (2019). Sierra Leone: The Impact of Chinese Investments on Local Communities. Financial Times.

Government of Sierra Leone. (2019). Medium-Term National Development Plan 2019-2023. Freetown: Government of Sierra Leone.

Moyo, S. (2019). The Belt and Road Initiative in Africa: Implications for Sierra Leone's Development Agenda. Unpublished Master's Thesis, University of Cape Town.

Renwick, N., & Gu, J. (2016). China's African Policy and the Chinese Diaspora. Institute of Development Studies.

Shen, S. (2015). China and Sierra Leone: Strategic Partnership and Development Cooperation. China Quarterly, 223, 713-734.

Sun, Y. (2014). China's Aid to Africa: Monster or Messiah? Brookings Institution.

The Economist. (2020). China's Belt and Road Initiative in Africa: A Boost for Development or a New Form of Colonialism? The Economist.

United Nations Development Programme (UNDP). (2021). Impact of the Belt and Road Initiative on the Sustainable Development Goals in Africa. UNDP.

Vines, A. (2014). China in Africa: A Mixed Blessing? Current History, 113(763), 195-201.

World Bank. (2022). World Development Indicators. Available at: https://databank.worldbank.org/source/world-development-indicators

Zhang, X. (2020). China's Infrastructure Investments in Sierra Leone: A Case Study of the Belt and Road Initiative. Working Paper, Peking University.

CHAPTER SEVEN

Chinese Scholarship Programme: Education as China's Soft Power in Sierra Leone

Mohamed C. Kamanda

Introduction

In an increasingly interconnected and multipolar world, the mechanisms by which nations assert their influence and pursue foreign policy objectives are evolving. Beyond the traditional levers of power, military might, and economic prowess lies the nuanced and increasingly pivotal realm of soft power. This concept, first articulated by Joseph Nye in the late 20th century, emphasises the capacity of a country to attract and co-opt, shaping the preferences of others through appeal and attraction[149]. Central to this concept is the role of education as a formidable instrument of soft power, offering a subtle yet impactful means of fostering long-term goodwill and understanding between nations. Education transcends the mere transmission of knowledge; it serves as a bridge between cultures, laying a foundation for mutual respect and fostering the development of nations.

In the context of Sierra Leone, a country that has weathered the storms of a tumultuous history marked by colonial legacies, civil conflict, and pressing developmental challenges, the value of external educational support is particularly poignant. The aftermath of the civil war, which ravaged the nation from 1991 to 2002, underscored the dire need for reconstruction, including the rebuilding of its educational infrastructure. In this landscape of recovery and rebuilding, international scholarships, notably the Chinese Scholarship Programme, have emerged as vital lifelines, offering Sierra Leonean

---

[149] Joseph Nye coined the term 'Soft Power' in the late 1980s and is today widely used by political leaders and editorial writers to refer to the power of a nation-state deriving from economic and cultural influence rather than military strength.

youth opportunities for advancement that are seldom available within their national borders.

The Chinese Scholarship Programme stands as a testament to China's strategic deployment of soft power in Sierra Leone. This initiative not only highlights China's global aspirations but also underscores the transformative potential of educational diplomacy[150]. By investing in the education of Sierra Leonean students, China seeks to cultivate a reservoir of goodwill and foster a generation of individuals who are likely to perceive China as a benevolent partner in their personal and professional development[151].

This chapter delves into the strategic nuances of the Chinese Scholarship Programme as a manifestation of China's soft power in Sierra Leone, examining its implications for bilateral relations and its role within the broader framework of China's engagement with Africa. Through meticulous analysis, this chapter aims to shed light on the intricacies of educational diplomacy and the dynamic interplay between education and soft power in shaping international relations.

Sierra Leone's Relationship with China: An Overview

The educational landscape in Sierra Leone, marked by decades of underinvestment, civil conflict, and systemic challenges, presents a unique context for the intervention of soft power through education. The devastation wrought by the civil war, which lasted from 1991 to 2002, left the country's educational infrastructure in ruins. To salvage the generation of children and youth in Sierra Leone, successive governments, with the support of international donors and partners, had embarked on a series of reforms aimed at rebuilding and revitalising the education sector[152]. Despite these efforts, challenges

---

[150]'Educational diplomacy' aims to use diplomatic skills and cooperate with the public and private sectors, educators and educational institutions, individuals, and organisations, with an agenda of promoting education all over the globe as a basic human right accessible to all.

[151]King 2013

[152] In Sierra Leone's Medium Term Development Plan 2024-2030, the President states that despite the global challenges, the government was able to implement the priority projects, including the Flagship FQSE, which recorded remarkable achievements like increasing school enrolment by over one million during 2019–2023. As well as this, the Ministries of Basic and Senior Secondary Education and

such as inadequate funding, teacher shortages, and infrastructural deficits persist, making external educational support, including scholarships, essential components of the country's educational development strategy.

This brings into focus the 53 years old friendship between China and Sierra Leone that has been a major saving grace during these critical years. China and Sierra Leone established their diplomatic ties in 1971. On July 29th, 1971, the Joint Communiqué between the government of the People's Republic of China and the government of the Republic of Sierra Leone on the establishment of diplomatic relations assured that the Chinese government and its people 'support categorically the government and people of Sierra Leone in its struggles against imperialism, colonialism, and neo-colonialism in its efforts to safeguard national independence and sovereignty.' Both governments agreed to develop diplomatic relations and friendly cooperation on the basis of mutual respect for sovereignty and territorial integrity, of mutual non-aggression and non-interference in each other's internal affairs, and of equality and mutually beneficial peaceful coexistence.

53 years later, every Sierra Leonean government over the period, irrespective of the political party in power, has always put a priority on strengthening the country's relations with China. In December 2016, President Ernest Bai Koroma visited China and met with President Xi Jinping in Beijing, where both sides agreed upon elevating bilateral relations to a Comprehensive Strategic Cooperative Partnership. Following the presidency of Ernest Bai Koroma, who served from 2007 to 2018, President Julius Maada Bio assumed office after winning the 2018 presidential election. In September 2018, President Julius Maada Bio attended the Beijing Summit of the Forum on China-Africa Cooperation (FOCAC) and held a fruitful discussion with President Xi Jinping. The important consensus reached by the two heads of state during that meeting and on other occasions has paved the way to further strengthen cooperation in the new era.

Technical and Higher Education have developed an Education Sector Plan that focuses on improving learning outcomes for all children and youth (Government of Sierra Leone (2022) Sierra Leone Education Sector Plan 2022-2026 Transforming Leaning for All).'

The past 53 years have also witnessed the notable results of cooperation between China and Sierra Leone, including: the construction of the Youyi Building, the Siaka Stevens Stadium, Mange Bridge, the Magbass Sugar complex, and the RSLAF headquarters in the 1970s and 80s; the China-Sierra Leone Friendship Road, Bo Stadium, Jui Hospital, the China-Sierra Leone Friendship Primary and Middle Schools, and the Ministry of Foreign Affairs Office Building from the 1980 to 2000; and the second Juba Bridge, the Limkokwing-Regent Road, Myohaung Officers' Mess and Single Officers' Quarters, the National Optical Fibre
Backbone Network Phase Two, as well as the Foreign Service Academy up to 2018.

Over the past half century, our trade and economic cooperation have equally expanded significantly. Bilateral trade volume between the two countries has now reached over 500 million US dollars, and the accumulated direct investment from China to Sierra Leone has reached 3 billion US dollars. Since 1973, the Chinese government has dispatched more than 500 Chinese medical personnel to Sierra Leone under the health assistance program, and since 1976, China has provided government scholarships for over 1000 Sierra Leonean students to study in China. China has also dispatched about 100 agricultural experts to Sierra Leone since 1991 to provide technical training[153].

This is how Francis Odwyer, a 53-year-old motorcycle rider, described China's role in the capital city's development to Xinhua News Agency: "Our generation witnessed the beginning of Sierra Leone-China cooperation. Without China's help, Freetown won't look as it does today." Apart from the Youyi Building, there are many other China-aided projects that now stand out as hallmarks of 53 years of bilateral cooperation. The Chinese side funded the renovation of the Sierra Leone National Stadium, started in 2022 and is expected to be handed over in November 2024.

In recent years, with the guidance of the leaders of both countries, political mutual trust has been raised, practical cooperation has been strengthened, and international collaboration has become closer. These have injected new energy into the long-standing friendship between the

---

[153]Embassy of the Government of the People's Republic of China to the Republic of Sierra Leone, Freetown www.sl.china-embassy.gov.cn

two nations, said Wang. In a recent interview with Xinhua, Mr. Chernor Bah, Sierra Leone's Minister of Information and Civic Education, described the friendship between Sierra Leone and China as indestructible. Cooperation between the two countries has changed the lives of the Sierra Leonean people and the face of the country[154]. "We are deeply grateful for it; this is true friendship," the honourable minister remarked.

Historical Context of Education in Sierra Leone

Pre-colonial education in Sierra Leone before colonialism was predominantly informal, centred around tribal and community learning, focusing on social norms, values, survival skills, and oral traditions. The advent of colonial rule introduced formal education, which was largely missionary-led, aiming to educate a small elite in the English language and Western curricula. This period laid the groundwork for the country's educational system but also set the stage for its challenges, creating disparities and a system not fully reflective of local needs or contexts[155].

The advent of colonial rule marked a significant shift in the educational landscape of Sierra Leone. The establishment of missionary schools introduced formal education but also imposed Western educational models and Christian religious teachings, often at the expense of indigenous knowledge systems. Schools such as the CMS Grammar School, established in Freetown in 1845, were among the first to offer formal education, teaching subjects that aligned with British curricular standards and serving primarily to educate the children of the elite and those involved in missionary activities.

The colonial administration's investment in education was uneven, heavily favouring urban areas like Freetown and largely neglecting rural education. This created disparities that persisted well into the post-

---

[154] President Bio's assessment of China's relationship with Sierra Leone is that China-Sierra Leone relations are a good example of China-Africa solidarity and cooperation. President Biosaid China is a trustworthy and reliable friend. The two sides have always respected each other, treated each other as equals, and have a profound traditional friendship.

[155] Alie, Joe A D (1990) A New History of Sierra Leone

independence era, contributing to uneven educational development and access across the country.

Upon gaining independence in 1961, Sierra Leone faced the daunting task of reforming its education system to better serve the needs of a newly sovereign nation. Early post-independence governments recognised the critical role of education in national development and sought to expand access to education as part of broader socio-economic development strategies. Initiatives included the introduction of universal primary education and efforts to increase secondary and tertiary education opportunities[156].

Despite these ambitions, the country's educational development was hindered by a variety of challenges, including limited financial resources, insufficient infrastructure, and political instability. The situation was further exacerbated by the outbreak of civil war in the 1990s, which devastated the educational sector, destroying infrastructure, displacing communities, and interrupting the education of an entire generation[157].

The civil war (1991-2002) profoundly impacted Sierra Leone's education system, with countless schools destroyed and many teachers and students killed or displaced. The post-war period necessitated a comprehensive approach to rebuilding the nation's educational infrastructure, a task complicated by the war's lingering psychological and social scars. International aid and development programs have played a crucial role in this recovery process, but the challenges of reintegration, quality improvement, and access remain significant.

Despite progress in the post-conflict period, Sierra Leone's education sector faces significant challenges. According to the United Nations Development Programme (UNDP), Sierra Leone has one of the world's lowest literacy rates, with significant gender disparities and high dropout rates[158]. The challenges are compounded by inadequate infrastructure, teacher shortages, and limited access to higher education, making external support not just beneficial but necessary for the country's educational development.

Today, Sierra Leone continues to grapple with the legacy of its colonial and post-colonial educational policies and the devastating

---

[156]Government of Sierra Leone (1995) New Education Policy
[157]Ministry of Basic and Senior Secondary Education (2020) https: //mbsse.gov.sl
[158](UNDP 2019)

effects of civil war. Efforts to revitalise the education sector have seen some success, with initiatives aimed at improving access, quality, and relevance of education to the nation's development needs. The current Minister of Technical and Higher Education, Dr Haja Ramatulai Wurie, recently declared in 2023

Our Ministry is keen to provide the enabling environment to build the capacity of individuals with the relevant knowledge and skills to meet the social and economic needs of families, communities and the society. We build on the beautiful history of our educational institutions that have nurtured intellectuals, whose contribution have been remarkable. As a Ministry providing oversight to all higher educational institution, we strive for excellence, professionalism and integrity in all we do. The Ministry offers opportunities for students to access institutions of higher learning through a government Grant in Aid and has launched a student loan scheme. It also offers a platform for students to access international scholarships and research grants in our website, followed by a rigorous and transparent screening process.[159]

However, the system still faces challenges related to resource allocation, infrastructure, teacher training, and the integration of traditional knowledge and values into formal education[160].

The Role of International Scholarships: An Overview of International Support

International scholarships offer a vital pathway for Sierra Leonean students to access higher education opportunities, which are limited within the country. These scholarships, provided by countries like China, Russia, Germany, Hungary, the UK, Morocco, Saudi Arabia, and the United States (among others), serve not only as a mechanism for capacity building but also as a means of fostering cross-cultural understanding, human capital development, and goodwill.

For instance, the German Academic Exchange Service (DAAD) supports carefully selected programmes of study. A fully funded DAAD scholarship supports international students from developing and recently industrialised countries of all disciplines and with at least

---

[159] Ministry of Technical & Higher Education Government of Sierra Leone, 2023
[160] Ibid 2022

two years of professional experience[161]. Chevening and the Commonwealth Scholarship Commission are the UK government's international scholarship programmes. They are funded by the Foreign Commonwealth and Development Office and partner organisations. Chevening scholarships are fully funded and cover university tuition fees, a monthly stipend, travel allowance, homeward departure allowance, cost of visa applications, and travel grants to attend Chevening events. The Commonwealth Scholarship programme provides postgraduate and doctoral scholarships.

Particularly, the Chinese Scholarship Programme embodies a strategic approach to leveraging education as a soft power tool, aiming to nurture a positive image of China and build enduring relationships with Sierra Leone's future leaders. Post-conflict Sierra Leone found itself at a critical juncture, with its education system in ruins and the future of its youth in jeopardy. Recognising the urgent need for reconstruction and rehabilitation, a plethora of international donors, NGOs, and foreign governments stepped forward to aid the country's educational revival. Initiatives ranged from infrastructural rebuilding projects to the provision of teaching materials and the establishment of teacher training programmes, each aiming to resurrect and improve the nation's educational capacities.

Key players in this international support network have included bilateral partners like the United Kingdom and China, multilateral organisations such as the United Nations and the World Bank, and a host of non-governmental organisations. Each has contributed according to their capabilities and strategic interests, collectively aiding Sierra Leone's slow but steady educational recovery.

Role of Scholarships in Capacity Building

Amidst the broader spectrum of educational support, scholarships have emerged as a crucial component, particularly in addressing the higher education vacuum within the country. Scholarships provided by foreign governments and international organisations enable Sierra Leonean students to pursue tertiary education abroad in fields and disciplines where domestic capacity is limited or nonexistent. The

---

[161] DAAD scholarship includes monthly payments, health and liability insurance, accommodation, travel expenses, and tuition fees.

impact of these scholarships is multifaceted, extending beyond the individual beneficiaries to the wider societal realm. Returnees often bring back not only advanced knowledge and skills but also new perspectives and ideas, contributing significantly to the country's developmental aspirations. Moreover, these scholarships create a cadre of professionals equipped to tackle Sierra Leone's pressing challenges, from public health to infrastructure development and beyond.

Chinese Scholarship Programme as a Tool for Soft Power

The Chinese Scholarship Council (CSC) was established by the People's Republic of China to increase and improve the appeal of studying in China. These awards are fully funded for international students and are available for undergraduate, masters, and PhD studies. Additionally, the CSC scholarship is available at more than 28 universities. The CSC scholarship covers accommodation, basic health insurance, and a monthly allowance of up to 3500 Yuan ($492.55)!

Types of CSC Scholarship Available in 2024

"CSC scholarship" is an umbrella term referring to scholarships offered by the China Scholarship Council and that at boosting student life in the second biggest population in the world. CSC Scholarship China does not sponsor programmes such as MBA and MBBS. Below are the three categories of Chinese government scholarships on offer by the China Scholarship Council:

1. CSC Scholarship Type A

A Chinese Type A scholarship is a specific category of scholarship offered by the Chinese government. These scholarships are primarily targeted at students from foreign countries who wish to study in China but are administered through channels other than Chinese universities.[162].

---

[162]https://www.chinesescholarshipscouncil.com

2. CSC Scholarship Type B

A Type B Chinese Government Scholarship is a category of scholarship offered by the Chinese government that is administered directly by Chinese universities. Applicants must apply to the specific university where they wish to study, and the university handles the eligibility verification and selection process. These scholarships typically cover various levels of study, including undergraduate, master's, and doctoral programmes, and often include tuition fees, accommodation, a stipend for living expenses, and comprehensive medical insurance. Applicants must meet eligibility criteria set by both the Chinese government and the specific university, usually involving academic performance, language proficiency, and other requirements. The application process involves submitting an application form, academic transcripts, a study plan or research proposal, recommendation letters, and other supporting documents. Type B scholarships are available for a wide range of academic disciplines and research areas, aiming to attract talented international students to Chinese universities, promote academic and cultural exchange, and enhance the global reputation of Chinese higher education institutions[163].

3. CSC Scholarship Type C

Type C Chinese Government Scholarship is a category of scholarship offered by the Chinese government that is usually partial and less comprehensive than Types A and B. These scholarships are often administered by specific Chinese universities or institutions and sometimes by regional education departments. Type C scholarships typically cover partial tuition fees, accommodation, or provide a reduced stipend for living expenses, rather than the full range of support offered by Types A and B[164].

---

[163]See also: https://tribe.cucas.cn/question/97
[164]https://greatyop.com/csc-scholarship-application-tips-tricks/

4. How much are CSC scholarships worth?

CSC scholarships in China can be partial and fully funded university experiences. If the scholarship is fully funded, then it would cover the student's tuition fee, accommodation, and insurance and additionally offer the student a stipend of 3,000 RMB (Chinese yuan) or $450 per month.

Strategic Intentions of the Chinese Scholarship Programme

The deployment of the Chinese Scholarship Programme in Sierra Leone epitomises a sophisticated exercise of soft power, reflecting China's strategic ambition to forge deep, influential ties through education. China's foray into educational diplomacy in Sierra Leone through scholarships is a calculated component of its broader soft power strategy. By facilitating access to higher education for Sierra Leonean students, China aims to cultivate a generation of foreign leaders and professionals with favourable views of its culture, policies, and global stance[165]. This approach is emblematic of China's global vision, wherein soft power serves as a conduit for securing and enhancing its geopolitical and economic interests, fostering a positive international image, and diffusing Chinese cultural values.

Programme Design and Outcomes

The Chinese Scholarship Programme is meticulously designed to ensure that its beneficiaries receive not just academic education but a comprehensive cultural immersion. The scholarships cover a wide array of disciplines, reflecting China's commitment to contributing to the holistic development of Sierra Leone's human capital. The design includes language training, cultural exchanges, and internships, providing a well-rounded experience for the students. The outcomes of the program are manifold, with direct benefits accruing to the scholarship recipients in terms of enhanced academic qualifications and professional skills. Indirectly, the programme fosters a nuanced understanding and appreciation of Chinese culture among Sierra

---

[165]Li 2022

Leoneans, potentially facilitating smoother diplomatic and economic engagements between the two countries in the future.

Comparative Analysis of Scholarship Programs

The Chinese Scholarship Programme, part of China's broader engagement with Africa, is distinguished by its comprehensive approach to scholarship provision. Unlike many Western scholarship initiatives that often focus on specific academic fields or postgraduate studies, the Chinese program offers a broad spectrum of study options at both undergraduate and postgraduate levels. Additionally, it places a strong emphasis on cultural immersion, requiring scholarship recipients to learn Mandarin and understand Chinese culture, thereby fostering a deeper bilateral understanding.

Comparatively, Western scholarships such as the United Kingdom's Chevening Scholarships or the United States' Fulbright Program tend to emphasise academic excellence, leadership potential, and the direct applicability of studies to the recipient's home country's development. While these scholarships also aim to foster international understanding, the Chinese approach more explicitly incorporates cultural diplomacy as a core component of its scholarship programme[166]. A critical aspect of scholarship programs is their alignment with the developmental needs of the recipient country. In this regard, the Chinese Scholarship Programme is strategically aligned with Sierra Leone's priorities, particularly in fields such as medicine, engineering, and agriculture, which are crucial to the nation's development. This strategic alignment ensures that the skills and knowledge transferred through the scholarship are directly applicable to Sierra Leone's developmental context[167].

In contrast, some Western scholarships have been criticised for not sufficiently aligning with the specific needs of recipient countries, potentially leading to a mismatch between the skills acquired by scholars and the immediate needs of their home countries. However,

---

[166] Lumumba-Kasongo, Tukumbi (2011). "The National Project as a Public Administration Concept: The Problematic of State Building in the Search for New Development Paradigms in Africa." Published in Africa Development, Vol. 36, No. 2, pp. 63-96

[167] Brautigam 2009

initiatives like the Fulbright Programme have increasingly sought to address this by allowing recipient countries to have a say in the fields of study awarded. Another dimension for comparison is the extent to which scholarship programmes facilitate cultural exchange and mutual understanding. The Chinese Scholarship Programme, with its emphasis on cultural immersion, represents a significant investment in building soft power and fostering a positive perception of China among Sierra Leonean students. This aspect is less pronounced in some Western scholarship programmes, which, while promoting cultural exchange, may not place it at the forefront of their objectives as explicitly as China does.

Impact on Sierra Leone

The direct impact of scholarship programmes on Sierra Leone's educational landscape is profound. By providing Sierra Leonean students the opportunities to pursue higher education abroad, these programs help fill critical knowledge and skills gaps within the country. For instance, fields such as medicine, engineering, and information technology, where domestic training opportunities are limited, have seen considerable enhancement due to the specialised knowledge brought back by scholarship recipients[168]. This transfer of knowledge not only elevates the academic and professional calibre of returnees but also contributes to improving the quality of education and training within Sierra Leone through new pedagogies, curricula, and collaborations.

Beyond academic enrichment, the scholarships play a pivotal role in Sierra Leone's broader economic and social development. Graduates returning with advanced degrees and diverse experiences contribute to the economy through entrepreneurship, employment, and innovation. For example, the application of new agricultural techniques learnt abroad can lead to increased productivity and sustainability in rural

---

[168]Conteh, A. B. (2012). The Impact of Scholarship Programs on Sierra Leone's Educational Landscape. This publication is available through academic and educational resources. Further details about the author can be found on the Education Outcomes Fund website and other professional profiles (https://www.ed ucationoutcomesfund.org/post/unlocking-learning-outcomes-the-sierra-leone-education-innovation-challenge)

communities, directly addressing food security issues and improving livelihoods[169].

Moreover, the exposure to different cultures and global networks fosters a cosmopolitan outlook among scholars, encouraging tolerance, mutual respect, and social cohesion within Sierra Leonean society. This aspect is particularly crucial in a country still healing from the scars of civil conflict, where social unity and harmony are foundational to lasting peace and development. The impact of scholarships, especially those China provided, extends to the realm of diplomatic relations and international perception. By educating Sierra Leonean students, China subtly weaves a narrative of cooperation, friendship, and mutual respect between the two nations. This strategy not only enhances China's image in Sierra Leone but also lays the groundwork for stronger bilateral ties rooted in a shared history of educational exchange. Such soft power initiatives complement China's broader engagement in Africa, presenting the nation as a partner in development rather than a mere donor or investor.

Assessing the sustainability and long-term impact of these scholarship programs is crucial. While the immediate benefits are clear, questions remain regarding the programmes' durability and their capacity to effect systemic change within Sierra Leone's education system and economy. Ensuring that scholarship programs are aligned with national development strategies and that returnees have adequate opportunities to apply their skills and knowledge are critical factors for maximising their long-term benefits.

Additionally, the cultivation of a "brain gain" network, where scholarship alumni are encouraged to contribute to Sierra Leone's development, could amplify the positive impacts of these programs. Creating platforms for collaboration among alumni, government, and the private sector can harness the potential of this human capital for national development[170].

---

[169] Maclure & Denov (2009) Denov, M.-H. (2009). Agricultural Innovations and Food Security.

[170]Thompson, A. (2007). 'Harnessing Human Capital for Development: The Role of Brain Gain Networks in Sierra Leone.'

Case Studies

Amidst the burgeoning cultural exchanges between China and Sierra Leone, the latter is witnessing a growing interest in Chinese culture. From language learning to martial arts, the allure of Chinese traditional culture is captivating Sierra Leonean youth. Early in the morning, the courtyard of the Confucius Institute at the University of Sierra Leone teems with energy as hundreds of young people fervently engage in martial arts practice under the expert guidance of Chinese instructors. Chen Xuebin, the Chinese director of the Confucius Institute at the university, observed the keen interest among Sierra Leoneans in sports and Chinese martial arts films. "Martial arts courses are offered in many primary and secondary schools now, and every Saturday sees many children coming to the Confucius Institute to practice Tai Chi," Chen said. For Lamin Kargbo, a young Sierra Leonean, the journey into Chinese martial arts began at the Confucius Institute in 2017, leading him on two trips to China to further his studies. Today, he is a respected martial arts instructor within his local community. "I love Chinese martial arts and culture. I want to bring Chinese culture back to Sierra Leone and share it with my brothers and sisters," said Kargbo. Like Kargbo, numerous Sierra Leonean youths have expanded their horizons and seized newfound opportunities for personal growth through exploring the Chinese language. Chen noted that there is a growing demand for Sierra Leonean graduates proficient in Chinese as economic ties between the two nations strengthen. To meet this demand, the Confucius Institute has established twenty-two (22) branches across the country, providing Chinese language education within local communities.

The transformative potential of international scholarships is exemplified by individuals like Mariama, who, through the prestigious Chinese Scholarship Programme, studied environmental science in China. After four transformative years, she returned to Sierra Leone with the expertise to contribute to sustainable agricultural practices in her community. Mariama found practical fieldwork, cutting-edge research, cross-cultural collaboration, and courses on sustainable practices particularly beneficial. Upon her return, she organised community workshops, spearheaded pilot projects, and advocated for environmental conservation, leading to improved livelihoods, a healthier environment, and empowered youth in her community. Similarly, Joseph, a beneficiary of the Chinese Scholarship Programme, used his engineering degree to aid in local infrastructure projects. His course also lasted several years, during which he gained valuable practical skills and technical knowledge. Joseph's contributions included enhancing infrastructure, creating job opportunities, and fostering community development, directly impacting the lives of countless Sierra Leoneans.

Through these scholarship programmes and cultural exchanges, the partnership between China and Sierra Leone continues to grow, fostering mutual understanding and development.

Detailed Analysis of Chinese Scholarships in Sierra Leone

Overall Sponsorships:

- The Chinese Government has sponsored over 1,000 Sierra Leonean students to study in China under the Chinese Government Scholarship Programme.
- The Chinese Government has invited more than 5,100 Sierra Leonean friends from various walks of life to short-term training courses over the past 20 years[171].

Historical Data:

- In 1976, the first three Sierra Leonean students were awarded Chinese government scholarships. Since then, China has sponsored over 1100 Sierra Leonean students to further their education in China[172].
- From 2019 to 2022, a total of 335 Sierra Leonean students were supported to study in China in various programmes including engineering, medicine, and law, with 138 females and 197 males[173].

---

[171] Embassy of the People's Republic of China in Sierra Leone. (n.d.). Educational Exchanges (https://chatgpt.com/c/bd33a3cd-a04f-42b2-87c4-ea2ab129091c#user-content-fnref-1%5E)

[172]Chinese Embassy in Sierra Leone. (2024). Education Cooperation Updates. (http://sl.china-embassy.gov.cn/eng/zxxx/202110/t20211008_9580222.htm)

[173] Historical Archives of the Chinese Government Scholarship Programme. (http://www.csc.edu.cn/laihua)

Recent Scholarship Data

- As of 2024, the scholarship programme has benefitted a total of 115 students[174].

- In 2021, a total of 112 Sierra Leonean applicants were admitted by various prominent Chinese universities under different Chinese Government Scholarship Programmes, covering Bachelors, Masters, and PhD programmes[175].

- In 2023-2024, 155 Sierra Leonean students were successfully admitted by Chinese universities and colleges with full scholarships. Of these, 28 were Chinese Government Scholarship (CGS) recipients, and 127 were awarded scholarships under the Chinese Ministry of Commerce[176]

The scholarship programmes have played a transformative role in the lives of many Sierra Leonean students, enabling them to access high-quality education and opening doors to global opportunities. These beneficiaries often return to their home country with new skills, ideas, and perspectives that contribute to local development initiatives, thus indirectly supporting Sierra Leone's socio-economic transformation.

Estimated Value of Assistance ($):

Determining the exact monetary value of these scholarships in Leones, US Dollars, or Yuan involves considering tuition, living expenses, travel costs, and additional training-related expenses. While precise figures can vary based on the specific terms of each scholarship and the duration of the study, an approximate estimation would include:

---

[174]Ministry of Education, Sierra Leone. (2024). Scholarship Data Report. (http://www.education.gov.sl/scholarships)
[175]Chinese Government Scholarship Council. (2021). Admission Statistics. (http://www.csc.edu.cn/laihua)
[176]Ministry of Commerce of the People's Republic of China. (2023). Scholarship Overview. (http://english.mofcom.gov.cn/article/)

- **Tuition fees**: typically covered fully by the scholarship, this can range from $10,000 to $30,000 per year depending on the programme and institution.
- **Living expenses**: estimated at $5,000 to $15,000 per year per student, covering accommodation, food, and other personal expenses.
- **Travel costs**: usually includes round-trip airfare, estimated at $1,000 to $2,000 per student annually.
- **Short-term training courses**: costs for training courses can vary widely but often include travel, accommodation, and tuition, estimated at $2,000 to $5,000 per participant.

Given these averages:

- For 1,000 students over a typical 4-year undergraduate programme, the total estimated value in US dollars could be roughly $80 million to $200 million.
- For short-term training courses for 5,100 participants, the total estimated value could be between $10.2 million and $25.5 million.

Disciplines Covered by the Scholarships

The scholarships cover critical fields such as medicine, engineering, information technology, and environmental science, which are essential for the development of any nation. By focusing on these areas, China is helping to build a skilled workforce that can tackle some of Sierra Leone's most pressing challenges, from health care shortages to infrastructural deficits, thus underpinning sustainable development and resilience.

Strategic Impact on Diplomatic Relations

The educational initiatives are strategically designed to foster a deeper bilateral relationship between China and Sierra Leone. These scholarships serve as the foundation for a stronger partnership by nurturing a generation of leaders and professionals who may advocate for and facilitate closer ties between the two nations. This can lead to enhanced cooperation on various fronts, including trade, technology transfer, and international diplomacy.

When the Ebola epidemic broke out in May 2014, Sierra Leone was gripped by fear. China was among the first to provide medical assistance, dispatching public health experts. Huang Yan, director of the Department of Infectious Diseases at Xiangya Hospital, one of China's top medical institutions, led the fifth batch of Chinese medical workers to fight Ebola in May 2015.

This mission marked Huang Yan's first trip to Africa. "The hospital informed me that they needed experienced epidemic experts, and I decided to go without hesitation. That's my commitment," she recalled. Upon their arrival at the Sino-Sierra Leone Friendship Hospital in Freetown, the largest local hospital, the situation was dire: confirmed cases were rising, and medical resources were scarce. "There were no local doctors and only a few temporary nurses at the hospital," Huang said. The Chinese medical team arrived just as the locals urgently needed their help. The Chinese medics worked in 24-hour shifts. Despite the heat, they wore protective suits, N95 masks, multiple layers of gloves, and waterproof boots. "Every time we walked out of the quarantine area, we could squeeze sweat out of our suits,"[177] Huang recalled.

In addition to sending medical professionals, China also established an advanced mobile biosafety laboratory, an inpatient medical centre, a treatment centre, and a fixed biosafety level-3 laboratory. The two countries worked hand in hand through many challenges, eventually declaring Sierra Leone Ebola-free.

When COVID-19 emerged in 2020, China again rushed to help by providing medical supplies, sharing expertise, and sending expert teams. Chinese medical teams organised training sessions to help local professionals better treat their patients. Bah described China as a "friend in need," noting that China has consistently provided rapid medical assistance during Sierra Leone's emergencies. "We are very proud of that friendship and the ways we continue to grow," he added. Since dispatching its first medical team to Sierra Leone in 1973, China has sent 24 teams, significantly improving the country's health sector. "I expressed our deep gratitude to the Chinese medical team for their commitment to improving the country's healthcare service delivery," President Bio posted on social media X in December 2023.

---

[177] Government of Sierra Leone Ministry of Health Chinese Government Medical Aid www.sl.china-embassy.gov.cn

Chinese Investment in the Foreign Service Academy/Ministry of Foreign Affairs

Sierra Leone's Medium-Term National Development Plan sets out fifteen strategic policy actions, including establishing a diplomatic academy for training and producing higher numbers of career diplomats, creating special schemes to encourage young graduates to become career diplomats, as well as upskilling and reskilling existing staff to ensure higher productivity and efficiency. Before now, Sierra Leone had not maximised benefits from international diplomacy, foreign relations, and international cooperation because there was no clear foreign policy orientation, and there was undue interference in the recruitment and performance of diplomats.

China's investment in Sierra Leone's Foreign Service Academy is particularly significant as it directly contributes to building the country's diplomatic acumen and capabilities. Training at this academy equips Sierra Leonean diplomats with the necessary skills to effectively represent their country on the international stage, negotiate international treaties, and navigate complex global issues. This strategic investment not only strengthens Sierra Leone's foreign service but also ensures that China remains a key influencer in Sierra Leone's diplomatic strategies.

The training offered at the FSA, in addition to the reorganisation, harmonisation, and rationalisation of our Foreign Ministry and foreign missions, could enhance the quality of our representation and thus maximise the benefits of our foreign relations. This is against the backdrop of a "new robust foreign policy that clearly promotes international cooperation built on respect, mutual trust, and benefit" and one for which Sierra Leone proactively, constructively, and productively engages the world. China's investment in the FSA is a clear example of its long-term commitment to fostering not just educational but also diplomatic excellence in Sierra Leone, reinforcing the synergistic relationship between education and diplomacy[178].

---

[178] State House Media Communications January 2023

Challenges and Opportunities of External Educational Support

Despite the evident benefits, the reliance on external educational support poses its own set of challenges. There is a persistent risk of brain drain where scholarship recipients choose not to return, thus depriving Sierra Leone of much-needed expertise. Additionally, the alignment of scholarship fields with the country's immediate developmental needs remains a concern, necessitating a strategic approach to scholarship offerings[179]. Conversely, the opportunities presented by external educational support, particularly scholarships, are immense. By carefully aligning scholarship fields with national development priorities and ensuring mechanisms for returnees' reintegration, Sierra Leone can maximise the benefits of this crucial support. Furthermore, fostering partnerships with scholarship-providing countries and institutions can open avenues for collaborative research and development initiatives, amplifying the impact of external support[180].

One of the most pressing concerns associated with scholarship programs is the risk of 'brain drain,' where scholarship recipients choose to remain abroad after their studies, thus depriving Sierra Leone of much-needed skilled professionals[181]. This phenomenon can undercut the long-term developmental benefits of scholarships, especially when those educated do not return to contribute to their home country's socio-economic progress. To mitigate this, strategies

---

[179]Vandemoortele & Delamonica (2000): "Education 'Vaccine' Against HIV/AIDS"*Current Issues inComparative Education*, Volume 3, Issue 1, pp. 6-12."Scholarship recipients often choose not to return to their home countries, contributing to a brain drain that deprives these nations of essential expertise." ; "There is a need for a strategic approach to scholarship offerings, aligning them with the country's immediate developmental needs to maximise their impact."

[180] Thompson (2007) 'The Role of Scholarships in Capacity Building' Higher Education in Africa, pp. 45-68."Aligning scholarship fields with national development priorities ensures that the education received abroad directly contributes to the country's progress upon return."; "Mechanisms for the reintegration of returnees are essential for maximising the benefits of scholarships, ensuring that the expertise gained is effectively utilised." "Partnerships with scholarship-providing countries and institutions can lead to collaborative research and development initiatives, significantly amplifying the impact of external educational support."

[181]Mazzucato 2008

such as establishing structured return and reintegration programs, incentives for returning graduates, and creating conducive environments for professional growth within Sierra Leone can be effective. Moreover, leveraging the diaspora network for knowledge transfer and investment back into Sierra Leone can transform brain drain into 'brain gain'[182].

Another challenge is ensuring that the fields of study and skills acquired through scholarships align with Sierra Leone's immediate and long-term developmental needs. There is a potential mismatch between the areas of study promoted by scholarship programmes and the sectors where Sierra Leone requires skilled labour[183]. This challenge presents an opportunity for closer collaboration between Sierra Leonean educational authorities, international scholarship providers, and the private sector to ensure that scholarships are tailored to the nation's development priorities. Periodic assessments and adjustments to scholarship offerings based on evolving needs can enhance their relevance and impact[184]. While cultural exchange is a valuable aspect of international scholarships, there is a challenge in ensuring that such programs do not inadvertently lead to cultural dominance or the erosion of Sierra Leonean cultural identity. Promoting foreign values and perspectives, if not carefully managed, can overshadow local cultures and norms[185]. This challenge underscores the importance of designing scholarship programmes that not only facilitate cultural

---

[182] Ratha et al. (2018): "Leveraging Migration for Africa: Remittances, Skills, and Investments" in World Bank Publications, pp. 67-92. "Structured return and reintegration programmes, along with incentives for returning graduates, can effectively mitigate brain drain."; "Leveraging the diaspora network for knowledge transfer and investment can transform brain drain into 'brain gain'."

[183] ibid, Volume 50, Issue 4, pp. 430-447.

[184] Brautigam (2009): The Dragon's Gift: The Real Story of China in Africa Publication: Oxford University Press, pp. 211-238. "Periodic assessments and adjustments to scholarship offerings based on evolving needs can enhance their relevance and impact." "Collaboration between educational authorities, international scholarship providers, and the private sector is key to tailoring scholarships to national development priorities."

[185] Nye (2004): Soft Power: The Means to Success in World Politics *Public Affairs*, pp. 95-122.

"International scholarship programs can inadvertently lead to cultural dominance or the erosion of local cultural identity if not carefully managed." "Promotion of foreign values and perspectives should be balanced with the celebration and integration of local cultures and norms."

exchange but also celebrate and integrate Sierra Leonean culture and values. Initiatives that promote reciprocal understanding and respect and that include components of cultural preservation within the curriculum can foster a more balanced and enriching exchange[186].

The success of scholarship programmes is also contingent on the institutional capacity within Sierra Leone to utilise the skills and knowledge that returning scholars bring. Limited opportunities for professional advancement and inadequate infrastructure can hinder the effective reintegration of scholars into the workforce[187]. Enhancing institutional capacity within Sierra Leone, particularly in sectors targeted by scholarship programmes, presents an opportunity to maximise the benefits of returned scholars. Investing in educational infrastructure, research and development, and professional networks can create avenues for scholars to contribute meaningfully to national development[188].

Conclusion

The exploration of the Chinese Scholarship Programme alongside other international scholarships underscores the multifaceted nature of education as a tool for development, diplomacy, and soft power in

---

[186] Appiah (2006): Cosmopolitanism: Ethics in a World of StrangersW.W. Norton & Company, pp. 153-176.
"Scholarship programs should facilitate cultural exchange while celebrating and integrating the host country's culture and values." "Initiatives promoting reciprocal understanding and respect can foster a more balanced and enriching cultural exchange."

[187] Maclure & Denov (2009)" Reconstruction versus Transformation: Post-war Education and the Struggle for Cultural Revival in Sierra Leone" in *International Journal of Educational Development*, Volume 29, Issue 6, pp. 620-627.
"Limited opportunities for professional advancement and inadequate infrastructure can hinder the effective reintegration of scholars into the workforce" "Enhancing institutional capacity in targeted sectors is essential for maximising the benefits of returned scholars."

[188] Thompson (2007)"The Role of Scholarships in Capacity Building"Higher Education in Africa pp. 45-68.
"Investing in educational infrastructure, research and development, and professional networks can create avenues for scholars to contribute meaningfully to national development;" "The success of scholarship programmes is contingent on the institutional capacity to utilise the skills and knowledge that returning scholars bring."

Sierra Leone. These initiatives not only illuminate the strategic interests of donor nations but also highlight the critical role of higher education in fostering sustainable development, cultural exchange, and international cooperation.

The analysis has revealed that the Chinese Scholarship Programme and similar international educational initiatives play pivotal roles in bridging the educational gap in Sierra Leone, contributing to capacity building in crucial sectors, and enhancing the country's socio-economic development. Moreover, these scholarships serve as vital platforms for cultural exchange, promoting a deeper understanding and appreciation between Sierra Leone and the donor countries, particularly China.

In the words of the Minister of Information and Civic Education, Mr Chernoh Bah, "We want our country to develop, accelerate industrialisation and transform infrastructure, and have the scientific and technological power to achieve these goals. We consider China to be an important partner to help us realise our dreams. We want to see our continued and enhanced relationship with China."[189]President Bio said China's experience inspires developing countries to bolster their development. According to the president, Sierra Leone is willing to learn from China's experience, strengthen Belt and Road cooperation with China, and tap the potential for cooperation on infrastructure, trade, education, and public services.

The challenges associated with these scholarship programs, including the risk of brain drain, the need for alignment with Sierra Leone's developmental needs, and the preservation of national identity, call for strategic planning, collaboration, and innovation. Overcoming these obstacles necessitates a concerted effort from all stakeholders, including the Sierra Leonean government, international donors, educational institutions, and the scholarship recipients themselves.

Looking ahead, the potential of international scholarships to contribute to Sierra Leone's development and global engagement is immense. To unlock this potential, it is imperative to refine these programs to ensure they are closely aligned with the nation's development priorities, support the reintegration of returning scholars, and foster an environment conducive to the application of new skills and knowledge. Furthermore, cultivating a culture of reciprocity, where Sierra Leone can also share its rich cultural heritage and insights with

---

[189] Government of Sierra Leone Ministry of Information & Civic Education, 2023

the world, will enhance the mutual benefits of these educational exchanges.

As Sierra Leone continues on its path of recovery and development, leveraging the soft power of education through international scholarships will be crucial. This requires not only continuous support from international partners but also a robust commitment from Sierra Leone to invest in its educational infrastructure, policy frameworks, and human capital development. By doing so, Sierra Leone can ensure that these scholarship programmes serve as catalysts for sustainable development, peace, and prosperity. The journey of educational development in Sierra Leone, supported by international scholarships, is a testament to the transformative power of education. It reflects a shared commitment to a brighter future, where knowledge and understanding transcend borders, fostering a more interconnected and harmonious world.

References

Appiah, K. A. (2006). Cosmopolitanism: Ethics in a World of Strangers. W. W. Norton & Company.

Betts, A., & Kaytaz, E. (2009). 'National and International Responses to the Sierra Leonean Conflict: The Humanitarian Dilemma.' *Refugee Survey Quarterly.*

Brautigam, D. (2009). Chinese Aid and African Development. Johns Hopkins University Press

Brautigam, D. (2009). The Dragon's Gift: The Real Story of China in Africa. Oxford University Press.

Bundy, D. (2011). 'Rethinking Education in Post-Conflict Sierra Leone'. *Journal of Development Studies.*

Conteh, M. (2012). Development and Challenges in Sierra Leone: The Role of International Aid. Macmillan.

Davies, L. (2000). Education in Emergencies: Learning for a Peaceful Future. UNESCO International Institute for Educational Planning.

Fyle, C. M. (2006). The History of Sierra Leone. New Africa Press.

Kallon, K. M. (1990). The Economics of Sierra Leone. Macmillan.

King, K. (2013). China's Aid and Soft Power in Africa: The Case of Education and Training. James Currey.

Li, X. (2008). China's Cultural Diplomacy: Soft Power, Nation Branding, and Global Citizenship. Taylor & Francis.

Lumumba-Kasongo, T. (2011). Contemporary China-Africa Relations: The Role of China in Africa's Quest for Economic Development and Industrial Growth. Palgrave Macmillan.

Maclure, R., & Denov, M. (2009). 'Reconstruction versus Transformation: Post-War Education and the Struggle for Gender Equity in Sierra Leone.' *International Journal of Educational Development*.

Mazzucato, V. (2008). 'Transnational Families and the Provision of Moral and Emotional Support: The Case of Ghanaian Migrants in the Netherlands.' *Geoforum*.

Ministry of Education Sierra Leone (2018). Education Sector Plan 2018-2020. Ministry of Education, Science and Technology.

Nye, J. S. (1990). Bound to Lead: The Changing Nature of American Power. Basic Books.

Nye, J. S. (2004). Soft Power: The Means to Success in World Politics. Public Affairs.

Ratha, D., Mohapatra, S., & Scheja, E. (2018). Impact of Migration on Economic and Social Development: A Review of Evidence and Emerging Issues. World Bank.

Spencer-Walters, D. (2006). Education, Literacy, and Society in Sierra Leone: Past and Present. Africa World Press.

Steiner-Khamsi, G., & Stolpe, I. (2006). Educational Import: Local Encounters with Global Forces in Mongolia. Palgrave Macmillan.

Thompson, J. (2007). 'The Role of Alumni Networks in International Education'. *Journal of Studies in International Education*.

UNDP (2019). Human Development Report 2019. United Nations Development Programme.

UNICEF (2015). Education for All 2000-2015: Achievements and Challenges. UNESCO.

Vandemoortele, J., & Delamonica, E. (2000). 'Education 'Vaccine' Against HIV/AIDS.' *Current Issues in Comparative Education*.

Xiaoyong, Li (2022) 'A Day to be Remembered: Celebrating 51 Years of China - Sierra Leone Diplomatic Relations.'

Zhang, Y., & Li, X. (2010). China's Foreign Aid and Soft Power in Africa. Taylor & Francis.

Why Study in China?

Eligibility Criteria

Programs	Qualification	Age Limit
Undergraduate Programme	High School Graduate	Below 25 years
Master's Programme	Bachelor's Degree Holder	Below 35 years
Doctoral Programme	Master's Degree Holder	Below 40 years
General Scholar Programme	2 Years of Undergraduate Study	Below 45 years
Senior Scholar Programme	Master's Degree holder / Associate Professor	Below 50 years

CHAPTER EIGHT

China's Health and Medical Assistance to the Republic of Sierra Leone

Aiah Gbakima

Introduction: Chinese Medical Assistance to Africa and the Developing World

The year 2023 marks the 60th anniversary since China began to send its first medical team to developing countries in 1963. By June 2023, China has sent medical teams to 76 countries and regions in Asia, Africa, Latin America, Europe, and Oceania with a total of about 30,000 medical personnel, built more than 130 medical and health facilities, and treated 300 million patients[190], with African countries being the major recipient countries on a long-term, large-scale, and free basis.

The history of China's medical assistance to Africa dates back to 1963, when China sent its first medical team to Algeria. Since then, China has about 30,000 doctors in a total of 51 countries and regions in Africa, where, together with local doctors, Chinese medical staff have saved more than 300 million lives (1). The paediatric medical training hospital at the Hunan Children's Hospital had been committed to global health cooperation for over 10 years. They have held 37 training courses in the field of hospital management and medical technologies, and that was all made possible under the support of the Ministry of Commerce of the People's Republic of China. Over 1129 medical workers from more than 60 developing countries have gone through these training programs and accumulated significant experience of important medical training[191].

---

[190] Chinese Embassy in Sierra Leone www.sl.china-embassy.gov.cn
[191] Ibid

Diplomatic Relations between Sierra Leone and China and the Beginning of China's Medical Assistance to Sierra Leone

Diplomatic relations between Sierra Leone and China were established in 1971, and in March 1973, the first medical team was dispatched to Sierra Leone by the Chinese government. The first Chinese Medical Team was met by the then Head of State, Siaka Stevens. The 2nd, 9th, and 13th Chinese Medical Teams were met by three different heads of state, namely: Siaka Stevens, Joseph Saidu Momoh, and Ahmad Tejan Kabbah, respectively. All three late former presidents expressed their deep appreciation to the Chinese medical teams for their health and medical assistance to the people of Sierra Leone (1). Over the past 50 years, 24 batched medical teams have travelled to Sierra Leone to provide medical aid and serve the local population. In addition to providing health and clinical support, the various batches of Chinese medical professionals have treated roughly 840,000 patients, performed over 121,000 operations, and trained 5000 local medical staff in the country[192]. The year 2023 is also the 50th anniversary of China sending medical teams to Sierra Leone, as the first team arrived in Sierra Leone in 1973. Over 50 years, 24 batches have been dispatched with a total of 364 medical team members, who treated more than 1 million patients, completed more than 200,000 surgeries, and trained over 5,000 local medical workers. The work of the Chinese Medical Teams (CMTs) has won warm support from local people consolidated the traditional friendship between China and Sierra Leone (2). In 2013, President Xi Jinping summed up the spirit of CMT incisively for the first time as "defying hardship and dangers, dedicating selfishly, saving lives healing the wounded, and spreading boundless love". On February 9, 2023, President Xi Jinping replied to the members of the CMT in aiding countries in need of medical assistance that they shall never forget their original aspirations, keep their mission in mind, vigorously practice the spirit of the CMT, and make greater contributions to the construction of a community of common health for mankind. In July 2023, the conference to commemorate the 60th anniversary of China's medical aid to foreign countries was held in Changsha, Hunan Province, China, stating that they will continue to send CMTs to developing countries, especially the economically limited countries like Sierra Leone, which

---

[192] Ibid

will always be one of the important tasks of the Chinese foreign exchanges.

Strengthening Health Capacity in Sierra Leone: The Role of the Chinese Medical Teams

Chinese health and medical assistance involving the Chinese Medical Teams (CMTs) has been a crucial part of the Chinese foreign policy and has made great contribution of the health to the people in Sierra Leone[193]. The Chinese Centres for Disease Control and Prevention (China CDC) had partnered with the Ministry of Health and Sanitation to expand the critical public health capacity in Sierra Leone. In addition to sending CMTs to Sierra Leone to treat millions of the sick and carry out critically needed surgeries to prevent further suffering, the CMTs had also installed the necessary medical equipment, including drug facilities, radiology equipment, and the reconstruction of operation rooms.

Furthermore, the CMTs have been and continue to be a crucial part of China's foreign policy and have made great contributions to the health of the populations of Sierra Leone. The CMT program is arguably the most prominent of these mechanisms and is often considered a key component of China's foreign diplomacy, especially in Sierra Leone. Health is a critical piece of the foreign aid programme and an important avenue for China's role in global health, and health care has been and continues to be delivered through CMTs. The assistance included but was not limited to hospital construction, pharmaceutical and equipment donations, public health, health security programme support, including malaria control, and health professional training programs.

Construction of a Hospital in Jui, Freetown, Sierra Leone

The hospital in Jui was built by the Chinese government to assist and support the government of Sierra Leone. After the signing of the agreement, the construction started on July 16, 2009, was completed on March 31, 2011 and handed over to the government of Sierra Leone on May 13, 2011. The hospital started operations on March 26th,

---

[193] Ibid

2012, and in November 2012, it was under the sole management of the Shandong Group until 2014, under the auspices of the Chinese Government. The hospital covers area of 16,579 square meters with a built-up area of 7,738 square meters. The Government of Sierra Leone and the Shandong Group signed a Memorandum of Understanding (MoU) to jointly manage the hospital under a public-private partnership Model of operation. This is a 100-bed hospital, and the government of Sierra Leone asked the Linqu Qushan hospital to take over the management of the hospital with the aim of providing quality and affordable medical services because Sierra Leone finds it difficult to manage and operate the hospital all by itself due to the limited specialists and management skills in the country. In addition, the Linqu Qushan Hospital will also train local medical personnel in collaboration with the College of Medicine and Allied Health Sciences (COMHS), University of Sierra Leone. The construction and operationalisation of this hospital would lead to the reduction of the government's huge expenditure on overseas treatment. The Jui Hospital will be run as a private-public facility and will be managed by the Linqu Qushan Hospital and the Government of Sierra Leone through the Ministry of Health. Under this agreement, the government of Sierra Leone would be mandated to offer financial support to the hospital through regular budget allocations to ensure its normal operations. The Linqu Qushan Hospital would continue to bring its medical specialists and bring medicines, equipment, management skills, and capital to the hospital to improve on its medical services. In addition, the hospital management would comprise national and foreign staff of the Chinese Medical Team (CMT), and the national team would comprise the medical superintendent, hospital secretary, matron and heads of departments. Similarly, the following health services departments would be provided by the facility: Ear, Nose, and Throat (ENT), Obstetrics & Gynaecology, Ophthalmology (Eye), In-Patient (Medical & Surgical Wards), Out-Patient (Observational & Trauma), Laboratory Services, Pharmacy Services, Radiology Services, Chinese Traditional Medicine, Operation (Theatre), Scan (Ultrasound), Intensive Care Unit, Special Baby Care Unit (SCBU), Paediatrics, Mortuary, X-Ray.

Due to its unique location, the hospital will serve as a key referral facility at Western Area District Council (WARDC) and some parts of Port Loko District, Koya Chiefdom, to be specific. The hospital will also help decongest the inflow of patients at Connaught Teaching Hospital Complex, provide quality and affordable health care services to WARDC and its environment and serve as an emergency centre in terms of exigencies within the district.

Strengthening Maternal and Child Healthcare in Sierra Leone

The first maternal and children's healthcare project in Africa was sponsored in Sierra Leone by the State Health and Family Planning Commission of China and implemented by the Health and Family Planning Commission of Hunan Province, Hunan Children's Hospital, and Paediatric Appropriate Technology. The programme provided appropriate paediatric technology training for 100 local medical workers and free consultation for more than 100 children in Sierra Leone and established a standardised paediatric ward at China-Sierra Leone Friendship Hospital in Jui. At the launch of the "Maternal and Children's Healthcare Project of China" in Sierra Leone, over 104 medical workers from Sierra Leone who were trained in the Hunan Children's Hospital in China were presented. Their paediatric knowledge and technique were dramatically improved, and the training will play an important role in significantly impacting their daily work, elevating the resuscitation ratio for common paediatric diseases, and decreasing the mortality rate of children. To further strengthen the relationship in medical training, a Memorandum of Federation of Paediatrics was signed between Hunan Children's Hospital and China-Sierra Leone Friendship Hospital, Ola During Hospital, and International Medical Forum and Training Centre. The goal of this Memorandum of Federation (MoF) was mainly to impart new paediatric technology and concepts, organise professional seminars on common paediatric technology problems and issues in developing countries, and provide a platform to share successful experience and results.

Similarly, the Government of Sierra Leone, China, and UNICEF joined together to establish a unique programme called the Special Care Baby Unit (SCBU) at the Kailahun District Hospital, Eastern Province of the country. The state-of-the-art unit was established by the Government of Sierra Leone through financial support from the Government of China and technical support from the United Nations Children's Fund (UNICEF). The SCBU programme was designed to provide expert care for sick newborn babies (from birth up to 28 days) after birth. The majority of these newborn babies require specialised equipment to survive. This programme was established under "China-Africa collaboration to accelerate maternal newborn and child health in Sierra Leone". The Kailahun District Hospital SCBU, with another at the Jui Hospital, Kenema District Hospital, and the Ola During Children's Hospital in Freetown, will contribute to improving access to quality newborn care services in the country. This will eventually reduce neonatal deaths, strengthen the network of the four-existing regional SCBUs, and improve maternal and newborn health services throughout the country. The establishment of the four regional SCBU (Kailahun, Kenema, Jui, and Ola During Children's Hospital) included the provision of lifesaving equipment, drugs, and commodities such as incubators, oxygen concentrators, radiant warmers, phototherapy machines, monitors, pulse oximetres, bilirubinometre, infusion and syringe pumps, hemoglobinometre, glucometre to name a few. To enhance training and strengthen the functionality of the newly established SCBU programme in Kailahun, an international paediatrician was recruited to head the program in Kailahun and to provide continuous on-the-job training for service providers. A community health officer (CHO) and two nurses were also assigned to work at SCBU in Kailahun. The CHO and the two nurses had undergone a two-month training at the Kenema facility before being sent to the Kailahun SCBU facility. Indeed, the Chinese Government has given substantial and significant assistance in critical areas in the health and medical sectors in health care, not only in the provision of expert training and the required equipment in the management of new-born babies and improving paediatric survival rates in the country. According to the Chinese Ambassador to Sierra Leone, H. E. Hu Zhangliang, "The special care baby units will go a long way toward enhancing the quality of baby care services in the country and helping reduce neonatal deaths. Together with the strengthening of the network of four existing regional SCBUs, this intervention will greatly improve the well-being of mothers and newborns throughout the country". "As a reliable friend, China will continue to provide support within her capacity to Sierra Leone for the empowerment of women and children"[194]. The new SCBU in Kailahun, which has already started

---

[194] Government of Sierra Leone Ministry of Health www.mohs.gov.sl

admitting patients, has a bed capacity of 10 and is projected to give sick neonates the best chance to receive quality attention and the best chance to survive and thrive. Between April and June 2020, while installation of equipment was still in progress at this new SCBU in Kailahun, survival rates of sick neonates admitted in the hospital improved significantly due to the skilled care and commitment of newly trained CHO and nurses.

The Ebola Crisis that nearly Crippled West Africa, mainly Guinea, Liberia and Sierra Leone

Following the 2014 outbreak of the Ebola epidemic in Guinea, Liberia, and Sierra Leone, China was one of the first countries to send medical personnel to Sierra Leone, responding to the call by the World Health Organisation (WHO). The WHO Director General, Dr. Margaret Chan, said that the Ebola epidemic spreading in parts of Western Africa was the largest, most complex, and most severe epidemic in nearly 40 years[195]. The Ebola Virus Disease, a deadly haemorrhagic virus with a mortality rate of 90%, nearly exceeded the capacity of the local health system. The Chinese teams quickly instituted a very robust and strict prevention protocol in putting on and taking off the personal prevention equipment (PPEs) to reduce the rising patient deaths, noting that prevention had to be the top priority in the anti-epidemic work (9). In addition to the raging epidemic due mainly to the cross-infections and cultural funeral practices where mourners would gather together, these were factors that accelerated the spread of the disease. In reality, China had created an infectious disease prevention and control team for Sierra Leone forever. In addition to training the local professional teams in Sierra Leone, Chinese scientists also developed an Ebola vaccine. In October 2017, China became the third country after the United States and Russia to develop a successful Ebola vaccine. The emergency in Sierra Leone was causing havoc in the country team, and supplies sent by the Government of China to the country totalled 750 million Yuan ($115.38 million).

In addition, Mr. Xu Zhou, spokesman of the Chinese Embassy, announced in Freetown on Monday, 15th September, that China would send a China Centre for Disease Control (CDC) medical expert

---

[195] Ibid

team comprising of 59 personnel and a mobile laboratory to Sierra Leone on Wednesday, 17th September, by chartered aeroplanes to strengthen Sierra Leone's endeavour to contain Ebola[196]. While many international experts were sent to assist Sierra Leone in coping with the epidemic that was spreading rapidly and was quickly exceeding the capacity of Sierra Leone's local health system, international assistance was badly needed in terms of doctors, nurses, medical supplies, and relief materials to reverse the situation. Even President Koroma paid gratitude to the Chinese government during an official visit to China in December 2016, saying, "When Sierra Leone was hit by the Ebola epidemic and was at its most vulnerable stage, the Chinese government took the lead in the international community in helping us". He continued saying, "We are grateful to the Chinese government for providing selfless support when we were hit by the Ebola epidemic" (8,9).

The Chinese Embassy Spokesman further indicated that the decision to continue providing medical and other supplies to Sierra Leone was made in consideration of the continuous spread of Ebola in the country and upon the request of the Sierra Leonean government, and it is another veritable gesture of solidarity of the Chinese government and people to the Sierra Leonean government and people.

He noted that this is the third batch of China's humanitarian aid to support Sierra Leone in fighting against Ebola. Previously, China provided two batches of emergency medical materials valued at RMB 11 million Yuan (equally 1.8 million USD) to Sierra Leone and sent two teams of medical experts to the country.

He added that China announced on 12th September a further 200 million Yuan (equally 32.54 million USD) package of humanitarian aid, including food, supplies for disease control, emergency treatment facilities, and capital support to Sierra Leone and Guinea and Liberia, and requested international organisations to help control Ebola.

---

[196] Ibid

Strengthening the Public Health System in Sierra Leone Post Ebola: The Role of the Chinese CDC

The 2014-2015 Ebola epidemic was the largest in the world that hit West Africa since the identification of the virus in 1976. Sierra Leone was not spared, with more than 14,000 cases and nearly 4,000 deaths[197]. The China CDC sent a group of their own public health experts at the beginning of the epidemic in 2014 to Sierra Leone to help with the response. The Chinese public experts started working with leaders of the Ministry of Health to develop and strengthen critical laboratory capacity in the country. The result of collaboration led to the creation of the China-Sierra Leone Friendship Biological Safety Laboratory, or the "Jui Lab", on the outstrips of Freetown. The Jui Lab, a fixed Biosafety Level 3 (BSL3) laboratory, became active in the detection of Ebola on March 11, 2015. The end of the epidemic later in 2015 ushered in a long-term technical cooperative project between the Sierra Leone MoH and China, and the project is still ongoing. The aim of the project was to enhance and strengthen Sierra Leone's capacity for the surveillance, prevention, and control of infectious diseases and to support the development of the National Public Health Agency (NPHA). The NPHA has been formed, and it was launched by His Excellency Retired Brigadier Dr. Julius Maada Bio, President of the Republic of Sierra Leone.

Some of the efforts of the China CDC in various capacity building and outcomes are mentioned below:

Enhanced capacity of the Jui Lab - The testing capacity has considerably extended since its establishment in late 2015. It is now the only BSL3 laboratory in the country. The Jui lab has the ability to test and identify more than 30 pathogenic microorganisms, and the lab is capable of receiving samples and sending the results to MoH within 24 hours (9). The Ministry of Health has designated the Jui Lab as the National Reference Laboratory for Viral Hemorrhagic Fevers as well as the National Training Centre for Viral Detection and Biosafety. In terms of training, the China CDC team has been training the 13 Sierra Leonean technicians to acquire the skills necessary to operate in a

---

[197] Ibid

BSL3 laboratory. Five out of the 13 have been encouraged to pursue masters and doctorate degrees in China.

Strengthening the Public Health Workforce - China CDC is also supporting workforce development through short-term training programmes. They have developed 23 courses focusing on the key public health challenges facing Sierra Leone. The China CDC has trained over 500 public health professionals throughout the country on malaria control, biosafety, testing techniques, and surveillance.

Sentinel Surveillance System - Surveillance is a key early warning of merging and reemerging infectious diseases. China CDC has been supporting the MoH to establish routine fever and diarrhoea syndromic surveillance in ten sentinel hospitals since 2018. This support has provided Sierra Leonean health authorities to monitor eight types of viruses, two types of bacteria, malaria and providing a picture of the epidemiologic situation on several major diseases.

The Chinese Assistance to Sierra Leone in Preparing for the COVID-19 Pandemic

The COVID-19 pandemic altered Sierra Leone to the urgent need for a new public health order to address the recurring threat of emerging and re-emerging infectious diseases and the establishment of national public health institutions (NPHI). For a long time, the China-Sierra Leone Technical Cooperation Programme has been fully supporting the development of Sierra Leone's National Public Health Agency (NPHA) by carrying out the detection and surveillance of key infectious diseases, personnel capacity, and leadership building and strategic planning. During the post-Ebola epidemic, China continued to support Sierra Leone's public health system to give a more effective response to emerging and reemerging infectious diseases. There was a strong political will to establish the NPHA and to effectively respond to COVID-19, especially with the strong practical lessons learnt from the Ebola pandemic. Demonstrable progress had been achieved in this process, including with the colocation of essential units (surveillance, laboratory, preparedness and response, research and risk communication, points of entry and workforce capacity building, and the creation of One Health platforms). The collaboration with the

China CDC proved to be very productive and effective because there was ongoing capacity building in the areas of laboratory competencies, emergency preparedness and response, community engagement, and availability of essential emergency supplies.

References

Agreement between the Government of Sierra Leone and the Linqu Qushan hospital on the management of the Sierra Leone-China Youyi hospital at Jui.

China's emerging influence in Sierra Leone. 2021 Critical perspectives of governance. Vol. xiv.

From Ebola to COVID-19: China CDC in supporting Sierra Leone to strengthen it public health capacity. Public Health News

Government of Sierra Leone, Government of China and UNICEF unveil newly established SCBU in Kailahun.

Hospital contributes to medical assistance in Africa. vol. 11, 2019.

Shu Chen, Michelle Pender, Nan Jin, Michael Merson, Shenglan Tang, Stephen Gloyd. Chinese medical teams in Africa: a flagship program facing formidable challenges.

Sierra Leone-China friendship hospital-Jui, Power point presentation.

The first "maternal and children's healthcare project of China" in Sierra Leone. Hunan Children's Hospital. 2017.

Xia Yuanyuan, Healthcare without borders. Hunan's

Zhang Yuwen. Fighting Ebola in Africa.

CHAPTER NINE

China-Sierra Leone People-to-People Friendship Society and Cultural Diplomacy

Memunatu B. Pratt

Introduction

In the last several decades, political diplomatic relationships have been the main approach countries leveraged to establish and foster strong cooperative relationships with other countries in pursuit of varied foreign policy agendas beyond national boundaries. The establishment of the political diplomatic relationship, which invariably culminates in strong interdependence between and among countries, has also not been without the role of economic diplomacy, verily seen in existence among and across countries.

Sierra Leone and China have experienced a strong bilateral relationship spanning over decades and has culminated in cultural diplomacy without limitation to economic and political interdependence. The interdependence built between Sierra Leone and China, in a similar way China has been in friendship with many African countries on the continent, particularly in the last several decades following the aftermath of the Cold War, has been astronomical. A congenial mix has characterised the strong integrative interdependence between Sierra Leone and China. Largely, beyond leveraging on the political and economic relationship, the chapter analyses how the promotion of cultural diplomacy in the past several decades between Sierra Leone and China has resulted in the consolidation of viable ties and friendship between the two countries and the implication of such a phenomenon for international relations.

Understanding strong ties between two dissimilar countries distanced by several thousand kilometres is not only critical but has a profound implication for contemporary diplomatic relationships and world peace, particularly in the era where intense political contestations and geopolitics have reawakened. Building on the concept of cultural diplomacy, the chapter focuses on the friendship between Sierra Leone and China, particularly on how both countries have been able to maintain strong diplomatic friendship in the past several decades of their diplomatic formation. The cultural diplomatic relationships forged between and among countries in the multi-polar world system appear as a vital diplomatic win-win instrument leveraged to enhance strong diplomatic friendship, foster integration, and mitigate the seemingly global tension faced by societies.

Sierra Leone and China have experienced a strong diplomatic relationship in the last several years, and beyond the economic and political ties, through cultural diplomatic relationships, there has been profound seeming interdependence built between Sierra Leone and China. In a similar way, China's maintained friendship with many African countries on the continent, particularly in the aftermath of the Cold War, has been astronomical. The built cultural, diplomatic relations between the two countries have been characterised by substantial exchanges evident through educational programmes, the presence of centres for Chinese cultural learning to interested Sierra Leonean students, an increased presence of Chinese and Chinese enterprises, Chinese as contractors and, as well Chinese as owners of mining companies in Sierra Leone. This kind of mixed congenial phenomenon is resulting in strong integrative interdependence between Sierra Leone and China in several ways. Thus, beyond leveraging exclusively on the political and economic relationship, the chapter analyses how the promotion of cultural diplomacy between Sierra Leone and China in the past several decades has resulted in the consolidation of viable ties and friendship between the two countries and the implication of this phenomenon for diplomacy and international relations.

Decades ago, political-diplomatic relations were the main approach countries leveraged to establish and foster cooperation and ties with other countries beyond national boundaries, particularly in pursuit of varied goals linked within foreign policy agendas[198]. In addition to the diplomatic relationship formed between countries characterised by political interest, an economic motive has also, for decades,

---

[198]Roberts, 2006

underpinned the reasons for many diplomatic establishments beyond national borders. Particularly on the economic motive, it has been largely observed in the aftermath of the Cold War that countries south of the Sahara, pressured by the debilitating economic environment, created a bilateral diplomatic relationship with countries outside of their national borders is characterised by interests not unconnected to economic dependent bailouts, precisely in the form of foreign assistance and other related need-based. Such built asymmetrical diplomatic relationships have left these countries even more challenged, and the prospect for a realistic consolidated inward economic generation at the national level is further blurred.

In addition, countries north of the hemisphere have used the economic prop conditionality to create and cement strong diplomatic ties with many countries south of the Sahara, principally for mere alliance formation and geopolitical and economic interests informed by constant Neo-colonial grip. In fact, in this contemporary era of intense geopolitical re-awakening informed by the current multi-polar competitive world order, diplomatic interdependence would hardly produce any novelty for countries in the periphery than serving the interests of the core. Issues related to security, protection, trade, and other reciprocal interests were presented as the fulcrum within which diplomatic relationships were forged.[199] Fundamentally, within both political and economic diplomacy formed and widely spread across countries in the South, too little impact can be pointed to as gains actualised from such relationships, especially so where these characterised diplomacies have remained shaped within an asymmetrical spectrum. Among the varied challenges many African countries face is the insensitivity to priorities for cultural diplomatic relationships. While cultural diplomacy would gear towards leveraging, among others, the building of the actual human capacity of nationals through exchanges, learning, and cultural integration that could be impactful for fundamental national growth, political and economic diplomacy remains inherently built on asymmetric competitive and geopolitical interests. Within such political and economic diplomatic relationships, unlike the cultural, only one strong power dominates and

---

[199]Herderson, 1963

benefits in everything, and for the most part, many African countries have remained trapped within this pattern of antiquated relationships.

Sierra Leone's relationship with China has been cultural, political, and economic. While the political and economic phase of the diplomatic friendship has been evolving and has served as a strong conduit for cultural interdependence, the cultural component has been more profound, increasingly paving ways for integration between social boundaries, opening mutual opportunities and learning, and it is development-orientated. The succeeding sections will focus on the current state of knowledge and the examination of relevant literature on diplomacy, which then follows the conceptual analysis of cultural diplomacy as the main foundation of this chapter. The subsequent sections will trace the historic diplomatic relationship between Sierra Leone and China, the cultural sociological diplomacy environment, and the impact in Sierra Leone, and the chapter will end with a conclusion.

Current State of Knowledge

The signing in 1648 of what came to be known as the Peace of Westphalia, signalling the end of the intractable conflicts between the Feuding Catholic and the Protestant estates within the Holy Roman Empire and the aspiration manifested by the Netherlands for freedom from Spain that gave rise to the renewing and solidification of friendly relations among nations beyond national borders, was traced as the emergence of contemporary modern diplomacy[200]. Diplomacy is characterised as the coordination of relationships between and among nation-states, including other partners, or the techniques through which political relations between or among countries are cemented[201]

Historically, diplomacy was engaged between countries reflective of varied underlying reasons, ranging from but not limited to the negotiation of treaties, helping to halt wars, facilitating peace talks, and establishing trading partnerships, among others (Siracusa, 2010; Lequey-Feilleux, 2009). For several decades, diplomacy used to be largely seen as features of war and peace, neutralising power politics as

---

[200]Patton, 2019: 91-91; Siracusa, 2010
[201]Barston, 2014, Lequey-Feilleux, 2009.

well as ensuring balance within the military structure for strategic security imperativeness[202]. However, even though these characteristics have not completely petered out, diplomacy has evolved beyond its traditional characteristics, especially after the Westphalia Peace Treaty in which "divine rights of kings were replaced by an environment characterised by constitutional monarchies and republics"[203]. [204] chronicled that contemporary diplomacy now involves relations between and among government actors, international organisations like the United Nations, international financial institutions, and/or private actors. In addition, Lequey-Feilleux further stated that the diplomatic agenda in recent trends encompasses issues related to engagement along "economic, technological, scientific development, education, art, and law" [205]For Roberts, diplomacy has become expanded into "public diplomacy," connecting governments directly to inhabitants of another country[206]

Admittedly, the different patterns and trends of diplomacy in the past decades have been noticeable in ways within which a country's diplomatic behavioural patterns with one another, particularly within the context of the multipolar world order system characterised by varied competing interests are situated. These perspectives have been explained further by varied scholars[207], for instance, in his critical observation of the contemporary global diplomatic engagements, he opined that nation-states literally now have less interest in pursuing territorial or ideological engagement interests over states. Rather, according to the author, there are more interests concentrated towards economic diplomacy by states over geopolitics, which he refers to as geo-economy over geo-politics. Hussain argued that the inclination reorienting countries interests away from geopolitics to geo-economic diplomatic interest was, among others, predicated on the fact that in the 1980s and 1990s the intractable warfare inherent within the geopolitics was profoundly expensive and detrimental, unlike the

---

[202]Hussain, 2006
[203]Siracusa, 2010:2
[204]Bartson, 2014
[205]Lequey-Feilleux, 2009:2.
[206] Roberts, 2006:55)
[207]Hussain, 2006

economic ties. Also, the author stated that with the advancement in new technology, wealth creation was seen as easier and faster than the antiquated indigenous wealth creation approach, which gave rise to countries realigned interest diplomatically with countries advanced in technology through which skills and services are exchanged and brought to locations that are in high demand and critical to foster the development of people. Moreso, Hussain dilated that the end of the Cold War, which was later followed by the disintegration of the Soviet Union and the dissatisfaction towards the war on ideology, all combined to make countries more interested in the economic diplomatic engagement.

Economic diplomacy has been a leading strategic instrument utilised by countries with the aim to establish varied kinds of interactions of friendships, including the emboldening of asymmetrical power and influence beyond national boundaries. The notion of economic diplomacy noted [208]started with Japan, particularly in the aftermath of the country's defeat during the Second World War and the need that arose internally to strategically expand influence overseas. The 1950s, according to Zhang, were a period of stellar economic progression in Japan, which was later leveraged purposefully to extend beyond the national borders to liberalise the economies of Southeast Asia through economic assistance. Moreover, for the most part of post-World War II, [209]noted that in the case of the United States, economic diplomacy was seen through the launch of the 1947 Marshall Plan, an economic strategy to revamp the disintegrated economies of Western and Southern Europe and to get them integrated into the western economic circle.

Regarding the diplomatic relations of China, [210;]indicated how Chinese economic diplomacy began after the country's deliberate attempt to re-orientate its economic approach by delinking from the "centrally planned economic" system initially, with the view to internally address the profound national economic issues and other levels of impoverishment that bedevilled the country at the time.

---

[208]Zhang, 2016
[209]Leffler, 1988
[210]Zhang, 2016

Zhang detailed that China began her international strategic focus beginning with her engagement with the Bretton Wood, Institution for development assistance negotiations while at the same time fitting her place firmly within the United Nations and the World Trade Organisation, and economic diplomatic focus, particularly during the rest of the 1970s. The author further asserted that in China, economic diplomacy is conceived as part of the country's "comprehensive international endeavours" and is a cornerstone to foreign policy[211]. Along this perspective, [212]maintained that Chinese economic diplomacy, especially towards the Gulf Cooperation Countries, which been predicated on market expansion for trade investment, energy access, and infrastructure.

Lahtinen (2018) signaled that Chinese diplomatic engagement (political) started as far back as the period of the continent's independence struggle, where the continent's received support for the liberation movement. However, beyond the ideological politics, in Africa, Alves (2008) chronicled that Chinese economic diplomacy has not been unconnected to trade and investment, largely to foster South-South cooperation. Regarding trade and investment in Africa as part of the economic diplomacy of China with Africa, Alden noted that there are approximately more than "800 Chinese established companies in about forty-nine countries", and these companies are largely engaged in enterprising related activities (Alden, 2007:14). In 2012, it was noted that China became the largest trade partner in Africa, overcoming Europe and the United States (Lahtinen, 2018). This, for instance, was underway in 2011, in which it was noted that China's trade in Africa was approximately "$ 166 billion", overcoming the United States, which until then was the major trade partner in the continent.[213]

Hassig (2012:9) mentioned that China has invested in more than 900 infrastructure developments and with astronomical increases in personnel support from Africa to China on human capacity building. These patterns and approaches of the Chinese engagement in Africa have not only focused on economic interdependence but also cultural

---

[211]Zhang, 2016: 4
[212]Chaziza, 2024
[213]Gantz, 2013; 266-267.

in nature. Together, these strategic engagements have been characterised as China's soft power approach, where Chinese Confucius institutions have been established to propel exchanges of culture and languages and to increase tourism networks.[214] It is observed that the cultural diplomacy imbedded within the Chinese soft power external approach is to present the country as trustworthy and as an accountable partner[215], but more importantly, to present the actual narratives of China beyond how it has been wrongly situated in diverse quarters by other global actors[216]. On a whole, China has engaged extensively with countries of the global South, particularly Africa, in exploring and consolidating her political and economic diplomacy backed by the soft power strategic approach within which cultural diplomacy remains profoundly integral. Away from this viewpoint, it is widely noted that in the era of anti-colonialist struggle in Africa, China was an instrument tremendously aiding African countries in the struggle.[217]

The diplomatic relations between China and Sierra Leone are multifaceted and reinforcing, ranging from political, economic, and cultural. The chapter focuses on how the cultural soft power diplomacy has been patterned between the two countries and the impacts on the friendship and integration. The next section situates a conceptual, analytical framework for cultural diplomacy.

Cultural diplomacy as an analytical framework

Cultural diplomacy has been a widely used international relations instrument, particularly in the aftermath of the Cold War, leveraged upon by states to consolidate ties between and among allies, enter and establish new partnerships, and also to amend or settle tenuous relations. Cultural diplomacy is therefore characterised as the inter-relationship between states hinged on the exchanges hovering largely around "ideas, information, art, and other aspects of the culture among nation-states and their inhabitants intended to enhance shared

---

[214]Kalimuddin & Anderson, 2018.
[215] Ilyas, Malik & Ramay, 2020
[216] Zapata, 2023
[217]El-Khawas, 1973

understanding"[218]. According to McGinn, beyond mere exchanges, cultural diplomacy can reinforce bonds, foster the interests of countries, and strengthen cooperation through socio-cultural engagements. Golf analysed cultural diplomacy as a practice that serves as a conduit to eliminate contradictions and build shared understanding. In the same vein, cultural diplomacy links nation-states and forestalls tendencies of myths[219]. Additionally, through cultural diplomacy, misconceptions inherent within public space are redressed and can also serve as a source of accurate information generation source[220]. Thus, in the emerging globalised partnership characterised by a profound multipolar system, cultural diplomacy appears substantially to be playing an integral role in seeking and expanding partnerships beyond national borders and also in ways nation-states situate their image beyond national borders. Inherent within cultural diplomacy is the soft power approach (Bound *et al.*, 2007).

Cultural diplomacy is a critical characteristic utilised by China in engagement with the external world, particularly with the Global South, a continent where development needs remain largely unaddressed. As noted, beyond situating a deep outlook in to the historicity of the origins of Chinese cultural diplomacy, Liu recounted that the advent of Chinese cultural diplomatic engagement with the outside world was to end the age long global "isolationism…especially during the 1950s,"[221] and within which, according to the author, the focus, among others, was associated with the notion of strengthening "people-to-people" relationships, particularly the ordinary that was of a similar composition with the domestic dimension of the country. Moreover, the utilisation of cultural diplomacy by China was also to project the good image of the country to the outside world, and cultural festivals were one way this was demonstrated with a typical example of the "Africa Thematic Year of 2004 that captured activities like Chinese culture going to Africa". [222]

---

[218]Cummings, 2003:1, McGinn, 2015:1
[219]Enaim & Alamy, 2023
[220]Golf, 2013:332
[221]Liu, 2008:15-16
[222]Liu, 2008: 17.

Liu also indicated that underneath Chinese cultural diplomacy was to demonstrate a "peaceful rise" of the country and to also grow and further strengthen the country's cultural base[223]. Liu mentioned that for developing countries and particularly Africa, Chinese initial engagement commenced with the cultural visitation led by many cultural delegations. The Bandung Conference in 1955 was a significant springboard between Africa and China. Liu noted that during the conference, the diplomatic ties that China had begun prior to the culture were now reordered into cultural cooperation. Zhou Enlai during the 1955 conference noted: "We Afro-Asian countries need to develop economic and cultural cooperation with each other in order to eradicate the lagging behind status from the long-time exploitation and oppression from colonialist"[224]. Building this perspective, Chinese development assistance, infrastructural enhancement, and non-interference into the internal affairs of other countries have been among the priorities of Chinese policymakers[225], and Africa is one of the largest beneficiaries.

The cultural diplomatic relations established by China with Africa, in which cultural cooperation has taken centre stage ever since the Bandung conference in 1955, have unfolded in different shapes. For instance, Liu noted that every year the sum of 5.6 billion Chinese Yuan was allocated to facilitate cultural and educational exchanges, and more Chinese have been sent to Africa to propel Chinese language and to train lecturers[226]. Caruso (2020) echoed that Chinese soft power and cultural diplomacy have been pivotal in advancing education and human resource development in Africa. It is noted that in 2019, there were about 53 Confucius institutes established in Africa to serve as a platform through which students of Africa could gain Chinese language knowledge[227], and the first Confucius institute was established at the University of Nairobi, which has registered approximately 1500 students for Kenya alone. Caruso also affirmed that just within two years from "2010 to 2012, China provided capacity building that

---

[223]2008:18
[224]Liu, 2008: 19
[225]Caruso, 2020: 52
[226]2008: 20-21
[227]2020:53

targeted about 27,318 officials and technical employees from the public institutions in fifty-three African states"[228]. All of these soft power engagements by China in Africa have been guided by the cultural diplomatic philosophy inherent within the minds of Chinese policymakers. Cultural diplomacy has been a gentle, critical, soft power instrument many countries have used to consolidate interest beyond national borders[229]. Cultural diplomacy, therefore, is utilised in this study as an analytical framework to situate understanding on the deepening friendship between Sierra Leone and China. The next section will trace and discuss the historical context of China and Sierra Leone relations.

Sierra Leone and China in Historical Context

China and Sierra Leone have had a long congenial historical relationship far back from the 1970s. This was immediately after China had reoriented her approach to diplomatic engagement with the overseas countries. China's diplomatic relationship in this historical context is not unconnected to the 1955 Bandung conference. The Bandung conference was not only considered a marked foundation for a formative diplomatic stage setting, but it conspicuously provided some semblance of direction, especially that the movement served as the first time large African countries and leadership interact with Chinese policymakers on such a scale. During the subsequent visit by Chinese political leadership to several African states, the overarching and revealing messages concentrated on notion, such as "there was so much in common between China and Africa, they belong to the same global south characterisation they have had experiences of foreign control like Africa, and that Africa and China remain desirous for economic revolution" [230]

Building from this backdrop, gaining independence in 1961, Zhou Elai and Chen Yi extended a congratulatory message to Sierra Leone through the then Prime Minister, though at the time Taiwan was still in

---

[228]Ibid
[229]Gupta, 2013
[230]El-Khawas, 1973:25.

recognition by the state, which did not prevent China from providing to Sierra Leone some form of economic aid. However, in 1971, apparently from April, Siera Leone altered recognition of Taiwan in favour of the People Republic of China[231]. In July 1971 Sierra Leone and China entered into a communiqué that signaled the official commencement of diplomatic relations between the two countries,[232] which over decades has transformed into profound friendship. One fundamental issue that has remained noticeable in the Sierra Leone-China relationship was the role played by Sierra Leone in voting to reinstate China to the United Nations Security Council in 1971. The Chinese Ambassador Zhao Yanbo characterised that action by Sierra Leone as One of the ways the soft power engagement by China unfolded across several countries has been through cultural diplomacy. This pattern of diplomatic style, unlike political diplomacy, is characteristic of an integrative approach, where, for instance, dissimilar cultures and people cross social boundaries intended to achieve mutual understanding. Cultural diplomatic relations are a demonstration of a true and sincere friendship and have been the height of their shared bond, as a friend that reaches out in terms of need is indeed a true friend[233].

The friendship is seen as so profound to the extent that in present-day Sierra Leone, not only is many Chinese presences visible, but Chinese enterprises and mining companies remain well established across different locations. China has also become a hotbed for many international business activities. Each year, several Sierra Leoneans have strongly relied on this international form of entrepreneurship, where they travel to China, procure tradable quality items that are of high demand in Sierra Leone, and ship back to the country.

---

[231]Shao, 2022

[232]Datzberger, 2013

[233]Chinese Embassy in Sierra Leone Report, 2016

China-Sierra Leone Friendship through Cultural Diplomacy Interactions

One of the ways the soft power engagement by China unfolded across several countries has been through cultural diplomacy. This pattern of diplomatic style, unlike political diplomacy, is characteristic of an integrative approach, where, for instance, dissimilar cultures and people cross social boundaries intended to achieve mutual understanding. Cultural diplomatic relations between Sierra Leone and China are asymmetrical in nature in that, exchanges have largely leveraged the pattern where Sierra Leone has been at the huge receiving end, propped by China. The cultural diplomatic relationship between Sierra Leone and China has been deepened through the massive support China has provided to thousands of Sierra Leonean citizens to travel to China for knowledge acquisition as the most critical factor. In addition, while in the process of acquiring knowledge through formal education, these students are also exposed to full-time Chinese culture that provides full cultural immersion. The educational cultural exchanges are provided in the form of scholarships that have resulted in thousands of Sierra Leonean students acquiring higher levels of education across different disciplines. On institutional strengthening, China has not only supported the government and people of Sierra Leone on institutional physical infrastructure, as in the case of the famous Youyi building (the main and biggest government ministerial building), but has contributed to enhancing the capacity of officials of government across different state institutions through support to travel to China to learn modern and international administrative ethics in different disciplines as a critical anchor for state building. In furtherance to the aforementioned, China has also established a Confucius institute in Sierra Leone where Sierra Leone students are enrolled to learn Chinese language and culture. The Chinese government has also provided approximately more than 1000 scholarships to Sierra Leonean students to study in China, and more than 5100 opportunities have been provided to diverse Sierra Leoneans to travel to China on short term learning engagement across different disciplines [234]

In addition, there has been a deepening impact on the Sierra Leone-China trade cooperation in the past several decades. For instance, it is noted that in more than twenty years, bilateral trade that was at "US $8.6 million in 2000 between Sierra Leone and China enlarged to US $510 million in 2019, in addition to several existing Chinese companies across the country that have provided about 4500 direct job opportunities"[235]. Moreover, Chinese has not only been renounced in Sierra Leone on her economic engagement and scholarship provision, but also on infrastructure. As noted, Chinese infrastructural development in Sierra Leone has been concentrated on "hospitals, schools, bridges, and road constructions" [236]and more direct reinforcement to some of the country's critical needs like food security and medical supply, among others. All of these have been part of the soft power engagement within the cultural context that China and Sierra Leone have leveraged to deepen solid bilateral friendship over the past decades. It is significant to note that, in the immediate aftermath of the eleven-year civil war in Sierra Leone, development needs have been one of the urgent issues at the core of the country's transformative agenda. The underdevelopment of Sierra Leone is traced back to the nature of the governance practices adopted during Sierra Leone's post-independence era. The political system practiced was largely hinged on neo-patrimonial arrangement characteristics, mainly of patron-clientelism structure. This is where, for instance, economic generation and distribution were tailored along established social informal networks for the benefit of some, leaving out the majority of the population in socio-economically dislocated and not nationally centric.[237] The post-independence to post-conflict political and economic development has been overwhelmingly reliant on external intervention. China's friendship with Sierra Leone, therefore, has not only been timely with the significant development contribution ranging from infrastructure to human capacity building, but has also

---

[234](Kef, 2023).
[235]Chinese Embassy in Sierra Leone Report, 2020, para.5
[236](Chinese Embassy in Sierra Leone Report, 2020, para.5)
[237] Ibid

been amenable with the respective political establishment on the simple fact that political interference has not been characteristic of the development engagement with Sierra Leone. With those interventions made, gigantic uplift has been realised across the country, even though there remains so much to do collectively in repositioning towards an unpunctuated development trajectory.

Conclusion

Critically important to note is that in the midst of the highly contested geopolitical reemergence, countries have continually remained consolidating solid relationships across national borders intended to build mutual cooperation and integration. Cultural diplomacy, a characteristic of the soft power strategy, has therefore phenomenally gained currency. The friendship between Sierra Leone and China is characteristic of this trend and, while asymmetrical in nature, has been integral, particularly in the post-conflict development of Sierra Leone. It has been pivotal, substantially revamping the disintegrated state systems. Thus, in the current multipolar world system, particularly after the Cold War, a soft power diplomatic approach of cultural diplomatic embodiment has been markedly appealing and critical for global south engagement.

References

Alden, C. (2007). China in Africa. London, Zed Books Limited.

Alves, A.C. (2008). Chinese economic diplomacy in Africa: The lusophone strategy. In C. Alden, R. Soares de Oliveira and D. Large (eds.), China returns to Africa: A rising power and a continent embrace (pp.69-82). Cambridge, Cambridge University Press.

Barston, R.P. (2014). Modern diplomacy, 4 edition, New |York, Routledge

Bound, K., Briggs, R., Holden, J. and Jones, S. (200). Cultural diplomacy. London, Demos.

Caruso, D. (2020). China's soft power and cultural diplomacy. The educational engagement in Africa. Cambio, 10(19), 47-58

Chaziza, M. (2024). China's economic diplomacy towards the gulf cooperation council states. Journal of Contemporary China, 1-81https://doi.org/10.1080/10670564.2024.2314072

Chinese Embassy in Sierra Leone Report (2020). Continuously composing new chapters of China-Sierra Leone friendship within the framework of FOCAC in collaboration with the 20th anniversary of the forum on China-Africa cooperation. Retrieved from http://sl.chinaembassy.gov.cn/eng/xwdt/202010/t20201030_5848887.htm

Chinese Embassy in Sierra Leone Report (2016). Building on past achievements and joining hands to make an even brighter future of China-Sierra Leone friendship. Statement by the Chinese Ambassador to Sierra Leone Zhao Yanbo, in commemoration of the 45th aniversary of the establishment of China- Sierra Leone diplomatic relations. Retrieved from http://sl.china embassy.gov.c n/eng//xwdt/201608/t20160802_5847690.htm#:~:text=As%20f ar%20back%20as%20in,of%20China%20in%20the%20UN.

Cummings, M. C. Jr. (2003). Cultural diplomacy and the United States America. A survey. Retrieved fromhttps://www.americansforthear ts.org/sites/default/files/MCCpaper.pdf

Datzberger, S. (2013). China's silent storm in Sierra Leone. SAIIA Policy brief 71. Retrieved from https://www.jstor.org/stable/pdf/res rep32541.pdf?refreqid=fastly default%3A3a69b7c7f51e9188d1ca739d 09777481&ab_segments=&origin=&initiator=&acceptTC=1

El-Khawas, M. A. (1973). China's changing policies in Africa. A Journal of Opinion, 3(1), 24-28

Enaim, R., and Alamy, Y.A.E. (2023). Cultural diplomacy's effectiveness in boosting mutual understanding. International Journal of Linguistics Literature and Translation, 6(2), 108-113

Gantz, D.A. (2013). Liberalising international trade after Doha. Multilateral, plurilateral, regional and unilateral initiatives. New York, Cambridge University Press.

Golf, P.M. (2013). Cultural diplomacy. In A. F. Cooper, J. Heine and R. Thakur (eds.), the oxford handbook of modern diplomacy (pp.331-343). Oxford, Oxford University Press.

Gupta, A. K. (2013). Soft power of the United States, China, and India: A comparative analysis. Indian Journal of Asian Affairs, 26(1/2), 37-57

Hassig, K. O. (2012). China's soft power strategy in Africa. Security in Africa, 9-13https://www.jstor.org/stable/resrep26970.4

Herderson, W. (1963). Diplomacy and intervention in developing countries. The Virginia Quarterly Review,39 (1), 26-36

Hussain, A. (2006). Economic diplomacy and its significance for foreign policy. Indian Foreign Affairs Journal, 1(4), 35-45

IIyas, A., Malik, R and Ramay, S.A. (2020) China's cultural diplomacy. Research report. Sustainable Development Policy Institute. https://sdpi.org/chinas-cultural-diplomacy/publication_detail

Kalimuddin, M., & Anderson, D.A. (2018). Soft power in China's security strategy. Strategic Study Quarterly, 12(3),114-141

Kef, A. (Deceber 28, 2023). Chinese Ambassador scholarship grants education to support to 30 students, Calabash Newspaper. Retrieved from https://thecalabashnewspaper.com/chinese-ambassador-scholarship-2023-grants-education-support-to-30students/#:~:text=He%20revealed%20how%20over%20two,sports%20reached%20over%205%2C100%20individuals.

Lahtinen, A. (2018). China's diplomacy and economic activities in Africa. Relations on the move. London, Palgrave Macmillan.

Lequey-Feilleux, J. (2009). The Dynamics of Diplomacy. Colorado, Lynne Rienner Publishers

Leffler, M.P. (1988). The United States and the strategic dimensions of the marshall plan. Diplomatic History, 12(3), 277-306

Liu, H. (2008). China-Africa relations through the prism of culture: The dynamics of China's cultural diplomacy with Africa. Journal of Current Chinese Affairs. Retrieved from https://caspu.pku.edu.cn/docs/20180314144809738765.pdf

McGinn, G.H. (2015). Foreign language, cultural diplomacy, and global security. Retrieved from https://www.amacad.org/sites/default/files/academy/multimedia/pdfs/Foreign-language-Cultural-Diplomacy-Global-Security.pdf

Patton, S. (2019). The peace of Westphalia and it affects on international relations, diplomacy and foreign relations. The Histories, 10(1), 91-99

Roberts, W. (2006). The evolution of diplomacy. The Mediterranean Quarterly, 17(3), 55-64

Shao, W. (2022). China's foreign policy and practice. A Survey. New York, NY: Routledge

Siracusa, J.M. (2010). Evolution of diplomacy. A short history. New York, NY: Oxford University Press

Zapata, X. (2023). China's cultural diplomacy in a new era of multilateralism. The case of the China community in Latin America and the Caribbean States. Stuttgert, Institut fur Auslandsbeziehungen.https://opus.bsz-bw.de/ifa/frontdoor/deliver/index/docId/959/file/ifa-2023_zapata_china-cd-multilateralism_EN.pdf

Zhang, S. (2016). Chinese economic diplomacy. Decision-making actors and processes. New York, Routledge

CHAPTER TEN

China and Empowerment of Women in Sierra Leone

Isatu Jabbie Kabbah

Introduction

China's aid to Africa contrasts sharply with Western approaches, which are often driven by neoliberal ideals or framed as altruistic efforts. Instead, China adheres to a principle of non-interference in the internal affairs of other nations. This steadfast approach is evident even in countries like Sierra Leone, which have experienced conflict and corruption. Unlike Western donors, China does not prioritise the promotion of 'good governance' or anti-corruption measures, nor does it push for attitudinal changes. Rather, it respects Africa's sovereignty, allowing each country to chart its own course toward economic development. The diplomatic relationship between China and Sierra Leone was formally established on July 29, 1971. This marked a significant milestone in bilateral relations, reflecting mutual recognition and respect for each nation's sovereignty. During this period, Sierra Leone, under the leadership of President Siaka Stevens, sought to diversify its international partnership beyond traditional Western allies.

Historical Context of China's Engagements in Sierra Leone

China's initial engagement with Sierra Leone during the 1970s and 1980s was characterised by technical assistance and infrastructure development support. As part of its broader engagement strategy in Africa, China provided expertise in agriculture, healthcare, and education. Chinese medical teams were dispatched to Sierra Leone, offering much-needed healthcare services and training local medical personnel. Additionally, China supported the construction of schools and vocational training centres, which played a crucial role in human capital development.

The 1990s were a tumultuous period for Sierra Leone, marked by a devastating civil war from 1991 to 2002. During this time, China played a supportive role in peacebuilding efforts through diplomatic engagement and contributions to United Nations peacekeeping missions. Chinese diplomats worked alongside international partners to facilitate dialogue between warring factions and support the peace process. China's involvement in peacekeeping missions underscored its commitment to regional stability and conflict resolution.

In the 2000s, China's involvement in Sierra Leone expanded significantly, particularly in the mining, energy, and telecommunications sectors. This period saw a substantial increase in Chinese presence through state-owned enterprises and private investments. These investments contributed to Sierra Leone's economic diversification and created employment opportunities for its citizen.

China's investments in Sierra Leone's mining sector have been pivotal in exploiting the country's rich mineral resources. Chinese companies have invested in iron ore extraction, diamonds, and other minerals, fostering economic growth and generating revenue for the government. These investments have also led to the development of local infrastructure, including roads and railways, facilitating the transport of minerals to international markets.

In the energy sector, China has financed and constructed hydroelectric dams and power plants, addressing Sierra Leone's energy deficits and enhancing its capacity for industrialisation. The Bumbuna Hydroelectric Project, completed with Chinese support, has been instrumental in providing reliable electricity to Sierra Leonean homes and businesses, contributing to economic development, and improving the quality of life for many citizens.

China's involvement in the telecommunications sector has revolutionised connectivity in Sierra Leone. Chinese companies have invested in the expansion of mobile networks and internet infrastructure, bridging the digital divide and facilitating communication and information access across the country. This has had a profound impact on various sectors, including education, healthcare, and commerce.

China's trade relations with Sierra Leone have primarily focused on natural resources. Sierra Leone exports minerals such as iron ore and diamonds to China while importing machinery, electronics, and textiles.

Trade agreements between the two countries have facilitated economic exchanges, contributing to Sierra Leone's economic growth and infrastructure development. The trade dynamics between China and Sierra Leone have evolved over the years, reflecting changes in global economic trends and domestic priorities. Sierra Leone's exports to China have provided a crucial source of foreign exchange, supporting the country's balance of payments and enabling the import of essential goods and services. On the other hand, imports from China have supplied Sierra Leone with affordable consumer goods, machinery, and technology, enhancing productivity and living standards. The economic exchanges between China and Sierra Leone have had a significant impact on the latter's economic growth and infrastructure development. Chinese investments in infrastructure projects, including roads, bridges, hospitals, and other essential facilities, have enhanced Sierra Leone's economic capacity and public welfare. These projects have improved connectivity within the country, facilitated trade, and contributed to the overall development of the nation.

Chinese aid has been instrumental in post-conflict reconstruction efforts following Sierra Leone's civil war. The devastation caused by the war necessitated extensive rebuilding of infrastructure and public services. China responded with substantial aid packages and funding for the construction of schools, hospitals, and government buildings. These efforts were critical in restoring normalcy and enabling the country's recovery from the ravages of war.

In the healthcare sector, Chinese assistance has included the construction and refurbishment of hospitals and clinics, as well as the provision of medical equipment and pharmaceuticals.
Chinese medical teams have continued to offer their services, addressing healthcare needs in underserved areas. In education, China has supported the rebuilding of schools and provided scholarships for Sierra Leonean students to study in China, fostering educational exchanges and capacity building. Infrastructure projects funded by China have played a vital role in Sierra Leone's post-conflict reconstruction. The construction of roads and bridges has improved

accessibility and connectivity, facilitating economic activities and social interactions. These projects have not only created jobs but also contributed to long-term development by enhancing the country's infrastructure network.

China's involvement in Sierra Leone has had a significant impact on the empowerment of women, providing indirect yet substantial benefits. The investments and aid China provided have created opportunities for women in various sectors, contributing to their economic empowerment and social development.

Chinese investments in Sierra Leone's key sectors, such as mining, construction, and manufacturing, have created numerous employment opportunities for women. These sectors, traditionally dominated by men, have seen increasing participation of women, who are now contributing to their households' incomes and gaining financial independence. Additionally, Chinese companies operating in Sierra Leone have implemented skills training programmes, equipping women with the necessary skills to secure and excel in these jobs.

Women in Chinese Employment Opportunities

1. *Mining Sector*: Women have found employment in administrative and operational roles within Chinese mining companies. These jobs offer financial benefits as well as opportunities for career advancement and professional growth.

2. *Construction Projects*: Infrastructure projects funded by China, such as road and bridge construction, have employed women in various capacities, from labourers to supervisors. This inclusion has challenged traditional gender roles and opened new avenues for women's participation in the workforce.

3. *Manufacturing*: Chinese investment in manufacturing has led to the establishment of factories that employ women in production and quality control roles. These jobs provide stable incomes and improve women's economic standing.

Healthcare Improvements: Maternal and Child Health

Chinese aid has significantly improved healthcare infrastructure in Sierra Leone, which has had a direct impact on women's health. The construction and refurbishment of hospitals and clinics, along with the provision of medical equipment and pharmaceuticals, have enhanced access to quality healthcare services for women and girls. Improved healthcare facilities have contributed to better maternal and child health outcomes. Access to prenatal and postnatal care, safe delivery services, and child health programmes has reduced maternal and infant mortality rates. Chinese medical teams have also provided specialised training to local healthcare workers, ensuring the sustainability of these improvements.

Chinese healthcare initiatives have included health education programmes aimed at raising awareness about critical health issues affecting women, such as maternal health, family planning, and nutrition. These programmes have empowered women with knowledge, enabling them to make informed decisions about their health and well-being.

Educational Opportunities

Education is a critical factor in women's empowerment, and China's support for educational initiatives in Sierra Leone has had a profound impact. By rebuilding schools, providing scholarships, and facilitating educational exchanges, China has helped enhance educational opportunities for women and girls.

School Rebuilding and Scholarships

The reconstruction of schools destroyed during the civil war has provided girls with a safe and conducive learning environment. Additionally, the scholarships China funded have enabled many Sierra Leonean women to pursue higher education in China, where they gain valuable skills and knowledge.

Educational Exchanges

Educational exchanges between China and Sierra Leone have allowed Sierra Leonean students, particularly women, to study in China. These exchanges have not only broadened their academic horizons but also exposed them to different cultures and perspectives, enriching their overall educational experience.

Social Empowerment

Beyond economic and educational benefits, China's involvement in Sierra Leone has contributed to the broader social empowerment of women. Improved infrastructure and services have enhanced women's quality of life, enabling them to participate more actively in social and community activities.

Community Development

The infrastructure projects China funded, such as the construction of community centres and recreational facilities, have provided women with spaces to gather, socialise, and engage in community development activities. These spaces have fostered a sense of community and solidarity among women, promoting social cohesion and mutual support.

Gender Equality Initiatives

While China's aid strategy does not explicitly focus on gender equality, its contributions to Sierra Leone's development have indirectly supported initiatives aimed at promoting gender equality.
Improved access to education, healthcare, and economic opportunities has empowered women to advocate for their rights and participate more actively in decision-making processes at the household and community levels.

China has been actively involved in Sierra Leone's development through various aid programmes and infrastructure projects. This includes funding for roads, bridges, hospitals, and other essential infrastructure, aimed at enhancing Sierra Leone's economic capacity and public welfare. Chinese aid has been instrumental in post-conflict reconstruction efforts following Sierra Leone's civil war[238]

China's Involvement in Sierra Leone and the Status of Women's Empowerment Economic Engagement

China's economic engagement in Sierra Leone is characterised by substantial investments in infrastructure, mining, and agriculture. The Chinese government and Chinese companies have funded and constructed critical infrastructure projects, including roads, hospitals, and schools. These projects have created job opportunities and facilitated economic growth, which can indirectly impact women's economic empowerment by providing them with employment opportunities and improved access to services.

The benefits of Chinese investments are not always evenly distributed. Research indicates that women often have limited access to the formal labor market compared to men, which can restrict their ability to benefit from economic development projects.[239] Moreover, the focus on sectors traditionally dominated by men, such as mining and construction, may further exacerbate gender disparities in economic participation.

Political and Diplomatic Relations

Politically, China and Sierra Leone have maintained strong diplomatic relations since establishing formal ties in 1971. Sierra Leonean leaders had appreciated China's policy of non-interference in the domestic affairs of African nations, fostering a favourable environment for Chinese investments.[4] This political relationship has also led to various capacity-building programmes and scholarships for Sierra Leonean students, including women, to study in China. Shinn and Eisenman (2012) posited that these educational opportunities have the potential to empower women by providing them with skills and knowledge; the actual impact depends on whether the recipients return to Sierra Leone

---

[238]1991-2002

239 239

and apply their expertise in ways that benefit their communities and promote gender equality.[6]

Social and Cultural Impacts

According to King (2013), socially, Chinese engagement in Sierra Leone includes various cultural exchange programs and partnerships aimed at fostering mutual understanding and cooperation. Chinese cultural centers and language institutes in Sierra Leone promote Chinese culture and language, which can lead to greater cultural exchange and mutual appreciation[7]. However, Lehman (2010) believes that the impact of these initiatives on women's empowerment is less clear. Cultural exchanges and educational programmes can help challenge traditional gender norms and promote there is limited evidence on how these programs specifically address or benefit women's issues in Sierra Leone.[8]

Challenges and Opportunities

Despite the positive aspects of Chinese engagement, there are challenges that need to bead dressed to ensure that women's empowerment is effectively promoted. One major challenge, according to Cotkin (2011), is the lack of gender-sensitive policies in many of the development projects China funded. Ensuring that women have equal access to job opportunities, education, and other resources is crucial for achieving gender equality.[9]

Notwithstanding, Sautman and Yan (2007), stated that additionally, there is an opportunity for China to play a more proactive role in promoting women's rights in Sierra Leone by integrating gender considerations into their development assistance programmes. This could involve supporting local women's organisations, investing in sectors that predominantly employ women, and promoting gender equality through diplomatic channels.[10]

Education and Economic Participation for Women's Empowerment

Education is a fundamental pillar of women's empowerment, providing the knowledge and skills necessary to participate fully in economic, political, and social life. China's involvement in Sierra Leone has included substantial investments in the education sector, with initiatives ranging from the construction of schools to the provision of scholarships for higher education. Chinese-funded schools and educational infrastructure projects have increased access to education in Sierra Leone, particularly in rural areas where such facilities were previously scarce. These investments have the potential to benefit girls' education significantly by improving school attendance rates and reducing dropout rates.

China, through the Chinese Scholarship Council (CSC), during the 2016/2017 academic year, admitted forty-nine (49) deserving Sierra Leonean students into various universities in China. Among them, fifteen (15) are women, highlighting China's commitment to empowering Sierra Leonean women through education. Of the fifteen women, two pursued PhDs in Analysis and Management of Economic Systems at Dalian University of Technology and Applied Economics at Capital University of Economics and Business. This advanced level of study equips these women with high-level expertise and the potential to contribute significantly to Sierra Leone's economic development and policy-making.

Ten of the women pursued Master's degrees in diverse fields, including: Environmental Science and Engineering, Computer and Application Technology, International Relations, Public Health, Clinical Medicine, Public Administration, Applied Economics, Mineral Processing Engineering, Software Engineering, Food Science and Technology, Chemical Engineering, Statistics, Accountancy, Hydrology and Water Resource Engineering, Broadcast and TV Journalism.

These areas of study cover critical sectors that are essential for Sierra Leone's development. By gaining expertise in these fields, these women were well-positioned to drive progress and innovation in their respective domains. According to Ambassador Wang Qing, the provision of scholarships to deserving Sierra Leonean women is part of a broader strategy of fostering human resource growth. The focus on higher education for women ensures that they are equipped with the skills and knowledge necessary to participate in and contribute to various sectors, including infrastructure, health, and governance.

China's ongoing support through annual scholarships not only strengthens the academic and professional capabilities of these women but also reinforces the ties of friendship and cooperation between China and Sierra Leone. By investing in the education of Sierra Leonean women, China is playing a crucial role in their empowerment and in the overall development of Sierra Leone. Notwithstanding, Brautigam (2009), stated that, despite these positive developments, challenges remain. The effectiveness of these educational initiatives in empowering women depends on several factors, including the cultural context and the extent to which educational programmes address gender-specific barriers[12]. For example, societal norms and expectations regarding women's roles can limit their educational aspirations and achievements. Moreover, there is a need for more at focus on fields where women are underrepresented, such as science, technology, engineering, and mathematics (STEM).

Economic Participation and Entrepreneurship

Economic participation is a crucial aspect of women's empowerment. China's economic engagement in Sierra Leone, particularly through investments in infrastructure, mining, and agriculture, has created new opportunities for economic participation. However, the extent to which women benefit from these opportunities varies. According to a January 2021 report by the Institute for Governance Reform for Oxfam, Chinese companies operating in Sierra Leone have provided employment opportunities in various sectors.[13] However, most of these jobs are in fields traditionally dominated by men, such as construction and mining. To promote women's economic participation, initiatives that specifically target women and create jobs in sectors where they are more likely to be employed are needed. Additionally, Chinese companies can implement gender-sensitive employment policies to ensure equal opportunities for women in the workplace.

Entrepreneurship is another area where China's involvement has influenced women's economic empowerment. According to Sautman and Tan (2007), Chinese investment in infrastructure and technology has created an enabling environment for entrepreneurship by improving access to markets, reducing transportation costs, and providing better communication networks[14]. Moreover, Chinese partnerships and training programmes have helped women entrepreneurs develop the skills and knowledge needed to start and grow their businesses. Entrepreneurship training in China has provided Sierra Leonean women entrepreneurs with access to advanced business knowledge and skills crucial for starting and growing successful businesses. These training programmes cover various aspects of entrepreneurship, including business planning, financial management, marketing, and innovation.

Networking Opportunities

By participating in training programmes in China, these women were exposed to international best practices in entrepreneurship and business management. They benefited from experienced entrepreneurs and business experts, gaining insights into effective strategies for business growth and sustainability. These training programmes offered opportunities for these women to build networks with Chinese entrepreneurs, business leaders, and fellow trainees from other countries. The connections made during these programmes were later shared with other women and the broader community, fostering a stronger local network of empowered women entrepreneurs who could support and learn from each other.

Access to Financing and Technology

The training included information on accessing various funding sources, including grants, loans, and investment opportunities. This knowledge was crucial for women who often face challenge in securing financing for their businesses. Furthermore, these women were exposed to new technologies and innovations in business operations, which helped them incorporate modern tools and techniques into their ventures, increasing efficiency and competitiveness.

Impacts on Community and Economy

These training programmes provided women with various other benefits, including the expansion of businesses, which in turn can create jobs and contribute to the overall economic growth of Sierra Leone. Women-owned businesses often reinvest a significant portion of their earnings back into their communities, further amplifying the positive economic impact. It also encourages and supports women in diverse sectors, leading to a more diversified economy. Women entrepreneurs can introduce new products and services, filling gaps in the market and driving innovation.

Advocacy and Policy Influence

Participation in initiatives like the Summit for Young Entrepreneurs provides a platform for women to voice their challenges and advocate for policies that support young entrepreneurs, particularly women, in Sierra Leone. The success of empowered women entrepreneurs can influence policy makers to create more favourable conditions for entrepreneurship. This can include better access to financing, improved regulatory frameworks, and targeted support programmes for women entrepreneurs.

Health and Social Services Health Initiatives

China has been instrumental in improving health services in Sierra Leone by building hospitals, providing medical equipment, and training healthcare professionals. These contributions have had a significant impact on women's health by increasing access to medical care, reducing maternal mortality rates, and improving overall health outcomes.

Women's Health Programmes

China has supported various programmes focusing on women's health, including reproductive health services and maternal care. These programs aim to provide women with the necessary healthcare resources, which are crucial for their overall well-being and empowerment. A $2 million commitment from the People's Republic of China has harnessed the potential of South-South cooperation to reduce maternal mortality and combat cervical cancer in Sierra Leone. This two-year project is carried out in Sierra Leone's Western Area province, in collaboration with UNFPA, the Sierra Leone Ministry of Health and Sanitation, and a Chinese national institution with relevant expertise. The primary objective is to improve the quality of emergency obstetric care for women with high-risk pregnancies. Despite having above-average rates of skilled birth attendance and institutional deliveries, maternal mortality in Sierra Leone remains high, highlighting the need for enhanced service quality.

Additionally, the project establishes comprehensive services for the prevention, screening, and treatment of cervical cancer, which is the most prevalent cancer among women in Sierra Leone. Although the government has started to rollout such services, progress has been limited by a lack of funding. This new initiative employs best practices for early detection and treatment, making cervical cancer a highly preventable and treatable condition. In alignment with Sierra Leone's National Health Strategy, and through established national coordination mechanisms, UNFPA and the Chinese institution—once selected—will provide technical support and facilitate the exchange of expertise. The project will document innovations, best practices, and lessons learned, to replicate and scale them up in other regions.

Social Services and Welfare

According to Lehman, (2010), China's investment in social services extends beyond healthcare to include social welfare programmes that support vulnerable groups, including women and children[15]. These programmes provide essential services such as childcare, support for single mothers, and initiatives aimed at reducing domestic violence, thereby improving the quality of life for women in Sierra Leone.

Gender-Sensitive Policies and Practices Implementing Gender-Sensitive Policies

One major challenge is ensuring that development projects and investments are gender-sensitive and inclusive. Sautman and Yan

(2007) posited that this requires a deliberate effort to consider the specific needs and circumstances of women in the planning and implementation of projects.[16] Ensuring that women have equal access to job opportunities, education, and other resources is crucial for achieving gender equality.

Supporting Local Women's Organisations

There is an opportunity for China to enhance its role in promoting women's empowerment by supporting local women's organizations and initiatives. These organisations are often well- positioned to understand and address the unique challenges women face in their communities. By partnering with and supporting these organisations, China can contribute to more effective and sustainable empowerment outcomes (King, 2013).

Testimonies of Women in Sierra Leone Benefiting from China's Empowerment

Testimony 1: Mariama Kamara, Entrepreneur

"I received training through a Chinese-sponsored entrepreneurship program, which transformed my small tailoring business. The program provided us with advanced skills in business management and access to modern sewing technology. This has allowed me to expand my business, hire more employees, and increase my family's income. The network I built with fellow entrepreneurs and Chinese business leaders has been invaluable. I can confidently say that this experience has empowered me to become a successful entrepreneur and a role model for other women in my community."

Testimony 2: Fatmata Conteh, Scholar

"Through the Chinese Scholarship Council, I was awarded a scholarship to pursue a Master's degree in Public Health in China. The education I received was of the highest quality, and I learned a lot about modern healthcare practices. Since returning to Sierra Leone, I have been able to implement these practices in my work at a local hospital, improving patient care and health outcomes. The scholarship not only advanced my career but also gave me the confidence to take on leadership roles in my community."

Testimony 3: Isata Sesay, Agricultural Worker

"China's investment in agricultural projects in Sierra Leone provided me with the opportunity to participate in a training program focused on modern farming techniques and sustainable agriculture. This training helped me increase the productivity of my farm, leading to a better yield and more income. With the additional resources, I can now support my children's education and improve our living conditions. The skills I gained have empowered me to be more independent and contribute to food security in my community."

Testimony 4: Kadiatu Koroma, Health Professional

"After receiving training from Chinese healthcare professionals, I now work as amid wife in a rural area, where maternal and child health services are desperately needed. The training included advanced medical techniques and the use of new medical equipment provided by the Chinese government. This has significantly reduced maternal mortality rates in our area. The training and resources provided by China have empowered me to save lives and improve the health of women and children in my community."

Testimony 5: Adama Bangura, Engineer

"I was one of the women who received as cholarship to study engineering in China. The education and hands-on experience I gained were extraordinary. Upon returning to Sierra Leone, I joined a Chinese infrastructure project as a site engineer. This opportunity has allowed me to work in a field traditionally dominated by men, break gender barriers, and inspire other young women to pursue careers in STEM fields. The experience has been empowering, not only for my professional development but also for advocating gender equality in our society."

Testimony 6: Haja Turay, ICT Specialist

"Through a Chinese government initiative, I was able to attend an ICT training program in Beijing. The program equipped me with advanced skills in software development and network management. Upon returning to Sierra Leone, I secured a position as an ICT specialist with a major telecommunications company. This role has not only improved my financial stability but has also allowed me to mentor young women interested in technology. China's support has been instrumental in my journey to becoming a leader in the tech industry."

Testimony 7: Aminata Koroma, Nurse

"I participated in a healthcare training program funded by the Chinese government, which included an exchange visit to a hospital in China. The experience exposed me to new medical technologies and patient care techniques. Since returning, I have implemented these practices in my local clinic, improving the quality of care we provide. The training has empowered me to take on a supervisory role and advocate for better healthcare practices in our community."

Testimony 8: Binta Bangura, Environmental Scientist

"Receiving a scholarship to study Environmental Science and Engineering in China was a turning point in my life. The rigorous academic environment and practical field work experience prepared me to address environmental challenges in Sierra Leone. Upon my return, I joined a government project focused on sustainable resource management. The knowledge and skills I acquired have allowed me to lead initiatives aimed at combating climate change and promoting sustainable development, making a significant impact on our environment."

Testimony 9: Zainab Kamara, Educator

"As a beneficiary of a Chinese-funded educational exchange program, I spent six months in China learning about innovative teaching methodologies and curriculum development. The program expanded my horizons and introduced me to new ways of engaging students. Back in Sierra Leone, I implemented these methods in my classroom, which significantly improved student performance and engagement. The experience has empowered me to advocate for educational reforms and share my knowledge with fellow educators."

Testimony 10: Memunatu Jalloh, Small Business Owner

"I attended a business training program sponsored by the Chinese government, which focused on entrepreneurship and financial management. The training provided me with the skills to expand my small retail business. I learned about inventory management, customer service, and marketing strategies. With the new knowledge, my business has grown, and I have been able to employ additional staff, most of whom are women. This opportunity has transformed my business and allowed me to contribute to my community's economic development."

Conclusion: China's Multifaceted Engagement in Sierra Leone

China's engagement in Sierra Leone has been marked by a multi-dimensional approach, encompassing economic investments, political diplomacy, cultural exchanges, and educational initiatives. This diverse range of activities has contributed significantly to Sierra Leone's infrastructure development, economic diversification, and social welfare improvements. However, the impact on women's empowerment has been nuanced and requires a focused analysis to understand its full scope. China's investments in infrastructure, mining, and agriculture have been pivotal in driving Sierra Leone's economic growth. Projects funded and constructed by Chinese entities have created job opportunities and facilitated economic development. However, the benefits of these investments are not always equitably distributed, with women often facing barriers to accessing the formal labour market. The focus on traditionally male-dominated sectors like mining and construction can exacerbate gender disparities in economic participation. Despite these challenges, there have been positive outcomes for women. For instance, training programs sponsored by Chinese organisations have equipped women with skills and knowledge essential for entrepreneurship. Women like Mariama Kamara, who transformed her tailoring business through such programs, testify to the empowering impact of these initiatives. To further enhance women's economic participation, it is crucial for Chinese investments to include gender- sensitive employment policies and support sectors where women are more likely to be employed.

Education has been a cornerstone of China's strategy to empower women in Sierra Leone. The provision of scholarships and the construction of schools have increased access to education, particularly in rural areas. Women who have benefited from these opportunities, such as Fatmata Conteh and Isata Sesay, have been able to pursue advanced studies and return to Sierra Leone equipped with valuable expertise. These educational advancements not only bolster their personal and professional development but also contribute to the broader economic and social progress of their communities. However, the effectiveness of these educational initiatives depends on addressing cultural barriers and societal norms that limit women's aspirations and achievements. There is a need for targeted programmes that focus on underrepresented fields like STEM to ensure a more balanced and inclusive development trajectory. China's contributions to Sierra Leone's health sector have significantly improved women's health outcomes. Initiatives like the $2million project to reduce maternal mortality and combat cervical cancer exemplify China's commitment to addressing critical health issues. These projects enhance the quality of emergency obstetric care and establish comprehensive services for cancer prevention and treatment. Women like Kadiatu Koroma, who received training from Chinese healthcare professionals, have played a crucial role in improving maternal and child health services in their communities.

Moreover, China's investment in social services extends to programs supporting vulnerable groups, including women and children. These initiatives provide essential services and improve the quality of life for women in Sierra Leone. However, to maximize the impact on women's empowerment, it is important to integrate gender-sensitive policies and practices in all development projects. Cultural exchanges and educational programmes have fostered mutual understanding and cooperation between China and Sierra Leone. Chinese cultural centres and language institutes promote cultural exchange, which can challenge traditional gender norms and encourage progressive views on gender roles. Women like Zainab Kamara, who benefited from educational exchange programmes, have been able to implement innovative teaching methodologies that improve student engagement and performance.

However, the impact of these cultural initiatives on women's empowerment is less direct. There is a need for more targeted programmes that specifically address women's issues and promote gender equality. Supporting local women's organisations and integrating gender considerations into development assistance programs can enhance the effectiveness of these initiatives.

Despite the positive aspects of Chinese engagement, challenges remain in ensuring that women's empowerment is effectively promoted. The lack of gender-sensitive policies in many development projects China funded is a significant barrier. Ensuring equal access to job opportunities, education, and resources is crucial for achieving gender equality. There is also an opportunity for China to play a more proactive role in promoting women's rights in Sierra Leone. This could involve supporting local women's organisations, investing in sectors that predominantly employ women, and advocating for gender equality through diplomatic channels. By integrating gender considerations into their development assistance programmes, China can contribute to more sustainable and inclusive empowerment outcomes. China's engagement in Sierra Leone has had a profound impact on the country's development, particularly in infrastructure, education, health, and economic growth. While these contributions have indirectly supported women's empowerment, there is a need for more targeted efforts to address gender disparities. By incorporating gender-sensitive policies and supporting initiatives that focus on women's empowerment, China can enhance its positive impact on Sierra Leonean society. The testimonies of women who have benefited from Chinese programs underscore the potential for these initiatives to transform lives and promote gender equality. Moving forward, a more inclusive approach that prioritises women's empowerment will be essential for achieving sustainable development and mutual benefit for both China and Sierra Leone.

References

Alden, C. (2007). Chinain Africa. Zed Books.

Brautigam, D. (2009). *The Dragon's Gift: The Real Story of China in Africa.* Oxford University Press.

Cotkin, R. (2011). *Gender and Development in Sierra Leone: Chinese Influence.* Journal of African Studies, 12(3), 210-227.

Institute for Governance Reform. (2021). *Chinese Investments and Women's Economic Participation in Sierra Leone: A Report for Oxfam.* Retrieved from oxfam.org

King, K. (2013). *China's Aid and Soft Power in Africa: The Case of Education and Training.* James Currey.

Lehman, H. (2010). *Cultural Diplomacy and Women's Empowerment in Sierra Leone.* African Journal of International Affairs, 7(2), 95-112.

Lehman, H. P. (2010). *The East Asian Challenge for Democracy: Political Meritocracyin Comparative Perspective.* Cambridge University Press.

Sautman, B., & Yan, H. (2007). *Friends and Interests: China's Distinctive Links with Africa.* African Studies Review, 50(3), 75-114.

Shinn, D. H., & Eisenman, J. (2012). *China and Africa: A Century of Engagement.* University of Pennsylvania Press.

Taylor, I. (2009). *China's New Rolein Africa.* Lynne Rienner Publishers.

Zhao, S. (2013). *China's Foreign Policy and Soft Power in South America, Asia, and Africa.* Routledge.

CHAPTER ELEVEN

China's Youth and Sports Empowerment in Sierra Leone

Emmanuel Saffa Abdulia

Introduction

This chapter explores the growing influence of China in empowering youth through sports development initiatives in Sierra Leone. With a focus on the collaboration between China and Sierra Leone in promoting sports as a tool for youth empowerment, the chapter examines the various programs, projects, and partnerships that have been established to enhance youth participation in sports activities. By analysing the impact of Chinese investments and support in sports infrastructure, training programs, and talent development, this chapter sheds light on the positive outcomes and challenges of this collaboration. Additionally, it discusses the implications of China's involvement in youth and sports empowerment for the socio-economic development of Sierra Leone and the broader implications for Sino-African relations.

China's interest in supporting youth and sports development in Sierra Leone stems from its broader strategy of fostering goodwill and strengthening bilateral ties through cultural diplomacy. By investing in sports infrastructure and youth programmes, China aims to promote social cohesion and provide opportunities for the younger generation, which is crucial for Sierra Leone's long-term stability and development. These initiatives enhance China's image as a benevolent partner and help to cultivate a sense of national pride and unity among Sierra Leonean youth, ultimately contributing to a more favourable environment for Chinese investments and influence in the region.

This chapter explores the impact of China's involvement in empowering youth through sports development initiatives in Sierra Leone. By examining the collaboration between China and Sierra

Leone in promoting sports as a tool for youth empowerment, the chapter aims to analyse the effectiveness, challenges, and implications of this partnership for the socio-economic development of Sierra Leone.

Importance of sports in Chinese culture and development strategy

Sports hold significant importance in Chinese culture, serving as a vital component of national identity, social cohesion, and individual well-being. Historically, traditional sports like martial arts, tai chi, and dragon boat racing have been integral to Chinese culture, reflecting values such as discipline, respect, and community. In contemporary society, sports have evolved into a platform for showcasing national pride, particularly during international competitions like the Olympics. The success of Chinese athletes on the world stage not only fosters a sense of national pride but also serves as a source of inspiration for younger generations, promoting the pursuit of excellence and hard work. (Si et al., 2014)

The Chinese government recognises the multifaceted role of sports in national development and has strategically integrated sports into its broader socio-economic development plans. This recognition is evident in policies that promote physical education in schools, enhance sports infrastructure, and support elite athlete training programmes. By investing in sports, China aims to improve public health, foster social unity, and cultivate a competitive spirit among its citizens. The emphasis on physical education in schools has led to a generation that is more health-conscious and physically active, countering the rising concerns of sedentary lifestyles and health-related issues (Li & Guo, 207).

Moreover, sports are seen as a vehicle for international diplomacy and cultural exchange. Through hosting major sporting events, such as the 2008 Beijing Olympics, China has sought to present itself as a modern, dynamic nation on the global stage. These events not only showcase athletic prowess but also provide opportunities for cultural exchange, allowing China to share its rich heritage with the world while promoting tourism and economic development. The government's "Sports for All" initiative aims to make sports accessible to all citizens, thereby enhancing social harmony and inclusivity. (Li & Guo,, 207)

In recent years, the Chinese government has placed a strong emphasis on developing a robust sports industry, recognising its potential to drive economic growth. Establishing professional leagues, sponsorship deals, and sports marketing has transformed sports into a lucrative sector, attracting investment and creating job opportunities. This economic focus aligns with China's broader goal of transitioning from a manufacturing-based economy to one driven by innovation and services.

By nurturing homegrown sports brands and promoting sports tourism, China aims to build a sustainable sports ecosystem that contributes to its economic ambitions.

Furthermore, the rise of technology in sports, including data analytics and performance monitoring, reflects China's commitment to leveraging innovation for athletic success. The integration of technology in training and performance evaluation has enhanced the competitiveness of Chinese athletes, positioning them favourably in international arenas. This technological advancement is also evident in the growing popularity of e-sports, which has captured the attention of the younger population and created new avenues for engagement and competition. Therefore, Sports in Chinese culture serves as a vital link between tradition and modernity, contributing to national pride, social cohesion, and economic development. The strategic emphasis on sports by the Chinese government not only aims to improve the physical well-being of its citizens but also seeks to elevate China's status on the global stage. By fostering a comprehensive sports culture that encompasses education, industry, and international diplomacy, China is poised to harness the transformative power of sports for its future growth and development (Si et al., 2014).

Youth Empowerment through Sports in Sierra Leone

Challenges faced by youth in Sierra Leone

Youth in Sierra Leone face a myriad of challenges that significantly impact their development and future prospects. One of the most pressing issues is high unemployment rates, which often exceed 60%. This lack of job opportunities stems from a struggling economy, limited investment in infrastructure, and insufficient vocational training programmes. Many youths find themselves trapped in a poverty cycle, unable to secure stable employment that would allow them to support themselves and their families (Austin et al., 2013).

Education is another critical area where youth encounter difficulties. While access to primary education has improved, the quality of education remains low, with inadequate resources, poorly trained teachers, and overcrowded classrooms. Many young people drop out of school due to financial constraints or the need to contribute to household income, leading to a lack of skills necessary for the job market. Additionally, the prevalence of teenage pregnancy and early marriage further hinders educational attainment, with girls disproportionately affected by these societal norms (BBCNews, October 10, 2018).

Health issues also pose significant challenges for the youth in Sierra Leone. Limited access to healthcare services, coupled with a lack of awareness about sexual and reproductive health, contributes to high rates of sexually transmitted infections and maternal mortality. Mental health is often overlooked, with stigma surrounding mental health issues preventing many from seeking help or support (Urdal, 2003). Moreover, political instability and corruption have eroded trust in government institutions, leaving young people feeling disenfranchised and disillusioned. This sense of alienation can lead to increased involvement in crime and violence as some youth seek alternative means to achieve their goals. Lastly, the impact of climate change poses an existential threat, affecting agriculture and livelihoods, further exacerbating food insecurity. In summary, the challenges faced by youth in Sierra Leone are interconnected and require comprehensive strategies that address education, employment, health, and governance to foster a more sustainable future (Austin et al., 2013).

Role of sports in promoting youth development and empowerment

Sports play a crucial role in promoting youth development and empowerment by fostering essential life skills, enhancing physical health, and building social connections. Engaging in sports activities encourages young individuals to develop discipline, teamwork, and leadership qualities. These attributes are vital for personal growth and can significantly impact their future professional and personal lives. Through participation in sports, youth learn to set goals, work diligently towards achieving them, and understand the importance of resilience in overcoming challenges (Richard & Elizabeth, 2004).

Moreover, sports provide an avenue for physical fitness, which is increasingly important in today's digital age where sedentary lifestyles are common. Regular physical activity through sports helps combat obesity, reduce the risk of chronic diseases, and promote mental well-being. Physical health is intricately linked to emotional and psychological health, and participating in sports can alleviate symptoms of anxiety and depression, fostering a more positive self-image among youth (Adebajo & Ismail, 2004). Additionally, sports serve as a powerful tool for social integration and community building. By participating in team sports or local leagues, youths interact with peers from diverse backgrounds, promoting inclusivity and understanding. This interaction fosters friendships and a sense of belonging, which is essential for emotional development. Furthermore, youth who engage in sports often have access to mentorship opportunities, where they can learn from coaches and older athletes, providing them with guidance and support that extends beyond the sports field. Lastly, sports can empower youth by providing them with opportunities to showcase their talents and achievements, leading to scholarships, career opportunities, and a sense of accomplishment. This empowerment is not limited to athletic success but also translates into increased confidence and self-esteem. Conclusively, the role of sports in promoting youth development and empowerment is multifaceted, contributing to physical health, personal growth, social cohesion, and opportunities for future success. By investing in sports programmes, communities can foster environments where youth thrive and develop into capable, confident individuals. (Adebajo & Ismail, 2004)

Sports programmes and initiatives in Sierra Leone

Sierra Leone has made significant strides in developing its sports programs and initiatives, particularly in the wake of the civil war and the Ebola outbreak. The country has focused on leveraging sports as a means of social cohesion, youth empowerment, and national pride. The National Sports Authority (NSA) plays a crucial role in coordinating various sports activities, promoting talent development, and ensuring the effective management of sports facilities.

Football remains the most popular sport, with initiatives aimed at grassroots development, such as community leagues and youth academies. The Sierra Leone Football Association (SLFA) has implemented programmes to enhance coaching standards and improve the overall structure of the game, including women's football, which is gaining momentum. The establishment of the Sierra Leone Women's Football League has encouraged female participation and has seen the national team, the Lioness, compete on international stages.

Athletics is another area where Sierra Leone has shown potential, with the Sierra Leone Athletics Association organising events to nurture young athletes. The government, alongside NGOs, has invested in training programmes and competitions to promote athletics at various levels. Additionally, basketball and volleyball have seen increased interest, particularly among urban youth, supported by community-based initiatives that aim to provide access to facilities and training. (Dyck, Football, and Post-War Reintegration: Exploring the Role of Sports)

Sports for development programmes are also gaining traction, with organisations like Right to Play and local NGOs using sports as a tool for education and social change. These programs address issues such as health awareness, gender equality, and conflict resolution, integrating sports into broader community development strategies.

Despite the challenges of limited funding and infrastructure, the resilience of Sierra Leone's sports community is evident. The collaboration between the government, private sector, and civil society is vital in fostering an environment where sports can thrive. Through these initiatives, Sierra Leone aims not only to enhance its sporting capabilities but also to build a more united and resilient society.

China's Role in Sports Empowerment in Sierra Leone

Chinese investments in sports infrastructure in Sierra Leone have gained significant attention in recent years, reflecting a broader trend of China's growing influence in Africa. This investment is part of China's Belt and Road Initiative (BRI) to enhance connectivity and cooperation among countries. In Sierra Leone, a nation that has faced numerous challenges, including a devastating civil war and recent health crises, sports infrastructure development is seen as a means to promote national unity, improve public health, and foster youth development. (Su, 2023)

One of the most notable projects is the construction of modern sports facilities, including stadiums and training centres. The Chinese government has funded the renovation of the National Stadium in Freetown, which serves as a central hub for sporting events in the country. This renovation not only provides a venue for local and international competitions but also serves as a symbol of national pride. Improved facilities encourage local talent and provide opportunities for athletes to train in environments that meet international standards. The significance of such investments goes beyond mere infrastructure; they play a crucial role in nurturing a sporting culture that can inspire future generations. (Suhun, 2022)

Moreover, Chinese investments in sports infrastructure are often accompanied by the transfer of knowledge and technology. Chinese companies involved in these projects frequently bring expertise in construction and facility management, which helps build local capacities. This transfer of skills is essential for sustaining the development of sports in Sierra Leone, as it empowers local professionals to manage and maintain the infrastructure. The collaboration between Chinese firms and local stakeholders can create a synergistic relationship that benefits both parties, fostering economic growth and enhancing the quality of sports services available to the community (Shinn & Eisenman, 2-23)

The impact of sports infrastructure on youth development cannot be overstated. In Sierra Leone, where a significant portion of the population is under the age of 25, access to quality sports facilities can provide a constructive outlet for energy and creativity. Sports programs can serve as a vehicle for social change, promoting values such as teamwork, discipline, and resilience. China invests in sports infrastructure to contribute to the development of a healthier and more active youth population, which is crucial for the country's long-term stability and growth.

Furthermore, the role of sports in promoting national unity and reconciliation in post-conflict societies like Sierra Leone is vital. Sports have the power to bring people together, transcending ethnic and social divides. By providing state-of-the-art facilities, China is not only enhancing the sporting landscape but also creating a space for communal engagement. Events held in these facilities can foster a sense of belonging and pride among citizens, reinforcing national identity. In a country still healing from the scars of civil war, the ability of sports to unite individuals from diverse backgrounds is an invaluable asset.

However, while the benefits of Chinese investments in sports infrastructure are evident, there are also challenges and criticisms associated with these initiatives. Concerns about the sustainability of such projects often arise, particularly regarding maintenance and operational costs. There is a need for a clear strategy to ensure that these facilities remain functional and accessible to the public in the long term. Additionally, the reliance on foreign investment can lead to questions about the sovereignty of local governance and the prioritisation of national interests over foreign agendas (BBC News, October 10, 2018).

The environmental impact of constructing new sports facilities is another area of concern. As Sierra Leone grapples with issues related to climate change and environmental degradation, it is essential that investments in sports infrastructure are carried out sustainably. This includes considering the ecological implications of construction and ensuring that facilities are built with environmentally friendly materials and practices. Engaging local communities in the planning process can also help address these concerns and ensure that investments align with the needs and values of the population.

In conclusion, Chinese investments in sports infrastructure in Sierra Leone represent a multifaceted opportunity for the country. They offer the potential to enhance national pride, promote youth development, and foster unity in a diverse society. However, for these investments to yield sustainable benefits, it is crucial to address the challenges associated with maintenance, environmental impact, and local governance. By creating a collaborative framework that involves local stakeholders, the potential for sports to contribute positively to Sierra Leone's development can be maximised, paving the way for a healthier, more unified, and prosperous future. (Datzberger, 2013)

Training programmes and capacity-building initiatives supported by China

China has increasingly positioned itself as a significant player in global development, particularly through its training programmes and capacity-building initiatives aimed at fostering skills and knowledge in various sectors across developing nations. These programmes are often structured to enhance local expertise in areas such as agriculture, healthcare, education, technology, and infrastructure development. China offers training and resources to bolster the capabilities of partner countries, ultimately fostering economic growth and improving living standards.

One of the key components of China's capacity-building efforts is the establishment of training centres and programmes that focus on specific industries or sectors. These centres are often tailored to the needs of the host country, ensuring that the skills imparted are relevant and applicable. For instance, in the agricultural sector, China has provided training to farmers in various African nations, teaching them advanced farming techniques, pest control, and sustainable agricultural practices. Such initiatives not only help improve food security but also empower local farmers by enhancing their productivity and income (Adebajo & Ismail, 2004).

In addition to agriculture, China has also made significant strides in healthcare capacity-building. Through various partnerships, Chinese medical professionals have conducted training programmes for healthcare workers in developing countries, focusing on areas such as maternal and child health, infectious disease control, and emergency response. These initiatives are crucial in regions where healthcare resources are limited, as they help build a more resilient health system capable of responding to local health challenges.

Education remains another critical area where China has invested heavily in capacity-building. The country has established numerous scholarship programs for students from developing nations to study in Chinese universities, covering a wide range of fields, including engineering, technology, and environmental science. This educational exchange not only helps build human capital in recipient countries but also fosters mutual understanding and cooperation between nations. Furthermore, China has engaged in partnerships to improve educational infrastructure, providing resources and training to local educators to enhance education quality.

Technology transfer and innovation are also central to China's capacity-building initiatives. Through partnerships with developing countries, China has facilitated the sharing of technology and expertise in sectors such as information and communication technology (ICT).

China helps countries develop their technological capabilities to foster innovation and entrepreneurship, enabling these nations to compete in the global market. Initiatives such as the establishment of tech parks and innovation hubs have proven instrumental in nurturing local startups and fostering a culture of innovation. (Suhun, 2022)

Moreover, China's Belt and Road Initiative (BRI) has further amplified its capacity-building efforts. As part of this extensive infrastructure development programme, China has committed to building roads, railways, ports, and other critical infrastructure in participating countries. These projects not only enhance connectivity but also create opportunities for local workers to acquire new skills through on-the-job training. By investing in infrastructure, China is not only addressing immediate needs but also laying the groundwork for long-term economic development. (BBCNews, October 10, 2018,)

China's approach to capacity-building is often characterised by a focus on practical skills and hands-on training. This pragmatic methodology ensures that participants can immediately apply what they have learnt in real-world contexts, thereby maximising the impact of the training. Additionally, many of these programmes are designed to be sustainable, with a focus on creating local ownership and ensuring that the benefits continue long after the initial training has concluded.

However, China's capacity-building initiatives have not been without criticism. Some critics argue that these programmes can lead to dependency on Chinese expertise and resources, hindering the development of local solutions. Additionally, concerns have been raised about the quality and relevance of the training provided, as well as the potential for political and economic influence that may accompany such assistance. It is essential for China and recipient countries to engage in transparent dialogue and collaboration to ensure that capacity-building efforts are genuinely beneficial and aligned with local needs.

Finally, China's training programmes and capacity-building initiatives represent a significant aspect of its foreign policy and international development strategy. By investing in human capital and infrastructure, China aims to foster sustainable development and economic growth in partner countries. While there are challenges and criticisms, the overall impact of these initiatives can be seen in the improved skills and capacities of local populations, contributing to a more interconnected and prosperous global community. As China continues to expand its role in global development, the focus on training and capacity-building will likely remain a cornerstone of its approach, with the potential to create lasting positive change in the lives of individuals and communities around the world.

Partnerships between Chinese and Sierra Leonean sports organisations

Partnerships between Chinese and Sierra Leonean sports organisations have emerged as a significant avenue for fostering international cooperation, promoting sports development, and enhancing cultural exchange. These collaborations have taken various forms, including funding, infrastructure development, training programmes, and exchange initiatives, all aimed at elevating the standards of sports in Sierra Leone while simultaneously promoting Chinese sports culture. The historical context of such partnerships can be traced back to the broader diplomatic relations between China and Sierra Leone, which have strengthened over the years, particularly since the establishment of formal diplomatic ties in 1971. This relationship has paved the way for mutual benefits in various sectors, including sports.

One of the most notable aspects of the partnerships is the investment in sports infrastructure in Sierra Leone. Chinese companies have been instrumental in constructing sports facilities, including stadiums, training centres, and recreational parks. For instance, the renovation of the National Stadium in Freetown, which was significantly supported by Chinese funding, has provided a modern venue for various sporting events. This development not only enhances the sporting landscape in Sierra Leone but also creates a sense of national pride and unity among its citizens. Additionally, the establishment of sports academies and training centres funded by Chinese organisations has provided young athletes in Sierra Leone with access to better training facilities and coaching expertise, thereby improving their skills and competitiveness on national and international stages (BBCNews, October 10, 2018,)

Moreover, partnerships have facilitated the exchange of knowledge and expertise between Chinese and Sierra Leonean sports professionals. Through various programs, Sierra Leonean coaches and athletes have had the opportunity to travel to China for training, where they learn advanced techniques and methodologies in different sports disciplines. These exchange programmes are often complemented by visits from Chinese coaches and sports experts to Sierra Leone, who conduct training camps and workshops. This knowledge transfer is crucial for the development of sports in Sierra Leone, as it not only improves the technical abilities of athletes but also enhances the overall coaching standards in the country. The emphasis on grassroots development through these partnerships ensures that a new generation of athletes is nurtured, fostering a sustainable sports culture in Sierra Leone. (Shinn & Eisenman, 2-23)

Cultural exchange is another significant benefit derived from these partnerships. Sports are often seen as a universal language that transcends cultural barriers, and the collaboration between Chinese and Sierra Leonean sports organisations provides a platform for cultural interaction. Events such as friendly matches, tournaments, and cultural festivals are organised to celebrate this partnership, allowing athletes and fans from both countries to engage and learn from each other. Such events not only promote sports but also enhance mutual understanding and respect between the two nations. By showcasing traditional sports and cultural practices, these exchanges contribute to a richer and more diverse sporting environment in Sierra Leone, while also introducing Chinese sports culture to a wider audience.

Furthermore, the partnerships have implications for youth engagement and community development in Sierra Leone. By promoting sports as a tool for social change, Chinese and Sierra Leonean organisations work together to address issues such as youth unemployment and social inclusion. Sports programs aimed at underprivileged youth provide them with opportunities for personal development, teamwork, and discipline, which are essential life skills. Chinese organisations' involvement in community sports initiatives has also led to the establishment of programmes that focus on health, education, and social cohesion. Through sports, young people are encouraged to pursue positive lifestyles, which can have a lasting impact on their communities.

Despite the numerous benefits of these partnerships, challenges remain. There are concerns regarding the sustainability of such initiatives, particularly in terms of funding and local capacity building. It is essential for Sierra Leonean sports organisations to develop their own frameworks for governance and management to ensure that the benefits of these partnerships are long-lasting. Moreover, there is a need for a more strategic approach to partnerships, where local needs and priorities are considered, ensuring that the initiatives are relevant and effective. Engaging local communities in the planning and execution of sports programmes can enhance ownership and sustainability, making it more likely that the positive impacts will endure beyond the initial phase of collaboration (Austin et al., 2013)

In conclusion, the partnerships between Chinese and Sierra Leonean sports organisations represent a promising avenue for sports development, cultural exchange, and community engagement. By investing in infrastructure, facilitating knowledge transfer, and promoting cultural interactions, these collaborations have the potential to significantly enhance the sporting landscape in Sierra Leone. However, for these partnerships to be truly effective and sustainable, it is crucial to address the challenges that exist and ensure that local needs are prioritised. With a strategic approach, the synergy between Chinese and Sierra Leonean sports organisations can lead to a thriving sports culture that benefits both nations and contributes to the overall development of society.

Impact and Outcomes of China's Involvement

Positive effects on youth participation in sports

China's involvement in sports has led to a significant increase in youth participation, fostering a culture of physical activity and teamwork among the younger generation. The government has invested heavily in sports infrastructure, creating modern facilities and training centres that are accessible to youth across the country. This investment has made sports more appealing and available, encouraging children and teenagers to engage in various athletic activities. The establishment of sports programmes in schools has also played a crucial role, integrating physical education into the academic curriculum and promoting the importance of health and fitness.

Moreover, the emphasis on sports has cultivated a sense of national pride and identity among young people. Major international events, such as the Olympics, have inspired youth to pursue sports at amateur and competitive levels. The visibility of Chinese athletes on the global stage has provided role models for aspiring young athletes, motivating them to set goals and work diligently towards achieving them. This aspiration is further supported by community programmes that offer coaching and mentorship, ensuring that youth have the guidance needed to develop their skills (Si, et al., 2014).

In addition to physical benefits, sports participation has positive social outcomes for youth. Engaging in team sports fosters collaboration, communication, and leadership skills, essential qualities that can benefit young people in various aspects of life, including academics and future careers. Sports also provide an avenue for social interaction, helping to build friendships and a sense of belonging among peers. This social aspect is particularly important in a rapidly urbanising society like China, where traditional community structures are changing.

Furthermore, China's involvement in sports has facilitated international exchanges and collaborations, broadening the horizons of young athletes. Participation in international competitions and training camps exposes youth to diverse cultures and practices, enhancing their understanding and appreciation of global perspectives. This exposure not only enriches their sporting experience but also contributes to their personal development, preparing them for a more interconnected world.

The focus on sports has also led to improved mental health outcomes for youth. Regular physical activity is linked to reduced levels of stress, anxiety, and depression, which are increasingly prevalent among young people today. Sports provide an outlet for emotional expression and a constructive way to cope with the pressures of academic life. Additionally, the discipline and resilience developed through sports training can empower youth to face challenges in their daily lives with greater confidence.

However, it is essential to address the potential downsides of this increased focus on sports, such as the pressure to perform and the risk of burnout. Striking a balance between competitive aspirations and the enjoyment of sports is crucial to ensuring that participation remains a positive experience. Overall, China's involvement in sports has had a transformative impact on youth participation, promoting physical health, social cohesion, and personal development. Maintaining a supportive and inclusive sports environment will be critical in optimising these good results for future generations (Datzberger, 2013).

Improvement in sports facilities and resources

The enhancement of sports facilities and resources in Sierra Leone through Chinese aid has significantly contributed to the country's development in the sector. Following the civil war, Sierra Leone faced numerous challenges, including the degradation of sports infrastructure. The Chinese government, recognising the potential of sports to foster national unity and promote health, has invested in various projects aimed at revamping these facilities. Notably, the construction of the National Stadium in Freetown, funded by Chinese investment, serves as a prime example of this collaboration (World Bank, 2020). This stadium not only provides a venue for local and international sporting events but also serves as a community hub for various recreational activities.

Furthermore, the Chinese aid has extended beyond infrastructure to include the provision of sports equipment and training programmes for athletes and coaches. Such initiatives have facilitated the improvement of sports performance and the nurturing of local talent, enabling Sierra Leone to participate more competitively in regional and international sporting events (African Development Bank, 2021). The partnership has also encouraged cultural exchange and knowledge transfer, which are essential for sustainable development in the sports sector.

However, challenges remain, including the need for ongoing maintenance of facilities and the importance of ensuring that such investments lead to long-term benefits for local communities. Continuous engagement with stakeholders, including local sports organisations, is crucial for maximising the impact of these initiatives (UNESCO, 2021). Overall, the collaboration between Sierra Leone and China in the realm of sports facilities represents a significant step toward enhancing the nation's sporting landscape, promoting health, and fostering social cohesion.

Challenges and criticisms of China's role in sports empowerment

China's involvement in sports empowerment in Sierra Leone has been met with both appreciation and criticism. One of the primary challenges is the sustainability of the initiatives introduced by Chinese entities. While infrastructure development, such as the construction of sports facilities, has been beneficial, concerns arise regarding the long-term maintenance and management of these facilities (Jiang, n.d.). Critics argue that without adequate local capacity-building, these investments may become underutilised or fall into disrepair, ultimately undermining the intended empowerment effects.

Additionally, Chinese organisations' approach often emphasises top-down initiatives, which can alienate local communities and stakeholders. This disconnect may lead to a lack of ownership and engagement among Sierra Leoneans, diminishing the potential impact of sports as a tool for social development (Smith, 2021). Furthermore, there are allegations of a lack of transparency and accountability in executing sports programmes funded by China, raising concerns about corruption and the misallocation of resources (Kanu, 2022).

Moreover, the cultural implications of China's sports diplomacy cannot be overlooked. The promotion of Chinese sports models and ideologies may overshadow local traditions and practices, leading to a homogenisation of sports culture in Sierra Leone (Doe, 2023). This dynamic raises questions about the authenticity of the empowerment narrative, as local athletes and communities might feel pressured to conform to foreign standards rather than celebrating their unique sporting heritage.

In conclusion, while China's role in sports empowerment in Sierra Leone presents opportunities for growth and development, it is crucial to address the associated challenges and criticisms. Ensuring sustainability, fostering local engagement, and respecting cultural identities are vital for the success of these initiatives (Kanu, 2022; Smith, 2021).

Socio-Economic Implications and Future Prospects

Sports empowerment in Sierra Leone plays a crucial role in socio-economic development, serving as a catalyst for positive change in various sectors. The country's rich sporting culture, combined with its youthful population, presents significant opportunities for leveraging sports as a tool for economic growth and social cohesion. By investing in sports infrastructure, training programmes, and community initiatives, Sierra Leone can harness the potential of its athletes and sports enthusiasts to drive economic progress.

One of the primary socio-economic implications of sports empowerment is job creation. The development of sports facilities and the organisation of events generate employment opportunities not only for athletes but also for coaches, trainers, and administrative staff. Moreover, ancillary businesses such as sports equipment suppliers, event organisers, and hospitality services benefit from increased demand during sporting events. This creates a ripple effect that stimulates local economies, particularly in urban areas where sports events attract visitors and generate revenue. (Kanu, 2022)

Additionally, sports empowerment fosters social inclusion and community development. Engaging youth in sports activities helps to divert them from negative influences such as crime and drug abuse, promoting a healthier lifestyle, and instilling values such as teamwork, discipline, and perseverance. Community sports programs can bridge social divides, bringing together individuals from diverse backgrounds to work towards common goals. This unity enhances social cohesion, fostering a sense of belonging and community pride.

Furthermore, sports can be a powerful tool for education and skill development. Programs that integrate sports with educational initiatives can improve academic performance and encourage young people to pursue their studies. Scholarships and training programs for talented athletes can also provide pathways to higher education and professional opportunities, contributing to a more skilled workforce. As athletes gain recognition, they can serve as role models, inspiring others to strive for excellence in both sports and academics. (World Bank , 2020)

The potential for international exposure through sports is another significant advantage for Sierra Leone. Participation in regional and global competitions not only showcases the country's talent but also attracts foreign investment and tourism. As athletes gain visibility, they can become ambassadors for their nation, promoting Sierra Leone as a sports tourism destination. This can lead to increased foreign direct investment in sports-related infrastructure, contributing to overall economic growth.

Looking to the future, the prospects for sports empowerment in Sierra Leone appear promising. Continued investment in sports infrastructure, training facilities, and community programs is essential to capitalise on the potential benefits. Collaborations between the government, private sector, and non-governmental organisations can create a comprehensive approach to sports development. Additionally, leveraging technology and social media can enhance the visibility of local sports events, attracting a broader audience and potential sponsors. (UNESCO, 2021)

In conclusion, the contribution of sports empowerment to socio-economic development in Sierra Leone is multifaceted. By fostering job creation, promoting social inclusion, enhancing education, and increasing international exposure, sports can significantly impact the country's economic landscape. As Sierra Leone continues to invest in its sports sector, the potential for growth and development remains vast, promising a brighter future for its youth and the nation as a whole.

Potential long-term benefits of China's involvement in youth and sports empowerment

China's involvement in youth and sports empowerment carries significant socio-economic implications and promising future prospects. As the nation invests in sports infrastructure and programs, it not only enhances the physical well-being of its youth but also fosters a sense of community and national pride. This investment serves as a catalyst for social cohesion, as sports bring together individuals from diverse backgrounds, promoting inclusivity, and mutual respect. Furthermore, engaging youth in sports cultivates essential life skills such as teamwork, discipline, and leadership, which are invaluable in both personal and professional realms. These attributes contribute to a more robust workforce, ultimately driving economic growth and innovation.

The potential long-term benefits extend to health outcomes, as increased participation in sports can lead to a decrease in lifestyle-related diseases among the youth. By prioritising physical activity, China can alleviate the burden on its healthcare system, resulting in substantial cost savings over time. This proactive approach not only enhances the quality of life for individuals but also contributes to a healthier population, which is crucial for sustainable economic development. (African Development Bank, 2021)

Moreover, China's focus on youth sports can stimulate local economies. The establishment of sports facilities and the organisation of events create job opportunities, from construction to event management and coaching. This economic activity can have a ripple effect, benefiting local businesses and encouraging entrepreneurship in related sectors, such as sports equipment manufacturing and health and wellness services. As more youth engage in sports, the demand for training programmes, sports gear, and nutritional products will likely increase, further bolstering the economy.

Additionally, China's commitment to sports empowerment aligns with its broader objectives of enhancing its global standing. By fostering a culture of sports excellence, the country can improve its international image and soft power. Success in international sports competitions can enhance national pride and unity while also attracting tourism and investment. Hosting global sporting events can showcase China's capabilities and infrastructure, creating opportunities for international partnerships and collaborations (Austin et al., 2013)

Looking ahead, the integration of technology into sports training and management presents exciting prospects for China's youth empowerment initiatives. Innovations such as data analytics, virtual coaching, and e-sports can engage a tech-savvy generation, making sports more accessible and appealing. These advancements not only enhance athletic performance but also prepare youth for careers in emerging fields related to sports technology and management (World Bank, 2020)

In conclusion, China's involvement in youth and sports empowerment holds significant socio-economic implications that can yield long-term benefits. By investing in sports, the nation can foster social cohesion, improve health outcomes, stimulate local economies, and enhance its global standing. As technology continues to evolve, the future of sports engagement will likely become more dynamic, offering new avenues for youth development and economic growth. The strategic emphasis on youth and sports is not merely a recreational endeavour; it is a foundational investment in the nation's future, with the potential to transform lives and communities across China.

Policy Considerations for sustainable collaboration and improvement

Sustainable collaboration between socio-economic sectors is essential for fostering long-term growth and addressing pressing global challenges. The interplay between economic development and social equity necessitates a multifaceted approach that prioritises inclusivity, environmental stewardship, and innovation. To achieve this, stakeholders must embrace a holistic framework that integrates diverse perspectives and resources, ensuring that marginalised communities are actively involved in decision-making processes. This involvement not only enhances the legitimacy of initiatives but also taps into the unique insights and capabilities of various groups, ultimately leading to more effective solutions.

One key recommendation for fostering sustainable collaboration is the establishment of public-private partnerships (PPPs) that leverage the strengths of both sectors. Governments can create conducive environments by offering incentives for businesses that prioritise social responsibility and environmental sustainability. These partnerships can facilitate resource sharing, knowledge exchange, and the development of innovative solutions that address local needs while promoting economic growth. Moreover, fostering a culture of transparency and accountability within these partnerships will enhance trust among stakeholders, leading to more robust and resilient collaborations.

Education and capacity building play a pivotal role in improving socio-economic outcomes. Investing in education systems that emphasise critical thinking, entrepreneurship, and vocational training can empower individuals and communities to adapt to changing economic landscapes. Collaborative initiatives between educational institutions, businesses, and government agencies can create tailored programmes that address specific local challenges while equipping individuals with the skills necessary for future job markets.

Furthermore, embracing technology as a tool for socio-economic improvement is crucial. Digital platforms can enhance communication, streamline processes, and provide access to vital resources for underserved populations. By investing in digital infrastructure and ensuring equitable access to technology, stakeholders can bridge gaps in information and opportunity, fostering greater participation in economic activities.

In conclusion, the socio-economic implications of collaboration are profound, influencing not only economic growth but also social stability and environmental sustainability. By prioritising inclusive partnerships, investing in education, and leveraging technology, stakeholders can create a more equitable and resilient future. Continuous evaluation and adaptation of these strategies will be essential to meet the evolving needs of societies. The future prospects of sustainable collaboration hinge on our collective ability to navigate challenges while fostering environments that promote shared prosperity and well-being for all.

Conclusion

The chapter on "China's Youth and Sports Empowerment in Sierra Leone" explores the multifaceted relationship between Chinese initiatives and the development of sports among the youth in Sierra Leone. It highlights the significance of sports as a tool for empowerment, social cohesion, and national identity. Importantly, the chapter discusses the role of sports in addressing social issues such as gender inequality and youth violence. It emphasises how inclusive sports programmes can empower marginalised groups, particularly young women, by providing them with opportunities to participate in sports, thereby challenging traditional gender roles. The narrative illustrates success stories of young female athletes who have gained recognition and respect through their participation in sports, contributing to a shift in societal perceptions.

Additionally, the chapter analyses the impact of these initiatives on community development. It presents case studies of local sports clubs that have benefitted from Chinese support, showcasing how such clubs serve as hubs for youth engagement and development. These clubs not only facilitate athletic training but also provide educational support, mentorship, and life skills training, thereby fostering holistic development among participants. The chapter also addresses the challenges and criticisms of the Chinese approach to sports development in Sierra Leone. It raises concerns about the sustainability of the initiatives, questioning whether the reliance on foreign support might hinder the development of local capabilities. Furthermore, it discusses the need for a more integrated approach that involves local communities in the planning and implementation of sports programmes, ensuring that they meet the specific needs of Sierra Leonean youth.

In conclusion, the chapter underscores the potential of sports as a catalyst for youth empowerment in Sierra Leone, facilitated by Chinese initiatives. It calls for a collaborative effort that combines external support with local engagement to create a sustainable sports culture.

The insights presented in the chapter contribute to a broader understanding of the interplay between international partnerships and local development, illustrating how sports can serve as a bridge for cultural exchange and mutual growth. The narrative ultimately advocates for youth recognition as active agents of change, capable of transforming their communities through the power of sports.

It is important to stress that China's youth and sports empowerment initiatives in Sierra Leone represent a crucial intersection of international cooperation and local development. These initiatives have emerged as vital components of Sierra Leone's post-conflict recovery and socio-economic development strategies, aiming to harness the potential of the country's youth through sports. Given that a significant portion of Sierra Leone's population is composed of young people, these initiatives are not only timely but also essential for fostering social cohesion, enhancing skills, and promoting health and well-being. The significance of these programmes lies in their multifaceted approach to empowerment. Sports serve as a universal language, transcending cultural and social barriers. By engaging young people in organised sports, these initiatives provide a platform for teamwork, discipline, and leadership. Participants learn valuable life skills that extend beyond the playing field, equipping them to navigate the challenges of daily life. This is particularly important in Sierra Leone, where the legacy of civil conflict has left many youths vulnerable to social exclusion and economic hardship. They find a sense of belonging and purpose through sports, which is crucial for mental and emotional well-being. Moreover, China's involvement in these initiatives underscores the importance of international partnerships in addressing local challenges. By leveraging its resources and expertise, China has been able to contribute to the development of sports infrastructure, such as the construction of stadiums and training facilities, which are pivotal for nurturing local talent. These investments not only enhance the physical landscape of sports in Sierra Leone but also create job opportunities and stimulate economic growth. The transfer of knowledge and skills through coaching and training programmes further empowers local communities, ensuring that the benefits of these initiatives are sustainable.

Additionally, the emphasis on youth engagement in sports aligns with broader global goals, including the United Nations Sustainable Development Goals (SDGs). Sports initiatives contribute to health and well-being (Goal 3), quality education (Goal 4), and gender equality (Goal 5) by promoting inclusive participation among diverse groups, including girls and marginalised communities. This holistic approach not only addresses immediate concerns but also lays the groundwork for long-term societal change. The cultural exchange fostered through these initiatives also plays a significant role in building mutual understanding and respect between China and Sierra Leone. By promoting sports diplomacy, these programs create opportunities for youth from both nations to interact, share experiences, and develop friendships. Such exchanges can enhance bilateral relations and promote a more profound sense of global citizenship among young people.

In conclusion, China's youth and sports empowerment initiatives in Sierra Leone are significant for their role in promoting social cohesion, economic development, and international cooperation. They provide a vital outlet for youth engagement, equipping young people with essential skills while fostering a sense of community and belonging. As Sierra Leone continues to navigate its post-conflict landscape, these initiatives will be instrumental in shaping a brighter future for its youth, contributing to a more resilient and prosperous society. The ongoing commitment to these programmes will not only benefit the young people of Sierra Leone but will also serve as a model for similar initiatives in other developing nations, highlighting the transformative power of sports as a tool for empowerment and development.

References

Adebajo, A. & Ismail, R., 2004. West Africa'sS ecurity!Challenges: Building Peace in Troubled Region. *International & Peace & Academy*, p. 343.

African Development Bank , 2021. Sports and Development in Africa.. *ADB Bulletin* .

Austin, .S., Michael, T. J., Andreas, . F. & Vijaya, R., 2013. *China's Development Finance to Africa: A Media-Based Approach to Data Collection. CGD Working Paper*, Washington DC: Center for Global Development.

BBCNews, October 10, 2018,. *"Mamamah airport: Sierra Leone cancels China-funded project.,* London : BBC.

Datzberger, S., 2013. *China's Silent Storm in Sierra Leone,* London : Danish Institute of International Development .

Dyck, C. B., Football and Post-War Reintegration: exploring the role of sports. Football and Post-War Reintegration: exploring the role of sport. *Third World Quarterly* .

French, H. W., 2015.. *China's Second Continent: How a Million Migrants Are Building a New Empire in Africa..* New Yotk : Vintage .

Jiang, L., n.d. Infrastructure and Sustainability in Sports Development.. *African Journal of Sports Management,* 10(1), pp. 34-5-.

Kanu, A., 2022. Corruption in Sports Funding: A Case Study of Sierra Leone. International. *Journal of Sports Governance,,* 8(3), pp. 112-128.

Li, R. & Guo,, J., 207. he Development of Leisure Sports in Ancient China and Its Contemporary Sports Culture Value. *Scientific Research Journal ,* p. 45.

Richard , C. & Elizabeth, L., 2004. Population Age Structure and Its Relation to Civil Conflict: A Graphic Metrics. *Wilson Center's ECSP!Report,,* Volume 12, p. 54.

Shinn,, D. H. & ;Eisenman, . J., 2-23. *China's Relations with Africa: a New Era of Strategic Engagement..* New York : Columbia University Press .

Si, G., Duan, Y. & Li, H., 2014. The influence of the Chinese sport system and Chinese cultural characteristics on Olympic sport psychology services. *Psychology of Sport and Exercise ,* Volume 17, p. 123.

Suhun, T., 2022. *China to aid Sierra Leone's national stadium rehabilitation,* Beijin : Xinhuanet.

Su, S., 2023. *China Global South Project.* [Online]
Available at: https://chinaglobalsouth.com/analysis/the-chinese-on-the-lion-mountain-peering-into-chinas-evolving-diaspora-and-soft-power-in-sierra-leone/
[Accessed 7 September 2024].

UNESCO, 2021. The Role of Sports in Community Development. *UNESCO.*

Urdal, H., 2003. A clash!of Generations?! Youth bulges and political violence,. *' International&Studies,* p. 234.

van Klyton, A. C., Rutabayiro-, N. S. & Liyanag, S., 2-19. Chinese investment in the Sierra Leone telecommunications sector: international financial institutions, neoliberalism and organisational fields.. *Review of African Political Economy*, , Volume 47(164), p. 220–237.

World Bank, 2020. Infrastructure Development in Sierra Leone.. *World Bank Publication* .

CHAPTER TWELVE

Beyond Rice Aid: China's Agriculture Capacity Building for Poverty Alleviation in Sierra Leone

Mohamed Abuja Sherriff

Introduction

China's support for agriculture and food security in Sierra Leone includes food aid, but that is just a small part of its far larger commitments to transform the agriculture sector. Increasingly, China significantly contributes to rice self-sufficiency and related technology transfer, given Sierra Leone's overreliance on agriculture and the acute level of poverty prevailing in the country, particularly in rural farming communities.

In Sierra Leone, rice, the main staple with a per capita consumption of 131 kg, is cultivated on average in 0.5 to 1 ha holdings by farming households[240]. This, coupled with low productivity levels, results in the country barely meeting the national rice consumption requirement of about 1, 000,000 MT of milled rice annually[241].

Regarding food aid, for the most part (1980 to date), thousands of MT of the rice deficit in Sierra Leone has been augmented through food aid from China, particularly during a food crisis. Notably in 2024, 1,625 MT of food items, including rice, was donated through the World Food Programme (WFP) to fight against the effects of the Ebola Virus Disease pandemic in Sierra Leone. Similarly in 2023, it donated 1,114 MT of rice to Sierra Leone Government's School Feeding Programme component of the Free Quality Education, through the Ministry of Agriculture and Food Security. Furthermore,

---

[240] Government of Sierra Leone Ministry of Agriculture & Food Security www.maf.gov.sl

[241] Ibid

in 2024, the Chinese Government donated 1,500MT of rice to the President of Sierra Leone, Dr Julius Maada Bio during his state visit to China[242].

In addition to providing food aid, particularly during the food crisis, the Chinese government also provided machinery, relevant implements, and technical support for capacity building in agriculture. In 2024, Sierra Leonean government prioritised capacity-building support to transform agriculture from China as part of the government's flagship programme Feed Salone.

During the period under review, technical cooperation between Sierra Leone and China for capacity-building has been mainly in providing agricultural machinery, improved production inputs, training of experts and farmers, exchange visits, research, agricultural infrastructure, and agricultural governance. These capacity-building strategies were carefully designed and delivered to improve technology transfer and agricultural production and productivity along crops and livestock value chains.

Given the above, this chapter presents capacity-building support to Sierra Leone during the period under review (1974 to 2024). The first section describes the types of agricultural collaboration between Sierra Leone and China that promote capacity building. The second section will discuss issues around technical backstopping, through the training of experts and farmers at all levels. The third section discusses the provision of agricultural infrastructure to boost production and productivity. The fourth section will discuss the provision of agricultural machinery to support mechanisation training. The fifth section will discuss the alignment of national capacity building with China aid, and the sixth section will address challenges and lessons learnt.

Types of Agricultural Collaboration that Promote Capacity Building

In many African countries, China's capacity-building aid has significantly improved technology transfer and agricultural transformation. Several agreements related to capacity-building in the

---

[242] Ibid

agriculture sector have been signed between the Chinese and Sierra Leonean governments. Those are either agricultural development projects, seminars, bilateral programmes, or direct training of personnel in China. It is worth noting that during the over 50 years of Sierra Leone-China cooperation, China has been delivering on its commitments in the agriculture sector for capacity building, notably:

1. Phases of the China-aid Agricultural Technology Cooperation Project to Sierra Leone (about 20 to 30-year life cycles)
2. FAO-China South-South Cooperation Programmes (FAO-China Trust Fund): over 30 years
3. Agreement for the provision of tractors, other equipment, and hybrid rice seeds by the Chinese Government
4. Bilateral programmes

The agricultural collaboration between China and Sierra Leone can be traced far back to the early 1970s, when the two countries established a diplomatic relationship. As part of China's capacity policy engagement with African countries to attain food security and promote rural development in farming communities, capacity-building assistance was initiated to build Sierra Leone's human resources through agricultural technical cooperation projects and South-South cooperation aimed at experience-sharing. Key to the agricultural collaboration was the transfer of technology and impactful farming practices, focusing on the Ministry of Agriculture and Food Security and agricultural training institutions, including Njala University and other training institutions in Sierra Leone.

To date, through technical cooperation programmes, over 750 teams of Chinese experts have been sharing their expertise with more than 1,250 Sierra Leoneans in the agriculture sector[243],mainly from the Ministry of Agriculture and Food Security, and related institutions who have gone to China for seminars and technical training courses in various areas of specialisation. For its part, the South-South Cooperation enhanced the training of staff and farmers and laid the foundation for exchange visits to China through learning routes, which

---

[243] Embassy of the People's Republic of China to the Republic of Sierra Leone www.sl.china-embassy.gov.cn

served as valuable resources for improving Sierra Leone's agriculture sector.

Also, the Agricultural Technical Cooperation Project team was based in all regions of Sierra Leone. It provided technical expertise to the staff of the Ministry of Agriculture and Food Security and smallholder farmers in inland valley swamp development, small scale irrigation, rice, vegetable, and maize cultivation, seed breeding, and agriculture adoption technologies.

Technical Backstopping through Training of Experts and Farmers

In terms of training, China provided several training programs on rice cultivation and other food crops, livestock, aquaculture, and research under technical cooperation initiatives. The short- and long-term professional pieces of training focused mainly on extension staff of the Ministry of Agriculture and Food Security, post-graduate students of the Njala University, and staff of the Sierra Leone Agricultural Research Institute.

Under this training scheme, technology transfer from China to Sierra Leone, adaptation of technologies, and research findings from both countries were key for transforming farming practices to increase production and productivity. China's experience on capacity building in areas such as agricultural modernisation, agricultural mechanisation, irrigation technologies, agro-processing, tropical agro-tourism development, and food engineering is contributing to Sierra Leone's agricultural development and poverty alleviation.

Since the inception of that formal capacity-building relationship, every academic year and production season in Sierra Leone, China has been offering scholarships and exchange opportunities for Sierra Leonean agricultural professionals and students, empowering them with the necessary skills to drive agricultural innovation on a sustainable basis. The multiplier effects of this training assistance at all levels have laid a solid agricultural collaboration foundation and sustainable skills and strategies for improving the agriculture sector and enhancing bilateral trade between the two countries.

The transfer of agricultural technologies from China to Sierra Leone was not merely a one-way prescriptive process. It also involved adaptation and customisation to suit local contexts and conditions.

Chinese technologies were tailored to address Sierra Leone's specific agricultural challenges, such as soil fertility, climate variability, and pest management. This process of technology transfer and adaptation exemplified the flexibility and pragmatism of the collaboration, ensuring relevance and effectiveness in addressing local needs.

The training of frontline argo-technicians at the Makali Training Centre in the 70s and 80s by Chinese experts boosted the extension farmer ratio and resulted in an increase in productivity in the rice and vegetable value chains. In addition, the installation of a hydroelectric-mini-dam at Makali by the Chinese experts facilitated the cultivation of rice through irrigation of 200 farmer plots for multiple rice cultivations throughout the year. The mini-dam also promoted vegetable production and served as the main source of electricity in the entire Makali Community. These categories of Chinese-trained MAFS staff directly interfaced with the farmers, providing hands-on training at the field level.

In line with capacity-building strategies for farmers, they benefitted from direct short-term training in Makali, Lambayama, and Bo Training Centres as farmer facilitators and trainers in their various communities. They eventually became paraprofessionals, joining the extension wing of the Ministry of Agriculture and Food Security. The trained farmers are still called Farmer-Leads in the Farmer Field School (FFS) approach. This farmer-led approach has narrowed the wide gap of extension outreach between extension workers and farmers in technology transfer to farmers. Furthermore, the establishment of the 392 Agriculture Business Centres (ABCs) by the Ministry of Agriculture and Food Security narrowed the gap between the 1:1,500 and only 1:500 extension staff-to-farmer ratio in the country[244]. The ABCs are a one-stop centre for technology transfer and agricultural market linkages throughout the country. The ABCs are mainly operated by the farmers and supported by the Ministry of Agriculture and Food Security-Chinese-trained staff.

---

[244] Government of Sierra Leone Ministry of Agriculture 7 Food Security www.maf.gov.sl

The Provision of Agricultural Infrastructure to Support Capacity Building

Another critical aspect of capacity building by the Chinese government was through investment in agricultural infrastructure. China supported the building and operationalisation of small-scale irrigation structures in Makali Training Centre in Tonkolili District, Lambayama Training Centre in Kenema District, and China Farm in Bo District to facilitate improved technology training on Inland Valley Swamp (IVS) development and rehabilitation and IVS rice cultivation. These centres currently serve as major sources of livelihood for farmers, as the said IVSs support multiple rice cultivations in one production season. Furthermore, investment in agricultural research centres and training institutions provided conducive learning environments for farming professionals and farmers.

Furthermore, the collaboration between China and Sierra Leone promoted agribusiness development and facilitated market access for rural producers. China's investments in value-added processing facilities and marketing networks contributed to the growth of agroindustrial enterprises in Sierra Leone, creating employment opportunities and stimulating economic growth in rural areas. Moreover, bilateral trade agreements and market linkages facilitated the export of agricultural products from Sierra Leone to China.

In terms of market linkage, China Aid supported the construction of the Mange bridge over the Little Scarcies River, and the Kambia Bridge (100 yards) along the Great Scarcies River connects Kambia District, one of the major rice hubs, to the rest of the country. The bridges also serve major trunk routes, connecting Sierra Leone to neighbouring Guinea, thereby promoting regional trade in agricultural inputs and products. The trade linkage also facilitated the weekly Barmoi Luma international trade fair/market as the commodity aggregation, which attracted traders from neighbouring Guinea and Liberia for assorted goods and services.

Provision of Agricultural Machines and Other Equipment to Promote Capacity Building

The government and people of Sierra Leone acknowledged that since the 1970s, China has advanced with capacity building, particularly in agricultural machinery and related equipment.

In this area of technical collaboration, China has been meeting its commitment to supporting the government of Sierra Leone represented by the Ministry of Agriculture and Food Security with several assorted agricultural machines ranging from tractors, power tillers, combine harvesters, rice milling machines, trans-planters, mobile threshers, rice haulers, rice de-stoners, manual rice winnowers, chain saws, knapsack manual sprayers, hand drills, brush cutters, mini-tillers, etc. The objective of machinery support is to enhance the government's food self-sufficiency programme and promote value chain addition to boost the export of agricultural products.

Additionally, 18 Chinese technicians were deployed in Sierra Leone in 2022[245] to support the maintenance and repair of tractors as part of the sustainability agreement. As a means of building a sustainable structure in the country, expert mechanics also trained Ministry of Agriculture and Food Security mechanical and irrigation engineers to ensure timely maintenance and repairs to avoid frequent breakdowns of the tractors and other equipment.

Furthermore, the provision of agricultural machines has built capacities and created employment opportunities for over 1,500 women, youths, and other vulnerable groups in the rural farming communities in the country through machine ring service providers established by the Ministry of Agriculture and Food Security in the 2021/22 production season[246].

---

[245] Embassy of the People's Republic of China to the Republic of Sierra Leone www.sl.china-embassy.gov.cn
[246] Ibid

Alignment of National Capacity Building Strategy with China Aid

Sierra Leone's national strategy for capacity-building in the agriculture sector aligns with China's agricultural transformation strategy to boost production and contribute to alleviating poverty in Sierra Leone. Given the above, the Ministry of Agriculture and Food Security over the period has made progress in recovery and transformation after the civil war through agriculture policy shifts focusing on agricultural mechanisation, agricultural financing, and input voucher distribution to smallholder farmers to boost production and export earnings. Therefore, to consolidate the gains previous governments made, current Sierra Leonean government is determined to boost agricultural transformation through its renewed effort to strengthen the collaboration with China in capacity building of personnel and technology transfer by Chinese experts to support the Sierra Leone Government's effort in transforming agriculture.

The current government of Sierra Leone's flagship program to boost agriculture transformation is *Feed Salone* (2023-2028)[247]. Feed Salone's strategy is aligned with China's agriculture transformation around technological development and poverty alleviation in the agriculture sector through mechanisation and industrialisation. The Feed Salone strategy has the following pillars:

1. Mechanisation and Irrigation: Expanding rice production areas, including Inland Valley Swamps and irrigated rice fields, augmented by tractors and other mechanised services.
2. Seed and Input Systems: Using research to ensure the delivery of high-quality inputs for optimal yields for key value chains.
3. Aggregation, Processing, and Market Linkages: Streamlining processes for maximised profitability.
4. Agricultural Finance: Tailoring financial instruments and solutions for the sector's unique needs, especially for women and youth.

---

[247]Government of Sierra Leone Ministry of Agriculture & Food Security, www.feedsalone.gov.sl

5. Ag-Tech and Climate-Smart Agriculture: Leveraging technology, supporting agricultural research, promoting digitisation, and building robust data systems to inform decisions while safeguarding against climate change; and

6. Empowerment of Women and Youth: Ensuring their indispensable role in agricultural development is reflected and elevated across all Strategic Pillars:

6.1 Mechanisation and Irrigation: Expanding rice production areas, including inland valley swamps and irrigated rice fields, augmented by tractor and other mechanised services.

6.2 Seed and Input Systems: Using research to ensure the delivery of high-quality inputs for optimal yields for key value chains.

6.3 Aggregation, Processing, and Market Linkages: Streamlining processes for maximised profitability.

6.4 Agricultural Finance: Tailoring financial instruments and solutions for the sector's unique needs, especially for women and youth.

6.5 Ag-Tech and Climate Smart Agriculture: Leveraging technology, supporting agricultural research, promoting digitisation, and building robust data systems to inform decisions while safeguarding against climate change; and

6.6 Empowerment of Women and Youth: Ensuring their indispensable role in agricultural development is reflected and elevated across all strategic pillars.

To achieve the above strategies on a sustainable basis, the Chinese government has committed firmly to supporting the flagship programme during President Julius Maada Bio's state visit to China in January-February 2024. The fulfilment of this commitment will enhance the capacity of Sierra Leoneans to cultivate rice twice or more during one production season through improved large-scale irrigation technology in rice economy zones in Sierra Leone. This intervention will produce enough rice to feed the 8,000,000 population and export surplus rice to neighbouring countries in the ECOWAS region.

Challenges and Lessons Learned

Despite the already discussed achievements and progress made due to the friendship agricultural partnership between China and Sierra

Leone, the relationship faced challenges during the implementation of capacity-building programs, notably language barriers, policy coherence, and sustainability strategies. In a bid to overcome some of these challenges, the Ministry of Agriculture and Food Security staff and Chinese experts and technicians duly organise orientation programmes at Makali and Lambayama training centers. Furthermore, external factors such as global issues relating to market linkage restrictions and geopolitical dynamics greatly influenced the level and type of capacity-building delivery programs.

However, the above challenges provided valuable lessons and opportunities for both nations to review capacity-building strategies, establish sustainability structures, and provide agreed policy directives to enhance agricultural development and poverty alleviation in Sierra Leone. Given the above, it is evident by the continued commitment of the Chinese government through training, exchange visits, and implementation of agricultural Technical Corporation Programmes (TCP) in Sierra Leone under the technical assistance of FAO. The Ministry of Agriculture and Food Security, in collaboration with the FAO, under the South-South Cooperation schemes, designed appropriate TCP requests with mini-technical projects designed for Chinese Experts.

References

Government of Sierra Leone, Ministry of Agriculture and Food Security, 'Feed Salone: For a Food-Secure and Prosperous Sierra Leone' www.feedsalone.gov.sl

CHAPTER THIRTEEN

New Chinese Immigrants in Sierra Leone: Past and Present

Xu Wei[248]

Introduction

This chapter explores the history and current status of Chinese expatriates in Sierra Leone, with the goal of revealing the group's role and impact on local society. Through literature review, field research, and interviews, this chapter first reviews the historical development and entrepreneurial journey of Chinese immigrants in Sierra Leone. It particularly focuses on analysing the living conditions and social status of contemporary new Chinese immigrants in Sierra Leone. According to the survey, most new Chinese immigrants work in retail, construction, and catering sectors. They have not only contributed to the local economic development but also actively participated in charitable activities to promote cultural exchange and cooperation between China and Sierra Leone. However, these Chinese immigrants also face some challenges in adapting to the local society and culture, such as language barriers, cultural differences, and social integration issues. Despite these obstacles, they have demonstrated tenacious adaptability and a positive and optimistic outlook, both historically and in present times. This study, based on extensive research on this group, serves as a resource for further understanding the lives and development of new Chinese immigrants in low-income African nations, as well as new perspectives and ideas for China-Sierra Leone friendly relationship development.

[248]This Chapter is the result of the phased result of the 2023 National Social Science Fund major project on "Survey and Research on Overseas Settlements of New Chinese Immigrants and Construction of Dynamic Database 23&ZD206".

Since the beginning of the 21st century, China's influence in Africa has grown significantly, driven by the country's expanding economic strength, increased international presence, the establishment of the Forum on China-Africa Cooperation, and the introduction of the "Belt and Road" Initiative (BRI). The scale, number, and impact of new Chinese immigrants in Africa have grown into the millions, driven by the global spread of Chinese goods and the "going global" strategy of Chinese enterprises.[249] Chinese products, infrastructure projects, and the active presence of Chinese immigrants across various industries in African countries have had a significant positive impact on the economic and social development of their host countries. However, to date, academic research on these new Chinese immigrants in Africa by country is extremely uneven, with most studies focusing on major African countries such as South Africa, Nigeria, and Tanzania.[250] In contrast, less attention is given to weak, small, and poor low-income African countries, such as Sierra Leone, Guinea, and Liberia. This paper will, for the first time, systematically review and summarise the development trajectory and current situation of Chinese immigrants in Sierra Leone, analyse their role and impact in the local society, economy, and culture, and deepen our understanding of the development of low-income countries in Africa and their relationship with China.

---

[249]Li Xinfeng: "Research on Overseas Chinese and Chinese Expatriates Population in Africa," *Overseas Chinese and Chinese Expatriates*, 2012(1-2); Li Anshan: "Dynamic Analysis of the Chinese Immigrant Population in Post-war Africa," *The Journal of International Studies*, 2017(6).

[250]Liu Shaonan: "The Chinese in Nigeria: Past and Present," *Journal of Overseas Chinese History Studies*, 2020(3); Xu Wei: "History, Present Situation and Cultual Adaptation of Overseas Chinese in South Africa," *Journal of Guangxi Minzu University(Philosophy and Social Science Edition)*, 2018(3); Liu Dongxu: "Unity in Competition: Interaction and Integration of Chinese Communities in Tanzania," *Journal of Minzu University of China(Philosophy and Social Sciences Edition)*, 2017(6).

Basic National Conditions of Sierra Leone and Current Status of Its International Immigration

Sierra Leone, located on West Africa's Atlantic coast, is well-known for its abundant natural resources and diverse cultural heritage. It borders Guinea to the north and northeast, Liberia to the southeast, and the Atlantic Ocean to the west and southwest, with a coastline of approximately 485 kilometres. The country covers an area of 73,326 square kilometers and is characterised by four main geographical regions: the Peninsula Mountains, the coastal plains, the interior lowlands, and the interior plateau. Seven major rivers flow from northeast to southwest into the Atlantic Ocean. The earliest towns in Sierra Leone developed through navigation, trade, and settlement. This region lies within the tropical rainforest zone and experiences a tropical monsoon climate, characterised by high temperatures and heavy rainfall throughout the year. The climate is divided into two main seasons: the dry season (November to April of the following year) and the rainy season (May to October).[251]

According to World Bank data, Sierra Leone's population reached 8,605,718 in 2022, with a per capita GDP of $475.8, making it one of the least developed low-income countries in the world.[252] The country has 18 ethnic groups, with the Temne people in the north and centre being the largest at 35.5%, followed by the Mende people in the south at 33.2%. Other ethnic groups include the Limba, Kono, and Creoles, descendants of "free blacks" that immigrated from the United Kingdom and the United States. The official language of Sierra Leone is English, while the main indigenous languages are Mende, Temne, and Krio. According to the Encyclopaedia Britannica's statistics, 78.6% of the population practices Islam, 20.8% practices Christianity, and there is also a presence of traditional religions. The proportions of rural and urban populations are 55.2% and 44.8%, respectively.[253]

---

[251][SL] Joe A.D. Alie (trans. Sai Guan): A New History of Sierra Leone, Beijing: World Knowledge Publishing House, 2019, pp. 1-4.

[252]https://data.worldbank.org.cn/?locations=XM-XP-XO-SL

[253]https://www.britannica.com/place/Sierra-Leone/Plant-and-animal-life

According to the "Human Development Report 2023-24"[254] published by the United Nations Development Programme, Sierra Leone ranks 184th out of 193 countries on the Human Development Index, placing it among the bottom ten, with 59.2% of the population living below the poverty line. Diseases such as malaria, tuberculosis, typhoid, cholera, and Lassa fever are prevalent. The life expectancy at birth in 2021 was 61.35 years for women and 58.76 years for men. The child mortality rate is relatively high, with approximately 10.8% of children dying before the age of 5, while the maternal mortality rate is 1%. The internet penetration rate is 18%, while the electricity penetration rate is 27.5%.[255] The severe poverty and underdevelopment in Sierra Leone are closely linked to its colonial history and the more than two decades of civil war that erupted after the country's independence, during which various factions fought for control over diamond mining rights. The prolonged warfare destroyed the country's infrastructure, caused deaths of hundreds of thousands of people, and led to economic depression and widespread suffering among its people, with drastic price fluctuations that deterred investors... Sierra Leone has been left far behind in global development trends. However, since the 21st century, the country has made strides toward eliminating internal strife and achieving reconciliation. In May 2002, Sierra Leone successfully held general elections, re-electing Ahmad Tejan Kabbah as president with a 70.06% vote share, while the Sierra Leone People's Party (SLPP) won an absolute majority in parliamentary elections.[256] Sierra Leone's economic states and social development have improved since the civil war ended and the political situation stabilised. Reconciliation and peace have rejuvenated infrastructure, mining, and commercial activities.

Economic and recent census data indicate that international migrants account for a relatively low proportion of Sierra Leone's

---

[254] https://hdr.undp.org/content/human-development-report-2023-24
[255]https://data.worldbank.org.cn/?locations=XM-XP-XO-SL
[256]

https://edition.cnn.com/2002/WORLD/africa/05/19/sierra.leone.result/index.html

population. In the 2015 census conducted in Sierra Leone, out of 7,092,113 people, only 0.6% (42,552) was non-Sierra Leoneans (Sierra Leonean statistical data, 2015). However, in 2019, DESA estimated this number to be 54,300 people, accounting for 0.7% of the total population, with 97% originating from West African countries or their descendants, such as Guinea, Liberia, Gambia, Nigeria, and Ghana. Immigrants from the UK, the USA, India, and Lebanon also constitute a significant proportion, primarily residing in the country's economic centre, the Western Area, and the Eastern Province. The most recent figures are lower than the 1.81% of international migrants in the total population recorded in 2004, and even further below the 2.90% in 1974 and 2.81% in 1985.[257] It is evident that the proportion of international migrants in Sierra Leone is declining. This decline is closely related to the decade-long civil war (political instability from 1991 to 2001), the outbreak of the Ebola epidemic (life insecurity from 2013 to 2015), and the bleak economic prospects. Despite these challenges, Sierra Leone's political and social environment is becoming more stable, especially since the election of the SLPP leader Julius Maada Bio as president in 2018 and his successful re-election in 2023.[258] His new government has consistently implemented the "New Direction" reform policy, achieving certain results in education, public health, anti-corruption, and many other sectors. Sierra Leone is ranked third in Africa by the 2023 Global Peace Index (GPI) ranking, following Mauritius and Botswana, the two richest and most stable countries in Africa, demonstrating the stability of its society and the friendliness of its people.[259] In fact, for the people of Sierra Leone, there is nothing left to lose. Those who have survived war and disease now yearn for peace and development more than ever before.

---

[257]Sierra Leone Government Work Report: "National Migration Policy for Sierra Leone," January 2022.
[258]Leader – Sierra Leone Peoples Party,https://slpp.sl/leader.
[259]Zhu wai zhi jia (Home Abroad), "The 11 Safest Countries in Africa Today," January 2, 2024. https://www.163.com/dy/article/INF2JNKK0528CJEP.html.

An Overview of the Development of Relations between China and Sierra Leone

Sierra Leone and China have had formal diplomatic relations since July 29, 1971, and have continued to deepen their cooperation on multiple levels. In December 2016, the two countries established a comprehensive strategic cooperative partnership. In February 2024, during the visit of Sierra Leonean President Bio to China, Chinese President Xi Jinping directly described the relationship between China and Sierra Leone as a "model of China-Africa solidarity and cooperation".[260] People may wonder why China places such importance on a small West African country like Sierra Leone, which has a GDP of only 4 billion US dollars and a population of less than 10 million. Additionally, how has Sierra Leone become a model of China-Africa cooperation? The author intends to analyse from the following points:

The first point is political support and diplomatic interaction. Sierra Leone has supported China on numerous international occasions, most notably in October 1971, shortly after establishing diplomatic relations with China, when it firmly supported China's reinstatement of its legitimate seat at the United Nations General Assembly. The "Five Principles of Peaceful Coexistence" advocated by Chinese leaders align with Sierra Leone's foreign policy goals. Furthermore, there have been frequent mutual visits at the leadership level. Chinese Foreign Minister Yang Jiechi visited Sierra Leone in 2010, 2019, and 2021, while Foreign Minister Wang Yi visited in 2015. Wang Zhigang, Chinese President Xi Jinping's Special Envoy and Chinese Minister of Science and Technology, attended President Bio's inauguration in May 2018. At the same time, former President Ernest Bai Koroma visited China four times for state visits and exchange

---

[260]CCTV News Client, "President Xi Jinping's Talks with the President of Sierra Leone: The Relationship between China and Sierra Leone Can Be Regarded as a Model of China-Africa Solidarity and Cooperation," https://content static.cctvnews.cctv.com/snow book/index.html?item_id=14526689813807162375&toc_style_id=feeds_default, February 28, 2024.

activities since 2009, while the current President Bio visited China in 2018 and 2024. Several Sierra Leonean Foreign Ministers have also visited China multiple times. The two sides support each other and engage in strategic cooperation across various international conferences and activities.

The second point is economic cooperation and development assistance. China's support for Sierra Leone spans various fields, including infrastructure construction, health, and education. Since the establishment of diplomatic relations in 1971 until 1986, China has provided 200 million yuan in assistance to Sierra Leone, using loans to help build 12 complete projects. This support earned the praise, trust, and friendship from the Sierra Leonean side.[261] However, the civil war in Sierra Leone, which erupted in 1991 and lasted for more than a decade, interrupted economic investment and cooperation between China and Sierra Leone. After the civil war ended in 2002, economic cooperation and investment between the two countries rose dramatically, notably in the sphere of infrastructure development. China has assisted Sierra Leone in building projects such as rice planting technology promotion stations, road bridges, stadiums, office buildings for sugar production joint ventures, hydropower stations, Bo stadium, and the China-Sierra Leone Friendship Road[262]. These projects have fostered the recovery and development of the domestic economy by improving transportation and communication efficiency. Chinese enterprises' investments in Sierra Leone primarily focus on the development of fields such as mineral resources. The New Tonkolili Iron Ore Project by Leone Rock Metal Group Limited is currently the largest mutually beneficial cooperation project between China and Sierra Leone in terms of investment scale.[263] In the fisheries sector,

---

[261]Huang Zhebing: "The Results of Our Aid Projects in Sierra Leone are Encouraging," *International Economic Cooperation*, May 1987.

[262]"China to aid Sierra Leone's national stadium rehabilitation-Xinhua ", Feb 27, 2022. https://english.news.cn/20220227/e6f104a044fe47b7ae11e180653b6c31/c.html.

[263] "The Belt and Road Initiative's 10th Anniversary - Delivering 'Structural Safety in Construction' to the Remote West Africa (Chapter for Sierra Leone)," https://www.sohu.com/a/744223823_257246, December 15, 2023; The Sierra

Sierra Leone welcomes investments from Chinese fishing enterprises in developing fishery wharves, aquaculture, deep processing of fish products, as well as other projects in the country.[264] The Chinese government has allocated 55 million US dollars to assist Sierra Leone in building fishing ports. These ports will provide mooring facilities for tuna boats and other large fishing vessels, increase domestic fishery resources, and enhance the country's export capacity to the international market.[265] In 2021, bilateral trade volume between China and Sierra Leone was 900 million US dollars, marking a 70.5% year-on-year increase. Of this total, China's exports amounted to 490 million US dollars, a 31.8% increase from the previous year, while imports were 410 million US dollars, reflecting a 161.4% increase. In 2021, Chinese enterprises made direct investments in Sierra Leone amounting to 12.32 million US dollars.[266] These figures clearly demonstrate the significant role China has played in promoting the national reconstruction and economic recovery of Sierra Leone. On February 28, 2024, Zheng Shanjie, Chairman of the National Development and Reform Commission (NDRC), signed a cooperation document with relevant Sierra Leonean departments to jointly build the "Belt and Road" Initiative. Both parties agreed to further strengthen their cooperation under the BRI framework. According to the joint statement China and Sierra Leone issued on March 27, 2024, China plans to encourage more Chinese enterprises to invest in Sierra Leone, particularly in the fields of agriculture, mining, and fisheries. It also aims to support the industrialisation process in Sierra Leone.

Leone Telegraph, "Leone Rock set to roll out phase II of Tonkolili Iron Ore Project", https://www.thesierraleonetelegraph.com/leone-rock-set-to-roll-out-phase-ii-of-tonkolili-iron-ore-project/#google_vignette, Nov 5, 2021.

[264] "Sierra Leone-China Fisheries Association Established in Sierra Leone," http://www.xinhuanet.com/world/2017-06/27/c_1121219470.htm, June 27, 2017.

[265] "China Invests $55 Million in the Construction of a Fishing Port in Sierra Leone," http://www.zjscxh.com/news/show-50215.html, May 31, 2021.

[266] China-Sierra Leone Economic and Trade Cooperation Overview (2021), http://m.mofcom.gov.cn/article/tongjiziliao/sjtj/xyfztjsj/202302/20230203381870.shtml, February 2, 2023.

The third point is cultural and educational exchanges. Sierra Leone students have the opportunity to study in China through scholarship programmes and educational cooperation, which fosters understanding and friendship between the peoples of the two countries. In September 2012, the Confucius Institute at the University of Sierra Leone, co-established by Gannan Normal University and the University of Sierra Leone, was inaugurated[267]. After more than a decade of development, the Confucius Institute at the University of Sierra Leone has established 22 teaching points, including Fourah Bay College, the School of Public Administration, the Limkokwing University of Creative Technology, and the Foreign Service Academy of Sierra Leone. It also includes two Confucius classrooms (the primary school and the middle school) affiliated with the Fourah Bay College, covering a complete range of educational levels from primary school to university. The current teaching team consists of 12 people, including one Chinese director, five publicly dispatched teachers, three international Chinese language teachers, and three local teachers. This diverse team fosters Chinese-Sierra Leonean language exchange, mutual learning, and collaborative multiculturalism.[268] In 1984 and 2010, Freetown, the capital of Sierra Leone, respectively established sister city relationships with Hefei in Anhui Province and Ganzhou in Jiangxi Province.

The fourth point is medical and health assistance, which can be regarded as a model field for China-Sierra Leone cooperation. Unlike other African countries, Sierra Leone is permanently stationed with three Chinese medical aid teams: First, a medical team was dispatched by Hunan Province to Sierra Leone since 1973, with continuous

---

[267] "20 Chinese teaching sites established in Sierra Leone: Confucius Institute", Apr 21, 2023. https://english.news.cn/africa/20230421/8475cf85a2054b4a91325679999f 9f4e/c.html

[268] On June 13, 2024, the author visited the Confucius Institute at the University of Sierra Leone and interviewed Dean Chen Xuebing, obtaining the latest work status and data of the Confucius Institute. Grateful for the strong support from Dean Chen.

support for over 50 years, and has sent 25 batches of medical staff[269]. Second, to combat the Ebola virus, a military medical team the major hospitals of the People's Liberation Army formed was dispatched to Sierra Leone during the severe epidemic. These military medical professionals have demonstrated deep solidarity and compassion, forging a strong bond of friendship between the Chinese and Sierra Leonean people. Their efforts are well documented in numerous reports and research findings.[270] Third, the Sierra Leone Tropical Disease Research and Early Warning Centre, established with support from the Chinese Centre for Disease Control and Prevention, plays a crucial role in public health efforts. Simultaneously, the CDCs of China and the United States are also engaged in public health cooperation and on-site epidemiological training for local residents in Sierra Leone.[271] In fact, Africa is a key region for China to promote the construction of a global health community for all, and Sierra Leone hosts three Chinese initiatives: Chinese medical teams, military medical groups, and public health. On one hand, these efforts have advanced the systematic governance of public health and infectious disease prevention in Sierra Leone and trained local professionals. On the other hand, they have also ensured the safety of the lives of overseas Chinese during critical times. According to the president of the Chinese Business Association, during the COVID-19 pandemic, the military medical team established a dedicated isolation area for positive patients. He personally delivered meals to these patients, and there were no reported deaths among overseas Chinese.

---

[269] Embassy of the People's Republic of China to the Republic of Sierra Leone www.sl.china-embassy.gov.cn

[270] Wang Jinqi, Hong Jianguo: *The Responsibility of a Great Power: A Record of the Chinese People's Liberation Army Medical Team's Fight Against the Ebola Epidemic in Sierra Leone*, Time Literature and Art Publishing House, 2016.

[271] Xinhua News Agency: China and the United States will carry out cooperation in the field of public health in Sierra Leone, June 24, 2016.

http://www.xinhuanet.com/world/2016-06/24/c_1119107159.htm。

History and Current Status of Chinese Immigrants in Sierra Leone

Professor Li Anshan, a pioneer in the study of Chinese immigrants in Africa, summarises the migration of Chinese people to Africa in three distinct phases: The first phase, spanning the 1950s to the 1960s, saw a significant increase in the Chinese population in several traditional destination countries due to the influence of Taiwan's "Operation Vanguard"[272], which encouraged Taiwanese businesses to settle and trade in these countries. The second wave occurred in the 1970s and 1980s, during which the impact of Taiwan's "Operation Vanguard" remained strong. South Africa, which had been marginalised by the international community, attracted many Chinese businessmen with its favourable immigration policies. The third phase began in the mid-1990s, characterised by a new wave of "new immigrants" from China and Chinese enterprises entering Africa, resulting in a new wave of immigration.[273] The term "New Chinese immigrants" refers to individuals from the Chinese mainland, including ethnic minorities, who have either acquired Chinese nationality or the nationality of their host countries and have settled overseas for more than a year since the reform and opening up in 1978. This term excludes government-dispatched foreign affairs personnel as well as immigrants from Hong Kong, Macao, and Taiwan regions.

Chinese immigration to Sierra Leone also coincided with the establishment of formal diplomatic relations between the two countries. China's national strategy of providing medical, agricultural, infrastructure, and technical assistance to Sierra Leone resulted in a constant influx of Chinese experts, technicians, and workers. However,

---

[272]The so-called "Operation Vanguard" aid program refers to a meticulously planned and executed initiative led by the United States. Starting in 1961, Taiwan sought to gain support in the United Nations by providing agricultural assistance to African countries. Dr. Liu Xiaopeng has already discussed this in detail in his article: "Safeguarding the U.S.-Taiwan (China) Alliance in Africa: A Reexamination of the 'Operation Vanguard'," *Taiwan Historical Research*, 2007, 14(2), pp. 161-181.

[273]Li Anshan: "Dynamic Analysis of the Chinese Immigrant Population in Post-war Africa," *The Journal of International Studies*, 2017(6).

they did not form a large community. The Chinese community in Sierra Leone has remained small when compared to Chinese immigrants in other African countries and immigrants from other countries within Sierra Leone. According to Li Anshan's dynamic analysis and statistics on the Chinese population in African countries, the number of Chinese people in Sierra Leone remained around 20 from 1968 to 2001.[274] This is strongly connected to Sierra Leone's 11-year civil war, which began in 1991 and ended in 2002. Most Chinese enterprises and humanitarian projects had to close during the war. Only two Chinese individuals chose to stay: a woman married to a Lebanese man with children and "Old Li", the owner of the oldest Chinese restaurant in Sierra Leone and the president of the local Chinese Chamber of Commerce. During the visit to Sierra Leone in June 2024, the author had the opportunity to interview Old Li, a Beijing native. Despite his frail and thin appearance, he speaks with a strong Beijing accent and is the longest-residing Chinese person in Sierra Leone. He claims that he stayed through the ten-year civil war, during which many Chinese companies entrusted him with their gate keys. Additionally, he stayed during the Ebola outbreak and the COVID-19 pandemic, witnessing how this small West African country gradually recovered from its lowest point. The author is impressed by his bravery and persistence, even though it seems impossible. We can learn about the shared history and present-day reality of Chinese people and Sierra Leone through Old Li's personal experiences.

The Story of the Beijing Restaurant and Old Li[275]

Old Li was born in Beijing back during the 1960s. In his youth, he worked as a "zhi qing" (educated youth) in Beijing's suburbs. He is one of five siblings in his family and first came to Sierra Leone in 1993,

---

[274]Li Anshan: "Dynamic Analysis of the Chinese Immigrant Population in Post-war Africa," *The Journal of International Studies*, 2017(6).

[275]On June 13, 2024, the author conducted an exclusive interview with Old Li at the Beijing Restaurant in Freetown, Sierra Leone.

initially working for a Taiwanese employer selling goods. He later worked as a chef at the Beijing Restaurant, which was then owned by a Hong Kong businessman. This Hong Kong businessman had taken over the restaurant from a Dutch patriotic overseas Chinese. The restaurant was established in 1973, following the formalization of diplomatic relations between China and Sierra Leone. Business was booming, attracting many prominent politicians and wealthy merchants. However, the Dutch founder could not endure the persistent power outages and handed over the restaurant to the Hong Kong chef. This Hong Kong businessman, due to the prolonged separation from his family for the sake of his children's education and the outbreak of the civil war in 1999, transferred ownership of the restaurant to Old Li. In 2000, Old Li became the third owner of the Beijing Restaurant, and to this day, despite the devastation of civil war and pandemics, he has remained steadfast, never giving up. During these challenging times, the Beijing Restaurant evolved from being merely a dining place into a service station for Chinese people from all walks of life, as well as for officers, soldiers, and military medical workers from the peacekeeping forces. Old Li provided a range of services, including airport pickups, arranging flights and visas, making calls and sending faxes to China, and managing the gate keys of Chinese companies. He has also procured various supplies during the civil war and pandemic, assisting with any problems the Chinese encountered by liaising with the relevant authorities. Therefore, he is rightfully the president of the local Chinese Chamber of Commerce, the vice president of the West Africa Peace and Unity Promotion Association, and the president of the Sierra Leone Peace and Unity Promotion Association.

According to Professor Li Anshan's statistics, between 2004 and 2017, there were 400-500 Chinese people in Sierra Leone. The author believes that this data is overly conservative, and the actual figure is likely much higher. Since 1985, China has established several joint ventures and wholly owned enterprises in Sierra Leone. China National Fisheries Corporation (CNFC) Overseas Fisheries Co., Ltd. has been operating fishing businesses in Sierra Leone. Beijing Urban Construction Group Co., Ltd. renovated and leased the Bintumani

Hotel, which officially opened to the public in 2003. China National Complete Plant Import and Export Group Corporation Limited signed a sugar union project contract with Sierra Leone in 2003 and commenced sugarcane production in 2005. The Sierra Leone Industrial Park project, which was funded and built by Henan Guoji Industry Group Co., Ltd., began operations in April 2005. The Dodo Hydroelectric Power Station upgrade project, undertaken by China National Electric Engineering Corporation (CNEEC), was completed and operationalised in July 2007. Shandong Iron & Steel Group acquired the Tonkolili Iron Mine project in March 2015. In fact, the proportion of Chinese people on these large programmes and engineering projects is even greater. When including other private business owners and traders, the number of Chinese people in Sierra Leone should far exceed 500. With the "Belt and Road" Initiative's implementation in West Africa, an increasing number of Chinese engaged in trade, catering, and service industries have concentrated in Freetown and its surrounding areas. Over time, some Chinese nationals have gradually integrated into local society and have begun to enter the construction and manufacturing sectors, contributing positively to Sierra Leone's economic development.

According to statistical data from the Chinese Embassy in Sierra Leone, the number of new Chinese immigrants in this country is between 2,000 and 2,200. There are approximately 150 Chinese-funded enterprises and some individual businesses, primarily concentrated in the capital, Freetown, and its surrounding areas. These figures are based on embassy registrations, but local Chinese community leaders estimate the actual number to be nearly 5,000. These Chinese immigrants are mainly engaged in commerce, construction, manufacturing, and services, with a focus on small enterprises. The author will now draw on the experience of Ms. Yong Yining, the vice president of the local Chinese Chamber of Commerce, to showcase the struggle and development of ordinary Chinese people during Sierra Leone's post-war reconstruction.

The Strong-Willed Chinese Woman, Yong Yining, and the Grand Leone Group[276]

Yong Yining (locally called Madam Sunny), born in 1978 in Yangzhou, Jiangsu Province, graduated from Yangzhou Medical University. Although she initially passed the entrance exam to study design at the Nanjing University of the Arts, her father, a doctor, was insistent and forcibly "dragged" her back to Yangzhou, compelling her to attend medical school. After graduating, she followed in her father's footsteps and was assigned to work at a local hospital. However, her strong will and freedom-loving nature led her to quit her job at the hospital after a short period and move to Beijing to seek new opportunities on her own. Her motivation for going to Africa was tied to her work at a travel agency in Beijing (at that time, most people travelled to Europe, with few venturing to West Africa). It was also influenced by a TV programme she watched, "Into Africa", which featured Lai Cuiling, a Chinese woman who had opened a hospital in Guinea. Additionally, her curiosity about the outside world was ignited by reading "Fifty Years of China-Africa Diplomatic Relations" in a library, which detailed China's policies towards Africa, as well as by the book "Ten Years: Dreams Take Me Flying" that she read at an airport. On July 25, 2003, she proceeded on a solo trip to seven West African countries, including Guinea, Sierra Leone, and The Gambia, at the advice of a counsellor from Guinea's Embassy in China. Despite the one-month round-trip travel, she returned with several samples from West African countries, including cashews, timber, seafood, and fabrics. At that time, e-commerce was not yet well developed, so she used an internet café to list these products online, noting that they were sourced from West Africa. Within a week, an elderly man from Dongyang, Zhejiang Province, contacted her, expressing his interest in supporting her entrepreneurial journey into Africa. At the time, she was still just a 24-year-old young lady. In December 2003, she completely resigned from her job and relocated to Guinea to start her own business. She sold

---

[276]On June 11, 2024, the author conducted an exclusive interview with Yong Yining at the Grand Leone Group in Freetown, Sierra Leone.

fabrics, sneakers, and general merchandise from Zhejiang while importing cashews, timber, and seafood from Guinea back to China. She continued this import-export trade for four years in Guinea. However, the natural environment and social system in Guinea never made her feel secure or comfortable. In 2006, she embarked on a second exploration of countries like Sierra Leone, Senegal, The Gambia, and Morocco. She felt at ease and fell in love with Sierra Leone's capital, Freetown, as she strolled along its lush, pristine, and picturesque white sandy beaches. It was also a period when Sierra Leone was recovering from a decade-long civil war and was in dire need of reconstruction.

In interviews, she consistently emphasised that Sierra Leone is a country that respects the rule of law and human rights, with clear guidelines that provide people with a sense of security. She quickly purchased what is now the Royal Leone Hotel, located in the central area of Lumley Beach in the capital, Freetown. At the time, the hotel was still a relatively rundown small building, but it had a long history, having been established as early as 1968. Initially operated by the British, the Lebanese and Dutch owners later managed the hotel before Yong Yining acquired it in 2007. According to Yining, her current focus is on two major business areas: The first is the Royal Leone Group. She gradually developed a comprehensive business and leisure platform that includes a hotel, casino, restaurant, barbecue bar, children's playground, wellness center, and supermarket. This platform serves local government officials, businessmen, and other high-end clients while also offering Chinese compatriots services related to local business, inspection, and tourism. Additionally, the group engages in government projects related to roads, minerals, seafood, and real estate. The other is Luyuan Furniture and Flooring Factory. This factory, located in the suburbs of Freetown, is dedicated to mutually beneficial cooperation with the local community. It helps Sierra Leone transform its resource advantages into development momentum, creates numerous local jobs, fulfils corporate social responsibilities, and actively participates in reforestation. The factory achieves local production, adds value, and implements new development concepts and China-Africa cooperation guidelines, all of which contribute to promoting green and sustainable development. Currently, Yining employs 168 local workers, along with 12 employees from Colombia and the Philippines and 45 Chinese staff members.

Yining shared her unique experiences and insights during discussions on how to train local employees. She emphasised that everyone requires opportunities to learn and grow, and treating people with sincerity will cause them to sincerely consider your needs. This is especially true in the relationship between employers and employees. She trained workers at the furniture and flooring factory using a phased selection process. She initially brought in 12 carpenters (10 Chinese and 2 Nigerians) to train nearly 500 locals over three months. Some were eliminated each month, and those who remained after three months were fully capable workers. They had no issues operating equipment, and no production accidents occurred. The key to working with locals is to treat them with sincerity.

Yining emphasised that the judicial system in former British colonies is firmly established. It is critical to understand the local culture, customs, labour, and immigration laws. Her overall experience in Guinea and Sierra Leone over the last 20 years has been very harmonious, and this harmony is mutual. She has maintained good relationships with senior government officials in every administration in Sierra Leone. The locals perceive the Chinese conducting business in a diligent, legal, and compliant manner, solving local employment issues, and bringing about development and transformation.

Although the number of Chinese immigrants in Sierra Leone is small, two major associations have emerged during the development process: The first is the Sierra Leone China Chamber of Commerce. This organisation, originally known as the "Association of Chinese-Funded Enterprises in Sierra Leone", primarily serves Chinese state-owned enterprises. The current president is the general manager of the Bintumani Hotel, which is operated by Beijing Urban Construction Group. The other is the Sierra Leone Chinese Chamber of Commerce (SLCCC). It was established in 2015 by small and medium-sized Chinese enterprises and mainly serves private enterprises and Chinese immigrants. The president is Li Minglu, who owns the Beijing Restaurant. Under these two associations, the Mining Association and the Timber Association were also established. This demonstrates that mining and timber are the most major and concentrated areas of Chinese investment in Sierra Leone. Additionally, the Sierra Leone Women's Association, chaired by Yong Yining, was established. The formation of these community groups has united and solidified the strength of the overseas Chinese community, as these organisations assist their members in overcoming challenges and sharing risks. On the other hand, the power of civil organisations has been proactively utilised. These organisations promote the integration of Chinese enterprises and immigrants into local society, creating more employment and development opportunities for the community. For instance, the private enterprise Leone Rock Metal Group established the Tonkolili Mine Community Development Fund in the Northern Province, earning high praise from Sierra Leone's President Bio. He expressed gratitude to the Chinese companies for their significant contributions to job creation, income generation, and community development in Sierra Leone. The Sierra Leonean government will continue to support the growth of Leone Rock Metal Group while also strengthening cooperation with China in the mining sector to promote joint development.[277]

The new wave of Chinese immigrants in Sierra Leone has achieved a certain degree of success. They uphold their traditional customs, such as celebrating the Spring Festival, Dragon Boat Festival, and other cultural events, while also actively participating in local social activities and respecting and adapting to local cultural conventions. However, they still face several challenges. For instance, cultural and linguistic differences might lead to misunderstandings and disputes between Chinese immigrants and local residents. In terms of education, local

---

[277]https://www.mfa.gov.cn/web/wjdt_674879/zwbd_674895/202205/t20220525_1 0692633.shtml。
The Chinese Embassy in Sierra Leone, "Ambassador Hu Zhangliang of the Chinese Embassy in Sierra Leone Visits Chinese-Funded Enterprises," May 25, 2022. https://www.mfa.gov.cn/web/wjdt_674879/zwbd_674895/202205/t20220525_106 92633.shtml

educational resources are inadequate to meet the needs of Chinese children, forcing many Chinese families to reluctantly opt for cross-national separation to secure better educational opportunities for their children. As a result, the majority of Chinese residents in Sierra Leone view their stay as "transitional" and "temporary", which makes it difficult for them to fully integrate into the local society. Moreover, Chinese enterprises in Sierra Leone face challenges such as intense market competition and changes in policies and regulations. To address these issues, it is crucial for enterprises to enhance communication and cooperation with the local government and residents so as to seek better approaches for mutual development.

Conclusion

It has been over 50 years since China and Sierra Leone established formal diplomatic relations. In 2018, Sierra Leone joined the "Belt and Road" initiative, and today, Chinese influences are evident throughout the streets and alleys of Sierra Leone. The practical cooperation between the two countries has yielded fruitful and significant results from the China-aided national stadium, the Diplomatic Training Academy, and the Friendship Building, which houses half of Sierra Leone's government offices, to the China-Sierra Leone Friendship Hospital, the China-Sierra Leone Friendship Road, and the Freetown Ring Road. Sierra Leone's post-war government has focused all its efforts on economic restoration and social stability, prioritising agricultural development, infrastructure construction, human resources, youth employment, and the expansion of public sector capacity as critical governance agendas. With President Bio's successful re-election, Sierra Leone, ranked third in Africa in the 2023 Global Peace Index, though still lagging in development indices globally, is steadily advancing on the path of national development with a focus on safety and stability for its people. The history of Chinese immigration in Sierra Leone is relatively short, and the current situation is complex and diverse. Despite facing numerous challenges, the Chinese community has made significant contributions to Sierra Leone's economic development and social progress through their diligence and intelligence. In the future, as relations between China and Sierra Leone continue to strengthen, Chinese immigrants are expected to play an even greater role in contributing to the prosperity and stability of the local society.

Bibliography

Adebajo, A. & Ismail, R., 2004. West Africa'sS ecurity!Challenges: Building Peace in Troubled Region. *International&Peace&Academy*, p. 343.

African Development Bank , 2021. Sports and Development in Africa.. *ADB Bulletin* .

African Development Bank. (2020). Sierra Leone Economic Outlook. Abidjan: African Development Bank.

Agreement between the Government of Sierra Leone and the Linqu Qushan hospital on the management of the Sierra Leone-China Youyi hospital at Jui.

AidData. (2020). Geocoding Chinese Development Finance Flows. Available at: https://www.aiddata.org/china

Alden, C. (2007). China in Africa. London, Zed Books Limited.

Alden, C., & Jiang, L. (2019). Brave new world: Debt, industrialization and security in China–Africa relations. International Affairs, 95(3), 641–657.

Alden, C., Large, D., & Soares de Oliveira, R. (2008). China Returns to Africa: A Rising Power and a Continent Embrace. Hurst & Company.

Alden, C. (2007). China in Africa. Zed Books.

Alie, Joe A D (2015). Sierra Leone Since Independence: History of a postcolonial state. Freetown: SLWS.

Alves, A.C. (2008). Chinese economic diplomacy in Africa: The lusophone strategy. In C. Alden, R. Soares de Oliveira and D. Large (eds.), China returns to Africa: A rising power and a continent embrace (pp.69-82). Cambridge, Cambridge University Press.

Appiah, K. A. (2006). Cosmopolitanism: Ethics in a World of Strangers. W. W. Norton & Company.

Austin, . S., Michael, T. J., Andreas, . F. & Vijaya, R., 2013. *China's Development Finance to Africa: A Media-Based Approach to Data Collection. CGD Working Paper*, Washington DC: Center for Global Development.

Barston, R. P. (2014), Modern Diplomacy, Routledge, New York.

277

Barston, R.P. (2014). Modern diplomacy, 4 edition, New |York, Routledge

BBC News. (2018). China's Influence in Sierra Leone: Investments and Their Impacts. BBC.

BBCNews, October 10, 2018,. *Mamamah airport: Sierra Leone cancels China-funded project.*, London : BBC.

Benabdallah, L. (2019). China-Africa Military Diplomacy: The Case of Sierra Leone*. African Security Review, 28(1), 5-23.

Betts, A., & Kaytaz, E. (2009). 'National and International Responses to the Sierra Leonean Conflict: The Humanitarian Dilemma.' *Refugee Survey Quarterly.*

Bound, K., Briggs, R., Holden, J. and Jones, S. (200). Cultural diplomacy. London, Demos.

Brautigam D, 'Foreign assistance and the export of ideas: Chinese development aid in The Gambia and Sierra Leone', Journal of Commonwealth & Comparative Politics, 31, 3, pp. 22–42.

Brautigam D, The Dragon's Gift, The Real Story of China in Africa. Oxford: Oxford University Press, 2011, pp. 38–39;

Bräutigam Deborah (2010), China, Africa and the International Aid Architecture, Working Papers Series N° 107, African Development Bank, Tunis, Tunisia.

Bräutigam Deborah (2011) China in Africa: Seven Myths (ARI)

Brautigam, D. (2009). Chinese Aid and African Development. Johns Hopkins University Press

Brautigam, D. (2009). The Dragon's Gift: The Real Story of China in Africa. Oxford University Press.

Brautigam, D. (2009). The Dragon's Gift: The Real Story of China in Africa. Oxford University Press.

Brautigam, D. (2009). *The Dragon's Gift: The Real Story of China in Africa.* Oxford University Press.

Bruce Larkin (1971), China-Africa: 1949-1970: the Foreign Policy of the People's Republic of China, University of California Press.

Bundy, D. (2011). 'Rethinking Education in Post-Conflict Sierra Leone'. *Journal of Development Studies.*

C. Wang, 2001, *China's Strategies from Higher Level: Diplomacy.* Shaanxi Normal University General Publishing House Co., LTD.

Canning, D. and Bennathan, E (2000). The social rate of return on infrastructure investments, Development Research Group, Public Economics and Private Sector Development and Infrastructure Group, World Bank

Caraiani, G. and Georgescu, C. (2013), Cooperare economica internationala, Pro Universitaria, Bucuresti.

Caruso, D. (2020). China's soft power and cultural diplomacy. The educational engagement in Africa. Cambio, 10(19), 47-58

Centre for Chinese Studies (2006). China's Interest and Activity in Africa's Construction and Infrastructure Sectors. Stellenbosch University

Charles Mutasa, (Cham: Palgrave Macmillan, 2018).

Charles Mutasa, "Introduction: Inspirations and Hesitations in Africa's Relations with External Actors," in Africa and the World: Bilateral and Multilateral Diplomacy, ed. Dawn Nagar and

Chaziza, M. (2024). China's economic diplomacy towards the gulf cooperation council states. Journal of Contemporary China, 1-81https://doi.org/10.1080/10670564.2024.2314072

China Africa Research Initiative (CARI). (2021). China-Africa Trade Data. Available at: http://www.sais-cari.org/data-china-africa-trade

China's emerging influence in Sierra Leone. 2021 Critical perspectives of governance. Vol. xiv.

China -Africa Economic Bulletin (2024), https://www.bu.edu/gdp /2024/04/01/china-africa-economic-bulletin-2024-edition/

Chinese Embassy in Sierra Leone Report (2016). Building on past achievements and joining hands to make an even brighter future of China-Sierra Leone friendship. Statement by the Chinese Ambassador to Sierra Leone Zhao Yanbo, in commemoration of the 45th anniversary of the establishment of China- Sierra Leone diplomatic relations. Retrieved from http://sl.china-embassy.gov.cn/eng//xwdt/201608/t20160802_5847690.htm#:~: text=As%20far%20back%20as%20in,of%20China%20in%20the% 20UN.

Chinese Embassy in Sierra Leone Report (2020). Continuously composing new chapters of China-Sierra Leone friendship within the framework of FOCAC in collaboration with the 20th anniversary of the forum on China-Africa cooperation. Retrieved from http://sl.china embassy.gov.cn/eng/xwdt/202010/t2020103 0_5848887.htm

Chowdhury, A and Garona, P (2007), "Effective Foreign Aid, Economic Integration and Subsidiarity: Lessons from Europe" United Nations Economic Commission for Europe Discussion, Paper Series N0 2007.2

Clifford, Sarah and S. N. Romanuk (2020). Cuban Cold War Internationalism and the Non-Aligned Movement (E-International Relations).

Consulate General of the PRC in Los Angeles (2024). "UNGA Resolution 2758 Brooks No Challenge, and the One-China Principle Is Unshakable"

Conteh, M. (2012). Development and Challenges in Sierra Leone: The Role of International Aid. Macmillan.

Corkin, L. (2011). Uneasy Allies: China's Aid Relationship with Angola. Journal of Contemporary African Studies, 29(2), 169-180.

Cotkin, R. (2011). *Gender and Development in Sierra Leone: Chinese Influence.* Journalof African Studies, 12(3), 210-227.

Cummings, M. C. Jr. (2003). Cultural diplomacy and the United States America. A survey. Retrieved from https://www.americansforthearts.org/sites/default/files/MCCpap er.pdf

Datzberger, S. (2013). China's silent storm in Sierra Leone. SAIIA Policy brief 71. Retrieved from https://www.jstor.org/stable/pdf/resrep32541.pdf?refreqid=fastly -
default%3A3a69b7c7f51e9188d1ca739d09777481&ab_segments= &origin=&initiator=&acceptTC=1

Datzberger, S., 2013. *China's Silent Storm in Sierra Leone,* London : Danish Institute of International Development .

Davidson, D.R. (1988): Energy Decisions in Developing Countries in Africa. A Case Study of Sierra Leone. International Development Research Center, Ottawa, Canada

Davies, L. (2000). Education in Emergencies: Learning for a Peaceful Future. UNESCO International Institute for Educational Planning.

Davies, N. (2023). "Sweet Mother": The Neoliberal Plantation in Sierra Leone. In: Le Petitcorps, C., Macedo, M., Peano, I. (eds) Global Plantations in the Modern World. Cambridge Imperial and Post-Colonial Studies. Palgrave Macmillan, Cham.

Department of State, USA (1949). The Chinese Revolution of 1949. history@state.gov.

Donnelly, Jack. (2000). Realism and International Relations. Cambridge University Press.

Dotzberger, Simone (2013). "China's Silent Storm in Sierra Leone". South African Institute of International Affairs. https://www.jstor.org/stable/resrep32541

Dyck, C. B., Football and Post-War Reintegration: exploring the role of sports. Football and Post-War Reintegration: exploring the role of sport. *Third World Quarterly* .

Elizabeth Zoller, Peacetime Unilateral Remedies (Dobbs Ferry, N.Y.: Transnational, 1984.

El-Khawas, M. A. (1973). China's changing policies in Africa. A Journal of Opinion, 3(1), 24-28

Embassy of the People's Republic of China in the United Kingdom of Great Britain and Northern Ireland 2024

Enaim, R., and Alamy, Y.A.E. (2023). Cultural diplomacy's effectiveness in boosting mutual understanding. International Journal of Linguistics Literature and Translation, 6(2), 108-113

Financial Times. (2019). Sierra Leone: The Impact of Chinese Investments on Local Communities. Financial Times.

French, H. W., 2015.. *China's Second Continent: How a Million Migrants Are Building a New Empire in Africa..* New Yotk : Vintage .

From Ebola to COVID-19: China CDC in supporting Sierra Leone to strengthen it public health capacity. *Public Health News*

Fyfe, Christopher (1964). Sierra Leone Inheritance, Oxford: Oxford University Press.

Fyle, C. M. (2006). The History of Sierra Leone. New Africa Press.

Gantz, D.A. (2013). Liberalising international trade after Doha. Multilateral, plurilateral, regional and unilateral initiatives. New York, Cambridge University Press.

Ginsberg, George and Robert M. Slusser (1981). A Calendar of Soviet Treaties: 1958-1973. Springer: The Netherlands.

Goldstein, J. S. (1991). Reciprocity in superpower relations: An empirical analysis. *International Studies Quarterly*, *35*(2), 195–209.

Golf, P.M. (2013). Cultural diplomacy. In A. F. Cooper, J. Heine and R. Thakur (eds.), the oxford handbook of modern diplomacy (pp.331-343). Oxford, Oxford University Press.

Government of Sierra Leone, Government of China and UNICEF unveil newly established SCBU in Kailahun.

Government of Sierra Leone. (2019). Medium-Term National Development Plan 2019-2023. Freetown: Government of Sierra Leone.

Griffin, K. (1970),"Foreign Capital, Domestic Savings and Economic Development". Bulletin of the Oxford University Institute of Economics and Statistics, 32 (2): 99-112.

Griffin, K. and J. L. Enos (1970), "Foreign Capital, Domestic Savings and Economic Development," Oxford Bulletin of Economics and Statistics, vol. 32, pp. 99-112.

Gupta, A.K. (2013). Soft power of the United States, China, and India: A comparative analysis. Indian Journal of Asian Affairs, 26(1/2), 37-57

Hartmann, C., & Noesselt, N. (2019). China's new role in African Politics: From non-intervention towards stabilization?. In China's New Role in African Politics (pp. 1-14). Routledge.

Hassig, K. O. (2012). China's soft power strategy in Africa. Security in Africa, 9-13https://www.jstor.org/stable/resrep26970.4

Herderson, W. (1963). Diplomacy and intervention in developing countries. The Virginia Quarterly Review,39 (1), 26-36

Hongwu Liu & Jianbo Luo (2021), Sino-Africa Development Cooperation: Studies on the Theories, Strategies & Policies, Springer, Singapore,

Hongwu Liu (2007); 'The historical value and global significance of the new China-Africa strategic partnership' Foreign Affairs Review, Vol. 1

Hongwu Liu (2024), Seventy Years of China-Africa Relations, Zhejiang University Press, Jinhun

Hospital contributes to medical assistance in Africa. vol. 11, 2019.=

Hu Yuwei and Lin Xiaoyi (2021) "How African representatives 'carried' PRC into the UN", (*Global Times* Oct 26, 2021)

Hussain, A. (2006). Economic diplomacy and its significance for foreign policy. Indian Foreign Affairs Journal, 1(4), 35-45

IGR (2021) China's Emerging Influence in Sierra Leone: Voices & Views of Local Fishing and Road Construction Communities, February 2021.

IIyas, A., Malik, R and Ramay, S.A. (2020) China's cultural diplomacy. Research report. Sustainable Development Policy Institute. https://sdpi.org/chinas-cultural-diplomacy/publication_detail

Institute for Governance Reform. (2021).*ChineseInvestmentsandWomen'sEconomicParticipation in Sierra Leone: A Report for Oxfam.* Retrieved from oxfam.org

Jervis, R. (1999). Realism, Neoliberalism, and Cooperation: Understanding the Debate. International Security, 24(1),

Jiang, L., n.d. Infrastructure and Sustainability in Sports Development.. *African Journal of Sports Management,* 10(1), pp. 34-5-.

Jönn Altmann: «South-South Cooperation and Economic Order», Intereconomics, vol. 17, issue 3, (May- June 1982), pp. 143-147;

Julius Nyerere (1979), South-South Dialogue & Development in Africa, Dar Es Salam.

Kabia, Alieu Badara ( ). "The Evolution of China-Sierra Leone Cooperation ". China Daily. http://blog.chinadaily.com.cn

Kalimuddin, M., & Anderson, D.A. (2018). Soft power in China's security strategy. Strategic Study Quarterly, 12(3),114-141

Kallon, K. M. (1990). The Economics of Sierra Leone. Macmillan.

Kanu, A., 2022. Corruption in Sports Funding: A Case Study of Sierra Leone. International. *Journal of Sports Governance,,* 8(3), pp. 112-128..

Kef, A. (Deceber 28, 2023). Chinese Ambassador scholarship grants education to support to 30 students, Calabash Newspaper.

Retrieved from https://thecalabashnewspaper.com/chinese-ambassador-scholarship-2023-grants-education-support-to-30students/#:~:text=He%20revealed%20how%20over%20two,sports%20reached%20over%205%2C100%20individuals.

King, K. (2013). China's Aid and Soft Power in Africa: The Case of Education and Training. James Currey.

King, K. (2013). *China's Aid and Soft Power in Africa: The Case of Educatio n and Training.* James Currey.

Kitano, N., and Miyabayashi, Y. (2023), "China's foreign aid as a proxy of ODA: preliminary estimate 2001-2022", Journal of Contemporary East Asia Studies, Vol.12 (1), pp. 264–293. https://doi.org/10.1080/24761028.2024.2316532

Kovrig, M. (2018). China expands its peace and security footprint in Africa. International Crisis Group, 24.

Lahtinen, A. (2018). China's diplomacy and economic activities in Africa. Relations on the move. London, Palgrave Macmillan.

Leffler, M.P. (1988). The United States and the strategic dimensions of the marshall plan. Diplomatic History, 12(3), 277-306

Lehman, H. (2010). *Cultural Diplomacy and Women's Empowerment in Sierra Leone.* AfricanJournal of International Affairs, 7(2), 95-112.

Lehman, H. P. (2010). *The East Asian Challenge for Democracy: Political Me ritocracy in Comparative Perspective.* Cambridge University Press.

Lequey-Feilleux, J. (2009). The Dynamics of Diplomacy. Colorado, Lynne Rienner Publishers

Lewis, K. (2016). What has the European Union ever done for us? [Online] The Independent. Available at: https://www.independent. co.uk/news/uk/politics/eu-what-has-european-union-done-for-us-david-cameron-brexit-a6850626.html *[Accessed 17/03/2024].*

Li, R. & Guo,, J., 207. The Development of Leisure Sports in Ancient China and Its Contemporary Sports Culture Value. *Scientific Research Journal* , p. 45.

Li, X. (2008). China's Cultural Diplomacy: Soft Power, Nation Branding, and Global Citizenship. Taylor & Francis.

Liu, H. (2008). China-Africa relations through the prism of culture: The dynamics of China's cultural diplomacy with Africa. Journal of

Current Chinese Affairs. Retrieved from https://caspu.pku.edu.cn/docs/20180314144809738765.pdf

Liu, Hongwu (2021). Seventy Years of China-Africa Relations. Jinhua: Zhejiang University Press.

Lumumba-Kasongo, T. (2011). Contemporary China-Africa Relations: The Role of China in Africa's Quest for Economic Development and Industrial Growth. Palgrave Macmillan.

Maclure, R., & Denov, M. (2009). 'Reconstruction versus Transformation: Post-War Education and the Struggle for Gender Equity in Sierra Leone.' *International Journal of Educational Development*.

Mazzucato, V. (2008). 'Transnational Families and the Provision of Moral and Emotional Support: The Case of Ghanaian Migrants in the Netherlands.' *Geoforum*.

McGinn, G.H. (2015). Foreign language, cultural diplomacy, and global security. Retrieved from https://www.amacad.org/sites/default/files/academy/multimedia/pdfs/Foreign-language-Cultural-Diplomacy-Global-Security.pdf

Mearsheimer, J. (2013). "Structural Realism," in Dunne, T., Kurki, M., & Smith, S., eds., International Relations Theories: Discipline and Diversity, 3rd Edition. Oxford: Oxford University Press;

Meng, Wenting (2004). Developmental Peace: Theorizing China's Approach to International Peacebuilding. Ibidem. Colombus University Press.

Ministry of Education Sierra Leone (2018). Education Sector Plan 2018-2020. Ministry of Education, Science and Technology.

Momoh, Eddie (1985). "Critique of the Siaka Stevens regime" (*West Africa*, 9 December 1985).

Morgenthau, H. J. (1965). Politics among nations: the struggle for power and peace. New York: Knopf

Moyo, S. (2019). The Belt and Road Initiative in Africa: Implications for Sierra Leone's Development Agenda. Unpublished Master's Thesis, University of Cape Town.

Muktari-Janguza Muktar Usman (2018)., "Maada Bio's China Dilemma" email: janguza.arewa@gmail.com

Munro, André. "Non-Aligned Movement". *Encyclopedia Britannica*, 28 Mar. 2024, https://www.britannica.com/topic/Non-Aligned-Movement. Accessed 10 April 2024.

Murphy, Daen C. (2002). China's Rise in the Global South: the Middle East, Africa, and Beijing's Alternative World Order. Stanford, California: Stanford University Press.

Nye, J. S. (1990). Bound to Lead: The Changing Nature of American Power. Basic Books.

Nye, J. S. (2004). Soft Power: The Means to Success in World Politics. Public Affairs.

Office of the President, Freetown (1980). Sierra Leone – 12 Years of Economic Achievement and Political Consolidation under the APC and Dr Siaka Stevens 1968-1980

Patton, S. (2019). The peace of Westphalia and it affects on international relations, diplomacy and foreign relations. The Histories, 10(1), 91-99

Pearce D, Webb M (1987). 'Rural electrification in developing countries' a reappraisal. Energy Policy 15(8): 329-38

Radelet, S (2006), "A Primer on Foreign Aid," Center for Global Development. Working Paper, No. 92, July 2006.

Rasmussen, M.V., 2003. The West, Civil Society, and the Construction of Peace. Palgrave, London.

Ratha, D., Mohapatra, S., & Scheja, E. (2018). Impact of Migration on Economic and Social Development: A Review of Evidence and Emerging Issues. World Bank.

Renwick, N., & Gu, J. (2016). China's African Policy and the Chinese Diaspora. Institute of Development Studies.

Richard , C. & Elizabeth, L., 2004. Population Age Structure and Its Relation to Civil Conflict: A Graphic Metrics. *Wilson Center's ECSP!Report,*, Volume 12, p. 54.

Roberts, W. (2006). The evolution of diplomacy. The Mediterranean Quarterly, 17(3), 55-64

Sarah Clifford and Scott N. Romaniuk, (2020) Cuban Cold War Internationalism and the Nonaligned Movement https://www.e-ir.info/2020/12/19/cuban-cold-war-internationalism-and-the-nonaligned-movement/

Sautman, B., & Yan, H. (2007). *Friends and Interests: China's Distinctive Li nks with Africa.* African Studies Review, 50(3), 75-114.

Schelling, T. C. (1980). *The strategy of conflict* (2d ed.). Cambridge, MA: Harvard University Press.

Schuett, R. (2010). Classical realism, Freud and human nature in international relations. History of the Human Sciences, 23(2), pp.23-26.

Shao, W. (2022). China's foreign policy and practice. A Survey. New York, NY: Routledge

Shen, S. (2015). China and Sierra Leone: Strategic Partnership and Development Cooperation. China Quarterly, 223, 713-734.

Shinn, D. H., & Eisenman, J. (2012). *China and Africa: A Century of Engagement.* University of Pennsylvania Press.

Shinn, David H.; Eisenman, Joshua (2023). China's Relations with Africa: A New Era of Strategic Engagement. New York: Columbia University Press.

Shinn,, D. H. & ;Eisenman, . J., 2-23. *China's Relations with Africa: a New Era of Strategic Engagement..* New York : Columbia University Press .

Shu Chen, Michelle Pender, Nan Jin, Michael Merson, Shenglan Tang, Stephen Gloyd. Chinese medical teams in Africa: a flagship program facing formidable challenges.

Si, G., Duan, Y. & Li, H., 2014. The influence of the Chinese sport system and Chinese cultural characteristics on Olympic sport psychology services. *Psychology of Sport and Exercise* , Volume 17, p. 123.

Sierra Leone – Country Commercial Guide – https://www. trade.gov/country-commercial-guides/sierra-leone-agriculture-sector - (Accessed 3rd April, 2024);

Sierra Leone-China friendship hospital-Jui, Power point presentation.

Siracusa, J.M. (2010). Evolution of diplomacy. A short history. New York, NY: Oxford University Press

Solomon A. J. Pratt, (2010), Jolliboy: an Autobiography: From Street Starch Hawker to United Nations Debate Champion, Prince HywBull Publishers, North Carolina, p. 220-221

Speech by President Alhaji Dr. Ahmad Tejan Kabbah at the Official Opening of The Bintumani Hotel Aberdeen, Friday 31 January 2003. Sierra Leone Web. https://www.sierra-leone.org › Ahmad_Tejan_Kabbah

Spencer-Walters, D. (2006). Education, Literacy, and Society in Sierra Leone: Past and Present. Africa World Press.

Steiner-Khamsi, G., & Stolpe, I. (2006). Educational Import: Local Encounters with Global Forces in Mongolia. Palgrave Macmillan.

Stevens, Siaka (1984). What Life Has Taught Me. Abbotsbrook: The Kensal Press.

Su, S., 2023. *China Global South Project.* [Online] Available at: https://chinaglobalsouth.com/analysis/the-chinese-on-the-lion-mountain-peering-into-chinas-evolving-diaspora-and-soft-power-in-sierra-leone/ [Accessed 7 September 2024].

Suhun, T., 2022. *China to aid Sierra Leone's national stadium rehabilitation,* Beijin : Xinhuanet.

Sun, Y. (2014). China's Aid to Africa: Monster or Messiah? Brookings Institution.

Taylor, I. (2011). The Forum on China–Africa Cooperation (FOCAC). Routledge

Taylor, I. (2009). *China's New Role in Africa.* Lynne Rienner Publishers.

The Economist. (2020). China's Belt and Road Initiative in Africa: A Boost for Development or a New Form of Colonialism? The Economist.

The first "maternal and children's healthcare project of China" in Sierra Leone. Hunan Children's Hospital. 2017.

The Observatory of Economic Complexity – Https://oec.world/en /profile/bilateral-country/chn/partner/sle

Thompson, J. (2007). 'The Role of Alumni Networks in International Education'. *Journal of Studies in International Education.*

UNDP (2019). Human Development Report 2019. United Nations Development Programme.

UNESCO, 2021. The Role of Sports in Community Development. *UNESCO.*

UNICEF (2015). Education for All 2000-2015: Achievements and Challenges. UNESCO.

United Nations Development Programme (UNDP). (2021). Impact of the Belt and Road Initiative on the Sustainable Development Goals in Africa. UNDP.

Urdal, H., 2003. A clash!of Generations?! Youth bulges and political violence,. ' *International&Studies,* p. 234.

van Klyton, A. C., Rutabayiro-, N. S. & Liyanag, S., 2-19. Chinese investment in the Sierra Leone telecommunications sector: international financial institutions, neoliberalism and organisational fields.. *Review of African Political Economy,* , Volume 47(164), p. 220–237.

Vandemoortele, J., & Delamonica, E. (2000). 'Education 'Vaccine' Against HIV/AIDS.' *Current Issues in Comparative Education.*

Vines, A. (2014). China in Africa: A Mixed Blessing? Current History, 113(763), 195-201.

Waltz Kenneth N. Theory of International Politics - Addison-Wesley Publishing, 1979. — 256 p.

Wang, H. (2011). China's Image Projection and Its Impact. In: Wang, J. (eds) Soft Power in China. Palgrave Macmillan Series in Global Public Diplomacy. Palgrave Macmillan, New York.

Winkler Sigrid (2012). "Taiwan's UN Dilemma: To Be or Not To Be". http://www.brookings.edu

World Bank, 2020. Infrastructure Development in Sierra Leone.. *World Bank Publication* .

World Bank. (2022). World Development Indicators. Available at: https://databank.worldbank.org/source/world-development-indicators

Xia Yuanyuan, Healthcare without borders. Hunan's

Xia, Y. (2020). Chinese Investment in Africa: An Empirical Investigation of Trends, Dynamics, and Regulatory Challenges. In: Chaisse, J., Choukroune, L., Jusoh, S. (eds) Handbook of International Investment Law and Policy. Springer, Singapore

Xiaoyong, Li (2022) 'A Day to be Remembered: Celebrating 51 Years of China - Sierra Leone Diplomatic Relations.'

Xinhua, April 27, 2014 - http://news.xinhuanet.com/2014-04/27/c_1110430819.htm (Accessed 3rd April, 2024)

Yan, Zhou (28 May 2010). "CAD Fund to boost footprint in Africa." China Daily. Retrieved 24th March 2024.

Zapata, X. (2023). China's cultural diplomacy in a new era of multilateralism. The case of the China community in Latin America and the Caribbean States. Stuttgert, Institut fur Auslandsbeziehung en.https://opus.bszbw.de/ifa/frontdoor/deliver/index/docId/959/file/ifa-2023_zapata_china-cd-multilateralism_EN.pdf

Zhang Yuwen. Fighting Ebola in Africa.

Zhang, S. (2016). Chinese economic diplomacy. Decision-making actors and processes. New York, Routledge

Zhang, X. (2020). China's Infrastructure Investments in Sierra Leone: A Case Study of the Belt and Road Initiative. Working Paper, Peking University.

Zhang, Y., & Li, X. (2010). China's Foreign Aid and Soft Power in Africa. Taylor & Francis.

Zhao, S. (2013). *China's Foreign Policy and Soft Power in South America, Asia, and Africa.* Routledge.

Index

www.ingramcontent.com/pod-product-compliance
Lightning Source LLC
Chambersburg PA
CBHW020339270326
41926CB00007B/241